Children of Reunion

Children of Reunion

Vietnamese Adoptions and the
Politics of Family Migrations

• •

ALLISON VARZALLY

The University of North Carolina Press   Chapel Hill

© 2017 The University of North Carolina Press
All rights reserved

Set in Charis by Westchester Publishing Services
Manufactured in the United States of America

The University of North Carolina Press has been a member of the
Green Press Initiative since 2003.

Library of Congress Cataloging-in-Publication Data
Names: Varzally, Allison, 1972– author.
Title: Children of reunion : Vietnamese adoptions and the politics of
　family migrations / Allison Varzally.
Description: Chapel Hill : University of North Carolina Press, [2017] |
　Includes bibliographical references and index.
Identifiers: LCCN 2016021188 | ISBN 9781469630908 (cloth : alk. paper) |
　ISBN 9781469630915 (pbk) | ISBN 9781469630922 (ebook)
Subjects: LCSH: Intercountry adoption—Vietnam. | Intercountry
　adoption—United States. | Vietnam War, 1961–1975—Children. |
　Vietnam War, 1961–1975—Evacuation of civilians. | Adopted children—
　United States. | Amerasians. | Vietnamese—United States.
Classification: LCC HV875.5 .V37 2016 | DDC 362.734089/95922073—dc23
　LC record available at https://lccn.loc.gov/2016021188

Cover illustration: Merrie Li and Tung Joe sitting in a play airplane at
　a park in Vietnam. Courtesy of Merrie Li Camp.

Portions of chapter 1 were previously published as "Vietnamese
Adoptions and the Politics of Atonement," *Adoption and Culture*
(December 2009): 158–99. Used here with permission.

For John and Zeke

Contents

Acknowledgments, xi

List of Abbreviations, xiii

Introduction, 1

1 Vietnamese Adoptions in the Early War Years, 13

2 After the Airlifts, 48

3 Amerasians' Families and Hopes of Homecoming, 77

4 Living Legacies, 117

Conclusion, 154

Notes, 161

Bibliography, 187

Index, 195

Illustrations

Nguyen Thi Thu (Trista Goldberg), Nguyen Hong Bich, and foster sister in Vietnam, 2

Trista Goldberg, adoptive brothers Trever and Troy, and sister, Tracee Jo, with Mickey and Minnie Mouse, 3

Trista Goldberg's family standing in a field, 4

Tom and Nhu Miller, just married, 40

Ri and Ken Armstrong at field hospital in Vietnam, 1969, 43

President Gerald R. Ford carries a Vietnamese baby from Clipper 1742, one of the planes that transported South Vietnamese children from Saigon, April 5, 1975, 50

Julie Andrews interacting with two Vietnamese children, 80

Merrie Li holding baby sister, Marie; brother Brandon; Tony; Tung and their mother, Lieu, 101

Jimmy Miller; his father, James; son; and father-in-law, Charlie, 108

Angelina Memon and her father, 109

Vikki and her parents, Henri and Dolores Sloviter, on Thanksgiving, 1975, 119

A group of children, including Stephen Lester Ngo Duling, sitting on a stoop in Vietnam, 1973, 122

Duling family (Stephen, his sister Teddie Anne, Henry, and Gretchen) and new kitten, 1973, 122

Ri and Ken Armstrong, 2015, 123

Jared Rehberg with his first guitar, 133

Tuyet Cam, "Misplaced Baggage," photo taken by Anh Dào, 135

Mike Ryan, "Misplaced Baggage," photo taken by Anh Dào, 136

Kim Delevett, her cousin Lan Phan, brother Lam, and mother, Nuoi, on the balcony of their Saigon home in April 1975 just before the children left for the United States, 149

Kim Delevett and her brother, Lam, with their adoptive American siblings, 150

Acknowledgments

A curiosity about wars in Southeast Asia, Vietnamese migrations, and the family as a location of social and political change motivated this book. As a child of 1970s Philadelphia—a city where a sizable population of Vietnamese refugees resettled, veterans' organizations mobilized, and the nation celebrated its bicentennial—I noted, if only indirectly, the import of American interventions abroad, their outcomes, and the difficulty of reconciling notions of freedom and obligation. In this book, I wished to explore these ideas and continue my efforts as a U.S. historian to reveal changing conceptions of community and citizenship in the most multiracial of nations.

During its infancy, this project received nourishment from a friendly set of interdisciplinary scholars, adoptive parents, and adopted Vietnamese, who belonged to the Alliance for the Study of Adoption, Identity, and Kinship. The organization accepted my paper for presentation at its annual conference and published my early exploration of the political discourse about Vietnamese adoption in its journal, *Adoption and Culture* (2009). Exchanges and conversations with academics most animated by topics of immigration, Asian America, transnationalism, gender, and the twentieth-century United States have greatly influenced the course of my research and writing. I am grateful for the insights and encouragement of Donna Alvah, Karen Balcom, Shana Bernstein, Catherine Cezina Choy, Mary Dudziak, Ellen Herman, Eleana Kim, Becky Kluchin, Phonshia Nie, Meredith Oda, Arissa Oh, Kim Park, Paul Spickard, Rachel Winslow, and Susan Zeiger. The book's reviewers offered encouraging and thoughtful criticism that improved the manuscript. At the University of North Carolina Press, Brandon Proia energetically guided this project to publication.

Patient and dedicated archivists at the Social Welfare History Archives; University of California, Irvine Southeast Asian Archives; Pearl S. Buck House; Swarthmore Library Peace Collection; University of California, Berkeley Ethnic Studies Library; and the National Archives at San Francisco responded quickly to questions, identified relevant, unexpected sources, and reassured me of the book's promise. I am grateful for the Clarke Chambers

Travel Fellowship, which permitted my foray into the Social Welfare History Archives.

Faculty at California State University, Fullerton, especially members of the History and American Studies Departments, have shaped the project, sharing their expertise and collegiality. Kristine Dennehy, Laichen Sun, and Lisa Tran brought my attention to scholarship, exhibitions, and documentaries in modern Asian history relevant to my investigations. A generous cohort of Americanists—Gordon Bakken, Margie Brown-Coronel, Kate Burlingham, Ben Cawthra, Natalie Fousekis, Volker Janssen, and Jessica Stern—offered invaluable comments on content and organization that have strengthened the book. By good fortune, Susie Woo, whose interests in Asian immigration and adoption so closely align with my own, joined our university three years ago. Collaboration with colleagues across the College of Humanities and Social Sciences in a film and speaker series commemorating Southeast Asian legacies allowed me to frame my research in a new way. I also appreciated the painstaking work of Jim Park and Justin MacMingus, two history graduate students at CSUF, who transcribed many of my oral histories.

Without the photographs and stories of my narrators—an unusually candid, generous, and eloquent set of individuals—this book would have less substance and little spirit. Rather than conceal their sometimes painful pasts, these adoptees, Amerasians, and their families revealed themselves in ways that inspired and complicated singular, simple narratives. My conversations with Ken Armstrong, Ri Armstrong, Bert Ballard, Merrie Li Camp, Jeffrey Corliss, Ahn Đào, Kim Delevett, Gretchen and Stephen Duling, Trista Goldberg, Tiffany Chi Goodson, Le Thi Hang, Virginia Littauer, Angelina Memon, Jimmy Miller, Nhu Miller, Tom Miller, Tung Joe Nguyen, Jared Rehberg, Jay Sheridan, Vikki Sloviter, Kimberly Nguyen Thompson, and Truc Tran reminded me of the joys and the necessity of oral history.

Longtime and new friends provided distractions and reassurances that lightened the labor of research. My family cheered me on and convinced me that I could complete a second book. I am most thankful for the love and laughter of John and Zeke. John remains my dearest companion, coach, and adviser. And Zeke makes my heart sing every moment of the day. His love of stories and insistence that his mom write more and more pages motivated me to continue.

Abbreviations

AVI	Adopted Vietnamese International
ARVN	Army of the Republic of Vietnam
CCR	Center for Constitutional Rights
COR	Committee of Responsibility
DRV	Democratic Republic of Vietnam
FCVN	Friends of the Children of Vietnam
FFAC	Friends for All Children
FMSVC	Friends Meeting for the Sufferings of Vietnamese Children
GAO	Government Accountability Office
INS	Immigration and Naturalization Service
ISS	International Social Service
LIRS	Lutheran Immigrant and Refugee Service
ODP	Orderly Departure Program
PRG	Provisional Revolutionary Government of Vietnam
PRPC	Philippines Refugee Processing Center
RVN	Republic of Vietnam
SRV	Socialist Republic of Vietnam
USAID	United States Agency for International Development
VAN	Vietnamese Adoptee Network
VNVA	Vietnam Veterans of America

Children of Reunion

Introduction

Born to an American man and Vietnamese woman in 1970, Trista immigrated to the United States and was adopted by a young American couple, Nancy and Chuck Kalan, in 1973 after she and her younger brother, Jeffrey, spent a year in the care of a Vietnamese foster family. Although Nancy would eagerly accept and manage the details of Trista's adoption, her husband, a veteran of the Vietnam War, had initiated their plans. Trista recalled her fear and shyness on meeting her new parents. "When I first saw my father, I cried," she explained, "because he had a full beard and I wasn't used to the facial hair." Moreover, as a four-year-old, "I still had memories of my family," she related. These memories would become less vivid over time as Trista learned English, became acquainted with American foods, and integrated into the mostly white community of Feasterville, Pennsylvania, but she retained cultural, political, and familial ties to Vietnam through regular contact with Jeffrey, who was adopted into the household of Trista's aunt and raised as her cousin, as well as her foster family, who departed Vietnam among a wave of refugees and resettled in the Kalans' household in 1975. Despite relationships and exposure that could have reinforced a Vietnamese identity, she admitted, "I probably actually repressed any of my culture and heritage growing up because I just wanted to fit in."[1]

In the 1990s, Trista reversed course, revisiting Vietnamese culture and refashioning relationships with Vietnamese relations. In doing so, she retraced the threads of Vietnamese migrations obscured by war and resettlement programs. After locating, networking with, and organizing with other adopted Vietnamese determined to piece together their own histories and disrupt the prevailing, politicized discourse about their rescue from Vietnam, the nation's obligations to Vietnamese, and the lessons of military interventions in Asia, she and Jeffrey began searching for their Vietnamese mother, Thanh Thi Nguyen.[2] Trista collected names, addresses, and other pertinent details from her Vietnamese foster family and Holt International, the agency that had arranged her adoption. Thanks to serendipity and perseverance, she discovered that her and Jeffrey's two sisters, two brothers, and mother had taken advantage of the Amerasian Homecoming Act,

Nguyen Thi Thu (Trista Goldberg), Nguyen Hong Bich, and foster sister in Vietnam. Courtesy of Trista Goldberg.

legislation passed to facilitate the migration of Amerasians and close relatives in 1987, and relocated to Lansing, Michigan, in 1991. The hunt continued within U.S. borders as Trista approached immigration authorities; tracked the dispersion of family members to Kansas, Texas, and Hawaii; and eventually arranged a reunion in California. She described the initial encounter as "surreal." Popular assumptions about the poverty and struggles of Vietnamese refugees prepared her to expect "a poor family that was going to need my assistance," but she soon realized "they were actually pretty settled." Her brother Que appeared at Los Angeles International Airport sporting Ray Ban sunglasses and a camcorder. When Trista's mother reached the scene, she embraced Jeffrey before reaching for her daughter. Although Trista could not understand what Thanh Thi said, "the mostly sobs and cries" communicated their shared feelings. Jeffrey described the encounter as "unique, but it was also strange," because although "it was nice meeting them, good to see resemblances and stuff," it "was too much

Trista Goldberg (*front*), adoptive brothers Trever (*left*) and Troy (*middle*) and sister, Tracee Jo (*right*), with Mickey and Minnie Mouse. Courtesy of Trista Goldberg.

at one time, almost like somebody forcing themselves on you. So you weren't sure if it was real or not."³

When the emotions of that initial reunion subsided, Trista and Jeffrey would learn more about the conditions and decisions that had separated them from their family, an education that reinforced their belief in their mother's affection and determination. Thanh Thi stated her surprise on discovering that the orphanage, where she had left the pair temporarily to ease the burden of caring for such a large family, had then placed them with a Vietnamese foster family and arranged for their adoption by Americans. She then detailed her efforts to reclaim her youngest children when she landed in the United States; she had told stories, shared pictures, and asked questions of everyone she met, to no avail. Now reconnected, Trista, Jeffrey, their mother, and their siblings sustained relations despite the strains of time and cultural differences. Trista regularly visited her mother in Hawai'i, while Jeffrey, who had recently divorced, had a self-described habit of wanderlust, and felt particularly drawn by the assembly of his Vietnamese family, chose to move to the island state. Jeffrey soon initiated a romantic relationship with a Vietnamese immigrant, Terri, to whom he was introduced by his mother and sister. The pair had two children together and

Trista Goldberg's family standing in a field. Courtesy of Trista Goldberg.

considered themselves married in practice if not in law. Yet, the realities of re-creating familial ties proved more difficult than Jeffrey anticipated. Although he considered Terri and their children his primary responsibility, his mother counted on his full financial support. And Terri, whom he depicted during an interview as a passionate person, refused to talk to Thanh Thi and disapproved of Jeffrey's Hawai'i-based siblings' business dealings. Mediating these familial tensions proved difficult, Jeffrey explained, because "I could never know what's actually going on because everything's being said in Vietnamese, and I have to rely on who's giving me the most correct translation, you know."[4]

This book is about the experiences and representations of Vietnamese like Trista and Jeffrey who have been adopted by Americans since 1965. It explores their lives and the stories told about them and their American and Vietnamese families to better understand the Vietnamese diaspora and changing ideas of U.S. citizenship in an era of heightened debate about national purpose in the world. Because of the timing of their arrival and the conditions that generated their departure from Vietnam, Vietnamese children became convenient sites and active participants in discussions about the meanings of the Vietnam War, the principles and practices of foreign policies, the process and consequences of Vietnamese migrations, and the nature of American family.

Almost 6 million U.S. troops served in Southeast Asia over the duration of the Vietnam War; 58,000 lost their lives, and more than 300,000 were wounded.[5] The U.S. military's practices, which included search-and-destroy missions, carpet-bombing raids, free-fire zones, and chemical defoliation, killed an estimated 3 million Vietnamese, disfigured countless others, leveled thousands of buildings, damaged the region's infrastructure, and contaminated its water, land, and air. The United States dropped more explosives on Vietnam than the Allies had on Germany and Japan combined during World War II. While armed combatants and unarmed civilians were clearly divided in North Vietnam, these differences blurred in South Vietnam, where villagers often fought as hard as their armed counterparts simply to survive. Disturbing episodes such as the My Lai Massacre in 1969, in which U.S. forces burned a South Vietnamese village and killed as many as 400 men, women, and children, highlighted the indiscipline of U.S. troops, the uncertain boundaries of conflict, and the suffering of South Vietnamese.[6] Before withdrawing troops and wrestling with regrets in 1975, the United States intensified and widened its efforts in Southeast Asia, causing further political, economic, and social damage.

The destructiveness of U.S. military and political interventions in Vietnam, the displacement of South Vietnamese, and the believed antipathy toward and neglect of war orphans by Vietnam's triumphant Communists produced the migration of Vietnamese children. Their relocation not only highlights the painful outcomes created and amplified by the exercise of American power in Southeast Asia, but calls us to revisit the distinctions usually drawn between immigrants and refugees to the United States. American officials, social workers, and families during the 1970s and 1980s typically envisioned the movement of Vietnamese children as a final passage. Based on this characteristic, the adopted Vietnamese were refugees, those forced by political persecution to depart. When framed as such, they appear worthy, but vulnerable and passive, featured in investigations that may overemphasize loss, difficulty, and alienation. However, the stories of Vietnamese families that attempted and sometimes succeeded in relocating to the United States, where they reclaimed and reintegrated their kin, suggests otherwise—that the adopted were actually purposeful migrants who had real futures with Vietnamese families or inside state-run institutions, but whose migration improved their conditions amid difficult circumstances and allowed the possibility of reunion or return to Vietnam. Conceptualized as immigrants seeking economic improvement and connections with family, the adopted recovered their agency *and* culpability, thus supporting broader, more nuanced interpretations.

Overall, adopted Vietnamese help us interrogate overlaps of and distinctions between two legal and lived categories during a period when the United States constructed more migrants as refugees than ever before (even while deemphasizing or denying its role in generating refugees) and increasingly justified their admission as a humanitarian rather than a political act. They allow us to recognize how race, war, and violence as much as mobility and opportunity have structured migrations since World War II. Finally, the arrival of adopted Vietnamese underscores the consequences of U.S. imperialism in Asia as well as the link between national confidence and the expectations imposed on newcomers.[7]

The entrance of Vietnamese children and their relatives beginning in the late 1960s further reveals the central but contested place of family in American immigration policy and society. The groundbreaking 1965 Hart-Cellar Act replaced discriminatory national quotas with more egalitarian preference categories and made possible dramatic growth in immigration from Asia and Latin America. The elevation of family connections, in particular, as a pathway to entry realized a long embraced belief that families strengthened and realized the nation's democratic principles. However, reaching for fairness by privileging family creation or reunification sharpened questions about what exactly constituted a family. How widely could or should the circle be drawn, and what happened when prospective immigrants designed families at odds with American blueprints? Both sympathetic and exasperated, Americans sometimes reprised racialized notions of who was most worthy to answer these questions.

Even though the majority of Americans opposed the migration and settlement of Vietnamese refugees through the 1970s, an opposition that reflected weariness about the war, anti-Asian prejudices, and economic anxieties stirred by recession, most supported the adoption of Vietnamese children by Americans. However, controversy erupted about the preparedness of primarily white, middle-class couples to assimilate Vietnamese or part-Vietnamese children to a society organized around racial difference. Should or would they attempt to inculcate cultural values of and historical knowledge about Vietnam? Could these interracial families overcome or overwhelm racial tensions by acting as if race made no difference, affirming the ascendance of a colorblind ideology against a more separatist, multicultural, race-conscious one? Many African Americans and Asian Americans voiced strong reservations about the absorption of Vietnamese children (especially those with black fathers) into white American families. Like many Asians and Africans, they deemed such families insensitive to the realities of racial prejudice at best and active colonizers of nonwhite peoples at worst. Even though African Americans and Asian Americans shared this concern, the simultaneous (and interrelated) inclusion of foreign-born Vietnamese children in and exclusion of native black children from white American families facilitated the emerging construction of Asian Americans as a model minority. Vietnamese children, especially girls, were domesticated and made familiar and dependent, destabilizing long-held assumptions about the perpetual foreignness of Asian immigrants; they became American.

The migration of adult Amerasians, a separate but related category of Vietnamese "adopted" into the American family, also emphasized a persistent lack of consensus about the American family and national identity even after the passage of civil rights and immigration legislation intended to align democratic ideals and social realities. As a result of the efforts of Amerasians and their families, the Pearl S. Buck Foundation, a few interested politicians, and journalists, Americans rediscovered a population of Amerasians who had grown up in Vietnam, sometimes wondered about their fathers, and wished to enjoy the prosperity and opportunities of the United States. The representation of these multiracial individuals as poor, desperate, and despised helped convince Americans to support the Amerasian Homecoming Act in the 1980s, a decade during which the Reagan administration welcomed anti-Communist refugees and proposed a conservative narrative of the Vietnam War intended to restore national confidence. This legislation permitted the migration of not only Amerasians who could prove or at least suggest American paternity but also select members of their Vietnamese family. The concern of American officials (grounded in actual observations) that some Amerasians and Vietnamese manipulated the system by pretending kinship demonstrates the nation's investment in a certain kind of affective, "natural" family. The idea that Vietnamese could or would define family as a utilitarian set of arrangements designed to gain entry to the United States undermined the fundamental reconceptualization of immigration policy and American attempts to present the United States as a benevolent and responsible actor in the world. It also showcased the creative adaptations of Vietnamese seeking opportunities and the repair of families splintered by war.

As evidence of a war that few Americans could or would put to rest, as youths presumed unable to speak for themselves, and as immigrants whose experiences of loss and disorientation paralleled the nation's own, these Vietnamese children became useful figures in discussions about the past and present of U.S. interventions abroad. Since the dramatic and dramatized first encounters between Americans and their Vietnamese adoptees, Americans have talked about Vietnamese children as a way to negotiate their regrets and uncertainties about the U.S. defeat in Vietnam. In debating the motivations and outcomes of these transnational adoptions, they have both defended and cursed U.S. actions. Although some credited the nation with taking responsibility for casualties of war and restoring its reputation internationally, others accused the nation of a continued will to dominate and disrespect the wishes of developing nations. This latter interpretation stressed obligations rather than rights as fundamental to American citizenship and defined national identity as an expression of limits and doubts rather than pride and conviction.

Competing ideas of gender and sexuality also inflected this discourse. Calls for the nation to fulfill war-accrued debts to the people of Vietnam by "rescuing" its children had heavy, paternalist overtones; the nation was conceived as a generous and responsible father figure. At the same time, Americans explored alternate notions of masculinity through their representations of actual relations between American soldiers (sometimes fathers) and Vietnamese children. Select media, social workers, and adoption advocates portrayed American soldiers alternatively as dedicated warriors, errant killers, or indifferent fathers. But GIs and their advocates countered such depictions with accounts of soldiers caring for orphans and searching for offspring. In doing so, these soldiers traveled a pathway toward belonging traditionally trod by women and sought to redeem the stature of men unsettled by the war and an ascendant women's movement. However, as social workers, agency organizers, and aspiring mothers, American women often fought to defend their conventional roles as citizens by proving their continued maternal powers and the civic significance of tending to the children of Vietnam.

To some extent, the sustained interest in Vietnamese children and young adults was beneficial, precipitating favorable immigration laws and social services. However, chronic and unresolved anxieties about the Vietnam War also complicated their assimilation. They attempted to find a sense of place when the terms of political and cultural belonging were more doubted and disputed than ever. Moreover, oftentimes their discursive value obscured their real experiences; they were infinitely talked about, spoken for, and looked at, but more rarely seen and heard. Over time, though, these individuals offered their own versions of and engagements with the Vietnam War and Vietnamese migrations as a necessary strategy of inclusion.

This history of entangled migrations and remembrance unwinds across five chapters. Chapter 1 studies the first wave of Vietnamese adoptions against the backdrop of military escalation and a vocal, soon-to-grow antiwar movement. It examines the language of responsibility, culpability, and multiculturalism that came to dominate defenses of adoptions in the Vietnam War era as Americans reconsidered the effectiveness and morality of U.S. foreign policy. Integral to such rhetoric was the imagined and real participation of American men and women as soldiers and social workers in Vietnam. This chapter not only elaborates the ways in which Vietnamese adoptions offered Americans an opportunity to engage with gendered notions of citizenship, but also examines questions about chances for racial equality at home, the extent of the nation's international obligations, and the power of intimate, familial relations to alter society and politics.

Chapter 2 focuses on the aftermath of Operation Babylift, the mass airlift of Vietnamese children to the United States on the eve of the nation's formal withdrawal. Arguably the most dramatic episode of the unfolding adoption and migration story, it received overwhelming media coverage, captured international attention, and pushed Vietnamese adoptees to the center of debates about the war's end and aftermath. Although architects of the airlift hoped it would benefit Vietnamese children and burnish America's tarnished image, it precipitated significant opposition among Americans and Vietnamese who accused the U.S. and Vietnamese governments of playing politics, and adopting families of privileging their own desires. The airlift and its controversy also displayed the creative ways in which Vietnamese families stretched across national boundaries, demanded reunions, and disputed American efforts to contain and control the legacies of war. As a failed effort to bring the era's negotiations about race, family, and national purpose to a close, the airlift anticipated the continued resonance of the Vietnam War and Vietnamese immigrants within American society throughout the rest of the twentieth century and into the twenty-first.

Chapter 3 examines Amerasians, those who could have been but were not adopted by American families in the 1970s. National concern for this population revived ideas about our responsibility for the unwanted children of Vietnam and our ability to absorb newcomers that had dominated earlier discussions about adopted Vietnamese. Advocacy of and eventual legislation for Amerasians suggested both the lingering uncertainties about the war and the continued desire to resolve them. Admitting national paternity and taking custody, Americans believed they could finally forgive, forget, and even repair relations with Vietnam. Amerasians understood their immigration differently, but also favorably. They envisioned rediscovering their fathers, winning social acceptance, and escaping poverty. However, charges of fraud and misrepresentation, the complexity and rarity of father-child reunions, and the difficulties of adjustment in a nation where one was presumed an American rather than guided to become one, compromised their sense of citizenship.

Chapter 4 investigates the experiences of Vietnamese children as they matured and maneuvered as reluctant legacies of the Vietnam War. Absorbed into and sometimes divided across American and Vietnamese families, adopted Vietnamese and Amerasians watched, listened to, and reflected on the many films, books, memorials, and U.S. policies toward Vietnam that expressed the nation's varied and unstable ideas of remembrance. Meanwhile, a prescription to preserve and celebrate cultural differences in the late twentieth century—a prescription that reflected the teachings of minority activists and their allies—pushed the adopted and their adoptive parents to learn Vietnamese traditions and find commonality with Vietnamese immigrants. However, oftentimes the distance created by their differences of language, location, economics, and education kept these groups apart. This chapter tracks the assimilation of the adopted Vietnamese and Amerasians through the 1970s and 1980s amid these contested memories, conceptions of cultural identity, and ideas of community. It also traces how they have interpreted their own histories since the 1990s. Through social media, memoirs, documentaries, reunions, conferences, tours of Vietnam, heritage camps, and calls to Congress they have changed their own and the public's thinking of the past. Moreover, their relationships and representations have helped expose a history of racial difference, violence, and dislocation that reveals their unique but central location within the larger diaspora of Vietnamese.

This book compliments and complements scholarship dedicated to the histories of immigration and multiracial relations. Such works have explored the construction of racial categories and notions of citizenship through the nation's evolving immigration laws, detailing how and why immigrants have creatively circumvented and accommodated these restrictions.⁸ They have also observed the importance of shifting U.S. interests in and relations with other world regions for patterns and experiences of immigration, observations that shape my investigation. Studies that revisit the idea and legal construct of "refugee" frame this book as well. As a category of alien distinguished from other immigrants, refugees have often served to deny or elide the role of U.S. military and political interventions in creating flows of migrants. As a privileged but understudied group, refugees potentially reveal contours of foreign policy and notions of national identity that differ from those revealed by other new entrants.⁹ The subject of Vietnamese refugees in particular—their process of migration, their strategies of community formation, their cultural productions, their forms of political engagement—has generated valuable research that informs my writing.

Works that consider the construction, experiences, and political uses of families to detect larger truths about gender, race, immigration, and citizenship during the second half of the twentieth century have also motivated this research. As the United States escalated and variegated its international involvements during the Cold War, it practiced forms of soft diplomacy that centered on American families. Scholars have chronicled how women and children especially were deployed in rhetoric and iconography or acted in programs and organizations to prove the strengths of U.S. democracy and assure the loyalties of foreign peoples. Although such efforts partially realized U.S. ambitions, they did not erase pressures created by Soviet propaganda and the demands of Asian American and African American leaders to improve interracial relations and promote racial equality at home. The increase and institutionalization of domestic and transnational adoption as forms of family formation also expressed the complex dynamics of anti-Communism, evangelicalism, neocolonialism, and racialism during the Cold War.¹⁰ Rather than a narrow and private act, historians have imagined adoption as a wide and public portal into American and global histories. Such journeys have taken them to Europe, Latin America, and Asia, especially Korea. As a focused study of adoptions and migrations from Vietnam since 1965, this book adds to these fields of knowledge, appreciating the interplay of local and global developments from the perspective of American families and as relevant to processes of assimilation and community formation.¹¹

The unique place of Southeast Asia and its wars in the nation's political discourse and imagination separates adopted Vietnamese and their families from other migrants, and *Children of Reunion* draws on literature that spotlights the region. Americans continue to debate the meaning, legacies, and preferred remembrance of U.S. military intervention there. The conflict remains the preferred example for discussing the efficacy of U.S. military actions abroad, most recently in Afghanistan and Iraq. Indeed, Vietnam War service records of candidates proved central to presidential campaigns until the election of Barack Obama introduced the prospect of a post-Vietnam generation of politicians. The abundant scholarly treatments of the war's origins, strategy, operations, and political outcomes matter to this book, but studies of the war's social and cultural outcomes and commemoration are most influential. These admirably examine Americans' efforts to rehabilitate, restore, and remedy a defeat through diverse forms and languages of commemoration. They expand our notions of remembrance by demonstrating the participation of nonelites and the objectification of Vietnam veterans and refugees.[12]

Children of Reunion seeks to fold this thinking about the nature of memory, war, and trauma into our understanding of migration. In defining and evaluating those factors that influence the reception and acceptance of immigrants and refugees, scholars have emphasized culture, education, financial resources, sustained connections to homelands, and the context of entry (for example, the presence of an ethnic community and family, racial views, and economic opportunities), but have paid less attention to how memories of wars, specifically wars as destructive and unresolved as those in Southeast Asia during the twentieth century, shaped the participation and incorporation of immigrants.[13] This work seeks to uncover this development, emphasizing the understandings and assertions of the adopted Vietnamese, Amerasians, and their transnational families.

By tracking the migrations of Vietnamese adoptees and Amerasians since 1965, this book answers questions about gendered power relations, obligations to refugees, and constructions of family during an era when our immigration laws have elevated the family's importance as a category of entry and anxiety about the consequences of U.S. global interventions have intensified. A desire to redeem defeat in Vietnam, faith in conventional forms of kinship, and commitment to capitalism guided American efforts on behalf of Vietnamese children and young adults. However, Vietnamese migrants countered these gestures, seeking and sometimes finding reunion with their children and thus pressing their claims as refugees in the United States. As Vietnamese and Americans debated the forms, duties, and privileges of family, they ultimately reworked ideas of responsibility and modes of belonging shattered by war.

1 Vietnamese Adoptions in the Early War Years

"We are well aware that children all over the world need love and care, but our focus is presently on Vietnam due to the horror which is being perpetuated in our name there," wrote Don and Augusta Sandstrom in a 1967 letter inquiring about opportunities to adopt a Vietnamese child. Fearing that their incentives might be misconstrued, the couple hastened to add, "Please don't be concerned that 'guilt' is our motivation, it isn't that simple when you have a great deal of love to share; but when you see an evil war being waged, it is hard to turn your eyes away without helping at least one little soul caught up in it. Unfortunately, the suffering of Vietnamese children continues, perhaps the child with whom we will eventually share our home and love is not even born yet!"[1] The Sandstroms were not alone in their desire to mitigate, by caring for a Vietnamese child, the destructiveness of a war whose purpose and prosecution they opposed. Although some Americans remained supportive of the U.S. campaign in Southeast Asia, challenges mounted as casualties increased, the war lengthened, and progress stalled.

The U.S. presence in Vietnam dated to Franklin Delano Roosevelt's efforts to control the decolonization of French Indochina during the 1940s. In the ensuing decade, the failure of these attempts prompted Harry S. Truman's slow but steady increase of American support for the French who battled against an emerging, independent Vietnamese state led by Ho Chi Minh. Like other populations who had long suffered the indignities of colonial rule, Vietnamese sought independence and had seized the opportunity of a weakening French empire during and immediately after World War II to do so. Ho Chi Minh helped make national independence rather than agrarian reform and class struggle the central objective of the revolution.[2] During the fateful Battle of Dien Bien Phu in 1954, French troops faltered and ultimately surrendered to Vietnamese nationalists, an outcome assured in part by Dwight D. Eisenhower's reluctance to provide even more military aid given the abundant financial support the United States had already extended. The Geneva Accords, which established the terms of peace, temporarily partitioned Vietnam into northern and southern regions. Rather than sever commitments, Eisenhower worked feverishly to build an anti-Communist, South Vietnamese state under the leadership of Ngo Dinh Diem. Certainly, Cold War concerns, namely a belief, or stated belief, that the United States must check an apparent expansion of Soviet influence in Asia, had motivated his actions. Yet, worries over the postwar reconstruction of Great Britain and Japan, a desire for markets and materials in Southeast Asia, the entreaties of Britain and France to help preserve their colonial empires, and the appeals of Vietnamese elites seeking support for their agendas also swayed his and his successors' decisions.[3]

The United States ignored calls to neutralize troubles in Vietnam before 1965 or have contact with the Democratic Republic of Vietnam (DRV, i.e., North Vietnam) once fighting broke out. Privileging military and political strategies over diplomatic ones, the United States and the DRV deflected international pressures and fought with little external involvement until 1968. The Tet Offensive—coordinated attacks by the North Vietnamese Army and National Liberation Front forces on more than one hundred cities in South Vietnam intended to spark rebellion among South Vietnamese and the immediate withdrawal of U.S. forces—altered the character of the war. Chastised, but not deterred, the United States adopted new methods of warfare, most notably counterinsurgency (the kidnapping, imprisonment, and assassination of likely insurgents) and Vietnamization (extending more support and increasing the combat role of South Vietnamese troops). Military stalemate regionalized the conflict as air and ground wars spread to Laos and Cambodia. Meanwhile, the opening of peace talks in Paris in 1968 between the United States and the Republic of Vietnam (RVN) on one side and the DRV and the Provisional Revolutionary Government (PRG) on the other not only raised the importance of diplomacy between these parties, but elevated the participation of third-party nations and international opinion. The Tet Offensive also energized transnational social movements that would successfully constrain negotiations and direct outcomes.[4]

Shaped by existing demands for peace and social justice, the antiwar movement in the United States organized expressions of the mounting frustration with war in Southeast Asia. Its political liberals, who constituted the movement's majority, respected the United States' tradition of championing human rights and distrusted the Soviet Union, but denounced the Saigon regime's authoritarian nature and believed U.S. resources were best invested elsewhere. Its pacifists put forward a stronger critique of American Cold War policy, equally faulting the Soviet Union and the United States for destabilizing global politics, while radical members of the movement identified Vietnam as simply a compelling example of more fundamental problems in U.S. society. Meanwhile, leftists, the smallest but an increasingly visible and noisy constituency, rejected both Marxism and the inequalities of capitalism. In 1965, a series of teach-ins at college campuses protesting Operation Rolling Thunder—a massive aerial bombardment of North Vietnam—helped crystallize and bring public awareness to these diverse voices against the war. Moreover, through the late 1960s, media coverage of mass demonstrations, the support for them expressed by Martin Luther King Jr., distaste for the military draft, the realization of an impasse after the Tet Offensive, and the launch of congressional hearings on the war strengthened the movement. Although he promised to end America's war in Vietnam when he assumed the presidency in 1968, Richard Nixon also wished to maintain Saigon's government and a non-Communist Vietnam. Such designs involved not only strengthening Chinese and Soviet participation in international negotiations, but intensified bombing campaigns and secret assurances to South Vietnam's leader, Diem Bien Thieu. Domestic dissent crested in the fall of 1969, persisting despite the tragic consequences of collisions between antiwar protesters with federal troops, and contributed to the end of the conflict. Although retaining a dislike for antiwar activists, the American public came to accept and assent to their message.[5] More generally, they stated suspicion about the competence of their political leaders and both the utility and morality of U.S. foreign policies.[6]

That suspicion directed some Americans, including the Sandstroms, to act on the behalf of Vietnamese children whose plight they discovered through the graphic accounts of humanitarian organizations and the media. In professing responsibility and proposing adoptive parenthood as the solution for needy children, they recommended the American family as a site of inclusion and redemption. Ideas about appropriate forms of family reveal an era's truths about national identity and purpose.[7] In the late 1960s and 1970s, Americans determined to aid Vietnamese children were also critiquing the state of U.S. foreign policy, proposing new gender roles, and testing the possibility of racial equality. In a revision of the rhetoric and reasoning that had governed American adoptions of Chinese, Japanese, and Korean children following U.S. interventions in other regions of Asia during earlier stages of the Cold War, American adoptions of Vietnamese children more often expressed a loss of faith in the containment policy specifically and the United States' ability to do good in the world generally. Thus, adoptions of the period were more explicitly, heatedly debated as political acts—with participants denying their own political motives while highlighting those of opponents—and increasingly represented as an apology for rather than the fulfillment and endorsement of the United States' expansionist, anti-Communist practices.[8]

Integral to such rhetoric was the imagined and real participation of American men as soldiers and civilians in Vietnam. In selectively provisioning, caring for, and adopting Vietnamese children, these men disputed their reputations as brutal warriors and undercut traditional assumptions about masculine national service.[9] Celebrating the compassion of its "gentle warriors," the U.S. military sought to prove the benevolence of its designs in South Vietnam, its determination to democratize and modernize the country.[10] Yet, these intentions were compromised not only by the irreconcilable contradiction that U.S. policies created the very harm select soldiers sought to repair, but by the decision of some American men to make permanent their commitments to Vietnamese children; these men would cease to be soldiers and become fathers who upended rules about nuclear family formation so central to the cultures of the home front and military. As primary caregivers, not simply providers for or protectors of children, these men made an assertion about national belonging usually professed by women, contributing to and reframing what historian Susan Jeffords has called the remasculinization of America, the revision and partial restoration of patriarchal power challenged by the assertions of the era's women's rights and civil rights movements.[11] Yet, as social workers, agency organizers, and aspiring mothers, American women pushed back against men's claims to Vietnamese children, reprising a familiar, maternal justification for their access to political influence.

Vietnamese adoptions offered Americans a chance not only to wrestle with gendered notions of citizenship, but also to consider the nation's obligations to peoples in newly independent nations, the prospects for racial equality and integration in an increasingly color-conscious era, and the role of family as a location of social and political change. Americans increasingly articulated an alternative vision of American identity and national purpose, one that included new anxieties about the integrity of their representative government, the possibilities for interracial harmony in a multiracial society, and the sources of national unity amid bitter cultural and political divisions.

American adoptions from Vietnam continued a pattern of assuming care for foreign children displaced by political and economic instability in Europe and Asia that dated to the 1930s and expressed the reach and depth of U.S. empire over the course of the twentieth century. U.S. voluntary agencies initiated child sponsorship programs in troubled regions, through which poor children received money, school supplies, clothes, and gifts from their American foster parents, some of whom were unable to legally adopt because they had not married or fell outside the white, Protestant mainstream.[12] During the 1940s, the U.S. military involvement in Europe and a refugee crisis prompted not only the expansion of such sponsorships, but temporary provisions for intercountry adoption. Although open to all European children, those unsettled by Soviet occupation in Germany, Poland, Czechoslovakia, Hungary, Greece, and Italy most often received the visas made available. In total, more than 4,000 were adopted by Americans between 1948 and 1953.[13] Their absorption by American families expressed not only the power of anti-Communist beliefs in shaping refugee policy but a shift in ideas of care and connection; rather than protect children overseas by investing in their families, communities, and institutions, Americans after World War II would increasingly chose to bring them to the United States. This idea of adoption as a solution to international political and economic crises showcased a confidence in family as the locus for change and the realization of U.S. geopolitical goals.

The confluence of falling domestic fertility rates and repeated U.S. interventions in Europe, Latin America, and especially Asia through the second half of the twentieth century accelerated the migratory practice. In addition, in the wake of the era's challenges to racial segregation, gender codes, and conceptions of youth, Americans came to believe that all children deserved the safety and affection of a family rather than the perceived indifference of an institution.[14] Meanwhile, American demand for European babies outstripped the dwindling supply as nations of the western continent recovered and rebuilt under the Marshall Plan—an American-funded program designed to ward off Communism and stabilize battered European economies. Moreover, although most Americans wished to adopt babies, the majority of available European children were adolescents. Jewish agencies, tending to Jewish youths, preferred to resettle them in Europe or Palestine rather than the United States. Finally, the renaissance of nationalism and relaxation of racial ideologies that had once stigmatized the offspring of black American GIs and European women persuaded European countries to withhold rather than deliver the next generation to expectant, foreign families.[15]

Still swayed by ascendant humanitarian principles of the Cold War era and a desire to parent, Americans looked elsewhere, specifically to eastern Asia, where the United States had attempted to establish its dominance since the late nineteenth century. Indeed, the former settler colony, which had practiced the art of empire by crowding out European rivals, subjugating Native Americans, enslaving Africans, and excluding Chinese laborers, first indulged its impulse to influence Asia in the Philippines. Systematically and brutally suppressing local resistance, the United States secured control over the archipelagos, corroborated its claims in the Pacific, and set a precedent for further expansion. Asian leaders, especially Chinese and Japanese, recognized and braced against the entry and ambitions of yet another imperial power.[16] Japan's rise in the region—marked by its defeat of Russia, takeover of Korea, and occupation of northeastern China—ran contrary to American interests and ultimately brought the two ascendant powers into direct and devastating conflict during World War II. Much to its disappointment, the United States' victory did not assure peace and the acceptance of its liberal vision in the postwar era. Instead, Soviet interests in northeast Asia, China's Communist revolution and resistance to the United States' Pacific designs, and nationalist movements sweeping through Asia assured conflict and instability. Confronted with these challenges, the United States recommitted rather than retreated, first fighting a war in Korea that caused massive combatant and civilian deaths, the ruination of landscapes, and the destruction of factories and cities. The war ended inconclusively and frustratingly in 1954 without relieving American desires for hegemony or anxiety about Communism. In Vietnam, Cambodia, and Laos, the United States made another, final and failed attempt to realize its vision of dominance in Asia, assuming the position of another colonial power, finding collaborators, and imposing pain and agony on millions of people.

This history of hubris, competing ambitions, and violence informed the reception of Chinese children. Chinese American and white families noticed and adopted refugee children from Hong Kong who had fled the mainland after the Communist revolution in 1949. Death and desperation on the crowded island pushed relatives to abandon or find alternative homes for their kin. One grandmother, Ling Wing Yung, described life in Hong Kong as "very hard. To make a living at my age in order to support myself and my two grandchildren . . . is unimaginable." Although she recognized the existence of freedom in Hong Kong, she feared the eventual advance of Communism. "I would not like to have my grandchildren grow up under such circumstances," she pleaded in a letter to friends, so "those are the reasons I want you to take them to the States. They could grow up with their minds free from fear. . . . Will you help me?"[17] By the early 1960s, under the authority of the Hong Kong Project, cooperating U.S. and Hong Kong organizations had recognized the concerns of Lin Wing Yung and placed as many as 500 Chinese children in the United States, first wooing Chinese American families, whom they argued best understood China's political situation and could best communicate its cultural traditions.[18] Many of those immigrants who answered the call were distant relatives or friends of the children's parents.

However, white Americans' interest in Chinese children invited experts to revisit the convention of racial matching, which had guided adoption practice by organizations as influential as the International Social Service,[19] a global group that assists families and individuals in matters such as desertion, immigration, repatriation, child custody, and especially adoption.[20] ISS social workers expressed reservations about the ability of white families and communities to accept the physical differences of "full" Chinese and tried to measure racial tolerance by querying their racial preferences. Although a repeatedly stated desire for part white, Asian girls rather than "pure" Asian boys by prospective white parents suggested a real and problematic attention to racial and gender differences, experts were ultimately persuaded by the insistence that love mattered most of all and that affectionate, patient parenting could transform Chinese children into good Americans; they endorsed the transracial placements.[21]

These conversations remained relevant as Americans turned their gaze to other locations of U.S. empire, namely Japan and Korea, where the United States more directly intruded into local politics, economics, and society and more conspicuously complicated the care of children and the security of families. Media reports of mixed-race GI babies ostracized by discerning locals, who insisted on racial purity, motivated Americans to respond. Sawada Miki, a Japanese heiress, and Pearl S. Buck, the daughter of American missionaries to China and a revered author, stepped to the forefront of the cause. Buck founded the Welcome House Adoption Agency in 1949 to help a population she termed "Amerasians," which included mixed-race Japanese and Okinawans born during and after the formal U.S. occupation of the island nation. One year earlier, Miki had opened the Elizabeth Saunders Home, the most well known of many orphanages in Japan that accommodated children with Japanese mothers and American fathers. In addition to feeding, clothing, and housing the children she believed suffered extreme prejudice, Miki sought to instill Christian values and locate adoptive families. This involved courting media attention and lobbying the U.S. Congress to find space within or outside immigration laws to permit the children's passage out of Japan. In the absence of precise regulations and procedures, which would develop as transnational adoptions became more commonplace, children from Japan were adopted via proxy and often delivered to American families without formal background checks. Although immediately after the dropping of atomic bombs on Hiroshima and Nagasaki some Americans had expressed outrage, declared the United States at fault for the pains of Japanese children, and demanded compensation on the youth's behalf, most did not specifically blame the United States for Japan's misfortune or construe adoption as an apology. Such critical pronouncements ran counter to the widely accepted, positive narrative that emerged after World War II in which the United States appeared a heroic nation whose just strategies had brought the war to a quick end and ensured a lasting peace. Thus, as Americans adopted more than 4,500 Japanese children in the decades after World War II, a mood of confident celebration rather than anxious responsibility underscored their actions.[22]

Similar strands of sentiment prevailed in discussions of adoptions from Korea, the favorite, most abundant source for Asian children during the early Cold War. Between 1950 and 1965, an estimated 5,500 children of full or partial Korean descent were brought to the United States.[23] Arissa Oh argues that on learning of the poverty and pain of Korean children, many of them orphans, and many fathered by American GIs, American families sought to "rescue" them by sending money or arranging for their adoption. The private efforts of Harry Holt, a veteran of the Korean War, and his wife, Bertha, to absorb eight mixed-race Korean orphans into their evangelical, rural family begat an adoption agency and an almost insatiable public appetite for stories about and adoptions of Korean children. In 1954, Holt watched a heart-wrenching documentary produced by World Vision—an international, Christian relief organization whose emergency services in crisis regions included sponsoring and helping to adopt Asian children—that portrayed the devastation of South Korea, especially the extreme sufferings of its orphans. Shocked and determined to help, Holt made the salvation of Korean children his life's work. The Holts built orphanages and a far-reaching agency that facilitated and popularized the adoption of thousands of Koreans over four decades. They succeeded in selling adoption as a form of American missionary work because they embodied the ideals of the period: the nuclear family, hierarchical gender roles, anti-Communism, conformity, and a version of Christianity that valued all of these commitments. Holt, a largely sympathetic media, and his government champions depicted adoptions as patriotic gestures by loyal Americans in the global struggle against Communism. Buck did not share

Holt's Christian fundamentalism, but she did agree with and help spread the belief that overseas adoption could promote American ideals. By making impoverished, displaced, often parentless Koreans their own, couples could refute Soviet propaganda that portrayed Americans as intolerant and indifferent to third-world peoples.[24]

The Korean government, which in the wake of liberation from Japanese rule celebrated a nationalist vision incompatible with racial diversity, had eased access to its multiracial offspring. Initially, limitations and underinvestment in its child welfare system also made exporting children acceptable.[25] However, U.S. servicemen, missionaries, and social workers—key agents in recovery plans following the Korean War—proved as important in promoting and facilitating adoption. They transferred American racial ideologies, adjusted local structures of childcare, and encouraged a singular, readily accepted script; Americans would rescue mixed-race children doomed to difficulty in Korea. The demand endured even as the supply dwindled, an imbalance that prompted a shift toward full-Korean orphans and such manipulative practices as baby hunting and compensation to Korean mothers who relinquished their offspring.[26] This American hunger for Korean children undermined official efforts to contain the nation's neocolonial objectives within Korean borders. The construction, even recommendation, of these interracial families composed of Korean children and primarily white parents also encouraged, Susie Woo has argued, new conceptions of race, gender, and family during a period of renewed civil rights challenges.[27] Most strikingly, the integration of Korean children dampened anti-Asian sentiment and guided immigration reforms that eased and systematized intercountry adoptions through the end of the twentieth century.[28] Such procedural and cultural precedents facilitated the eventual immigration of children from other nations, including Vietnam.[29]

Americans who adopted from Vietnam in the late 1960s and early 1970s were not the first generation to think more positively about families constructed through adoption and act on a sense of obligation for children who had suffered through war. Nor were they the first to conflate personal desires for the security, affection, and contentment of parenthood with their views of international relations. However, the meanings and uses of the discourse of responsibility deployed during these early confrontations with Asia changed in the context of the Vietnam War. Although some Americans continued to frame their desire to adopt in terms of patriotism, anti-Communism, and humanitarianism, more critical, subversive, and explicitly political explanations prevailed. When Americans spoke of their obligations to the children of Asia, they no longer conceived of that obligation as a theoretical proposition arising from the inevitable violence of war and the mission of a rich, freedom-loving nation, but as the concrete consequence of failed U.S. policy. They articulated their responsibility in the negative language of guilt and blame rather than the positive rhetoric of uplift and rescue. Moreover, Americans acknowledged adoption's politicization, even as they disputed its morality and propriety. Competing views of the Vietnam War and the nation's foreign affairs had made political the seemingly apolitical act of caring for and adopting Vietnamese children. This public awareness marked a turn toward a more skeptical and divisive political culture and a break from the relative optimism of the early Cold War. This revised conception of the debt Americans owed children of war highlighted heightened doubts, despondency, and dissent about the U.S. government and Cold War doctrine. It also reflected shifting social movements and mores, especially the inroads of nationalism in the developing world. The predominantly white American couples who inquired about and adopted Asian children during the 1940s and 1950s certainly defied prevailing racial attitudes and even the recommendations of most social workers, who believed religious and racial matching in adoptive placements best served the interests of the child and society alike. By the late 1960s and early 1970s, however, hopefulness about the prospects of color blindness to correct a history of racial intolerance and to include the long-excluded had faded in the face of widespread race riots and the mobilization of the third-world Left. Americans discovered the limits of racial integration and increasingly considered the value of preserving distinct minority cultures.[30]

Americans adopted an estimated 3,267 children from Vietnam between 1963 and 1976. Annual figures steadily climbed over this period, peaking at 655 in 1975 before falling slightly to 424 in 1976 and descending precipitously through the close of the decade. Many of them were the sons and daughters of American GIs, whom the media, adoption agencies, and U.S. government represented as social outcasts with bleak futures, a portrait that convinced many Americans that adoption was a moral and political imperative. This had not always been the consensus position; in the early days of the U.S. military intervention in Vietnam, some predicted more positive outcomes. During his Vietnam tour on behalf of the Friends Meeting for the Sufferings of Vietnamese Children (FMSVC), Morgan Sibbett noted that "no one really seems to know whether these children are accepted or not." Some "wishful thinkers" he encountered believed that "these children are being much more easily assimilated into the culture than they were in Korea," even going so far as to suggest that Amerasian children—at least those with Caucasian fathers—were regarded as status symbols. Others expressed similarly upbeat prognoses for Vietnamese children with white fathers. ISS general director Wells Klein explained that "as a result of Vietnam's colonial experience, the Caucasian-Vietnamese child is not a new phenomenon," and thus "Vietnamese culture does not place great emphasis on racial purity." In 1966 the *Philadelphia Evening Bulletin* echoed this representation of Vietnam as a traditional melting pot where more progressive views about racial mixture and thus the successful integration of mixed-race progeny prevailed.[31]

However, by the early 1970s an expanded population of GI babies, poverty, dislocations, death, and diminished respect for the United States among the South Vietnamese seemed to have reduced whatever chances might have existed for the easy acceptance of multiracial children. Despite early assertions that the lives of children fathered by Americans might unfold differently in Vietnam than they had in Korea or Japan, reports of their abandonment and mistreatment abounded. Those who had already heeded the call to help multiracial children during previous U.S. campaigns in Asia renewed their commitment. Members of the Welcome House Adoptive Parents Group created in 1968, most of whom had adopted Korean children years earlier, mobilized to raise money for a reception center in Vietnam that would serve mixed-race children whom they described as "outcasts," suffering "a plight most excruciating for no one wants them." Their inspiration was the persuasive and popular Buck, who cleaved closely to the narrative of GI abandonment, maternal innocence, and American authority that she and her associates had first spun in the context of postwar, occupied Japan. In the early 1970s, as a spry seventy-nine-year-old, Buck was still making headlines as an advocate for mixed-race children. During a visit to Washington, D.C., she lobbied Congress to combine, refine, and pass bills to help GI babies. While estimating that "one out of every ten American soldiers fathers an Amerasian child," she emphasized that "the mothers are not prostitutes." Yet, the persistent impression that they were, and the legal reality that a child belonged to his or her father in Vietnam, meant "nobody wants them."[32]

But Americans insisted that they wanted them. Connie and Harvey Bartz, a couple who had at first proclaimed their indifference to race when FMSVC asked about their preferences, stating, "We don't care if the child is green," confessed a strong interest in mixed-race children. "As Americans, we feel more responsible to these children than to full blooded Vietnamese. Their predicament is greater because in addition to deprivation due to homelessness, their mixed racial heritage caused them social ostracism,"[33] they noted. This belief in the vulnerability of multiracial Vietnamese and a concurrent sense of commitment to them dominated the testimonies of adoptive parents and those wishing to adopt, as well as popular media coverage. Statements and headlines such as "They didn't stand a chance," "GI War Babies Face Grim Future," "Hunger, disease and neglect are a way of life to the countless orphans left behind by the GIs," "Countless Orphans Abandoned in South Vietnam Gain Support from Highland Park Committee," and "These are the kids in big trouble. Especially the half-black ones," were common.[34]

However, nationalist pride and capacious ideas of family precipitated conservative adoption policies and procedures in Vietnam that complicated the release of *all* its children.[35] Vietnamese conceived of family—even if economic and political instability made the conception difficult to practice— as a collection of generations living within a single household. In defining members, they recognized the totality of their maternal and paternal relatives. This expansive sense of belonging meant that when death or difficulty separated parents from their offspring, the child's aunts, uncles, cousins, or grandparents typically and readily assumed charge. Thus, as Welcome House director Mary Graves noted in explaining local opposition to American adoptions of Vietnamese children, Vietnamese struggled to understand why "people who are not related to these children, people outside the family group," would ever choose to adopt them.[36] These concerns informed child welfare and adoption policies. Beginning in 1970 in response to the dramatic growth of orphanages within Vietnam since 1955, South Vietnam's Ministry of Social Welfare placed a limit on the establishment of new ones and introduced forms of assistance for Vietnamese who cared for orphan relatives within their homes. They also coached poor mothers not to abandon their babies, provided vocational training and money to launch small business ventures for widows with young children, and supported a Foster Parents Plan in which foreign parents could support a child within his or her Vietnamese home by sending letters, pictures, and money. Vietnamese and foreign voluntary agencies played a central role in financing and implementing these varied efforts.[37]

To assist orphans who did not find Vietnamese homes, the South Vietnamese Ministry of Social Welfare implemented adoption laws that the Committee of Child Welfare[38] described as having "many complicated and strict conditions." All adoptions by foreigners were to happen within the country, and the party had to be at least thirty-five years old or more than two decades older than the child being adopted. If a couple, they had to have married at least ten years prior.[39] Securing a waiver of these criteria required perseverance, connections, and patience. Even adoptions by those who met these conditions proved difficult. At the International Conference on Children and National Development held in January 1975, Rosemary Taylor noted some of the obstacles, urging the Ministry of Social Welfare to make procedures more "relevant to the welfare of the child," expedite agency over nonagency adoptions, discourage lawyers from involvement in the process, and promise that "no political, military or financial consideration will be permitted to separate a homeless child from a loving family."[40] Morgan Sibbett also detailed procedural shortcomings, noting a lack of clear standards in the selection of families, and a haphazard, even competitive process of selecting children eligible for adoption.[41]

American couples sought a separate, expedited process for the adoption of GI babies. At first, the Vietnamese government expressed some willingness to part with those fathered by Americans. Jan De Hartog shared his impression with the Office of the Prime Minister of South Vietnam in 1967 that "there is some doubt in government circles about the wisdom and desirability of sending full-Vietnamese children out of their homecountry." Appreciating these reservations, he promised that FMSVC would confine its early outreach to children of mixed race. De Hartog made clear that his organization did not simply comply but agreed with the government's position, citing a supposed agreement among professional social workers in Korea, who ruled "that international adoptions to a Western national should be confined to this type of children."[42] However, by the early 1970s, the Vietnamese government had grown more resistant. Although the "government is not insensitive to the special problems that racially mixed children may face," observed ISS director Klein, it was "reluctant to see them further differentiated from their siblings and other children by being treated as a group apart."[43] Officials insisted that the needs, not the paternity, of orphans should determine their eligibility and speed of placement. Disputed estimates of the number of orphaned children further muddied the adoption process. According to Klein, as of 1972, 120 registered orphanages in Vietnam cared for 19,000 children, with another 6,000 children housed in approximately forty unregistered institutions. Of this 25,000, fewer than 1,000 were the offspring of American GIs and a majority were not truly orphans, but placed temporarily in orphanages by families who planned to retrieve their relatives once their economic circumstances had improved and their physical setting stabilized.[44]

If uncertainty about the status of Vietnamese children and the Vietnamese government's policies often frustrated well-meaning, prospective parents from the United States, so did the protocols created by U.S. governmental and private agencies integral to the adoption process. Couples complained that outdated immigration laws, rigid social welfare professionals, and religiously biased orphanages stymied their efforts. Most orphanages in Vietnam were operated by Catholics, who often rejected adoption applications submitted by Americans of other faiths. ISS also frustrated American hopes to adopt with ease. The critique most commonly made of the nonpartisan agency was one long voiced by adoption agencies: ISS's deliberate, bureaucratic approach, or what aspiring adopters Don and Augusta Sandstrom derisively called its "elaborate social machinery," unnecessarily slowed the process of matching children and willing families.[45]

Moreover, Americans faulted their own government for policies that delayed and complicated their familial ambitions. Prospective adoptive parents of the Vietnam era benefited from a 1961 federal law that established permanent provisions for the admission of alien orphans, effectively codifying temporary measures issued in the previous thirteen years.[46] To initiate an adoption, a couple had to file an I-600 form, or Orphan Visa Petition, contact an adoption agency willing to act on their behalf, and discover their state's adoption laws and regulations. Most states required a home study—an intensive investigation of a family's neighborhood, employment, finances, and child-rearing and educational philosophy—to be conducted by their department of social services and then shared with the Immigration and Naturalization Service (INS). Assuming these parents received a positive review, they next had to prove to U.S. officials that a specific Vietnamese child was available. U.S. law defined orphans as children under the age of fourteen whose parents had died, disappeared, deserted, or abandoned them. Those petitioning to adopt a child with surviving parents needed to procure a written release statement or, in cases where the identity and whereabouts of the child's parents could not be determined, file a waiver. If and when INS received and approved all the required documentation, it would ask the U.S. consul in Vietnam to conduct its own investigation; this included a medical exam and confirmation that the child had no afflictions or disabilities unstated in the petition. Finally, and assuming the consul uncovered no "adverse information," it would process the visa application. Although a congressional research report estimated that these steps typically took no more than one year to complete, in practice the process often lasted longer. Besides, many anxious applicants convinced that adoption would save lives and promote the end of a problematic war believed twelve months was an insufferably long period to wait.[47]

Many Americans aching to adopt a Vietnamese child continued to view the act as a fulfillment of rather than a challenge to democratic principles and foreign policy objectives. They often acted within a framework of evangelical Christian faith, believing that God willed them to help Vietnamese orphans. As a missionary, devout anti-Communist, and defender of the American presence in Vietnam, Stuart Harverson worked to save the souls and lives of Vietnamese orphans in the 1960s. And he understood with certainty the origins of these children's misfortune: the Vietcong. In his 1971 account, he made his case, depicting a tragic episode in which five Communist guerrillas appeared unexpectedly one day outside the home of Ang, a young Vietnamese boy. As Ang looked on helplessly, the men seized and brutally murdered his father.[48] Devout American couples seeking to adopt orphans such as Ang described their quest as a journey guided by God, elevated from the messy world of secular politics. Carol Dey related, in her memoir about the adoption of her Vietnamese daughter, that she "was deeply affected by posters of starving children during the church's Thanksgiving clothing drives and school's UNICEF's appeals."[49] She angrily dismissed those who questioned her decision to adopt a Vietnamese child. "And what are *you* doing to help the American children?" she retorted when a ticket taker at the local airport asked why she chose to adopt a foreign rather than domestic infant. "What difference does it make what country the orphans are from? What does geography have to do with it? Poverty and starvation know no boundaries. Shouldn't we help everyone in need, regardless of race or location?"[50] Attuned though she seemed to political circumstances and Vietnamese families' preferences for and patterns of togetherness, Graves of Welcome House insisted that their resistance to adoption should give way, because "in those orphanages there is nothing but death. They talk culture, tradition, philosophy while the children are dying."[51] Although Dey and Graves invited Americans to aid Vietnamese children, they offered no explanation of the sources of the youth's hunger and poverty, avoiding references to American troops in Vietnam, debates about the efficacy of the containment doctrine, and, most important, a precise assignment of responsibility. Thus, they, like other Americans who portrayed adoption as a purely humanitarian and Christian act, promoted a version of national obligation that did not condemn but celebrated U.S. activities in the world.

However, between 1965 and 1975, American leftists asserted an alternative vision of accountability and national purpose, a highly critical one that became increasingly influential and accepted as the war wore on. In doing so, they reinterpreted the prevailing discourse about American responsibility in the Cold War. These Americans acted out their antiwar principles, linking their political beliefs and family aspirations. Middle-class, white women figured prominently in this resistance, articulating a gendered form of protest that foregrounded and celebrated maternity. They did so with the help of a newly woven network of organizations including the Welcome House, the Friends of the Children of Vietnam (FCVN), FMSVC, and the Committee of Responsibility (COR). As leaders and members of these child-focused organizations, American women expressed kinship with and derived inspiration from groups such as Women Strike for Peace, which entered the Cold War conversation about freedom, security, and U.S. actions abroad in 1961 when 50,000 women gathered and demanded the end of the nuclear arms race. Eschewing the hierarchy and exclusiveness associated with male-led organizations, these activists shifted their focus from test bans to the Vietnam War in the late 1960s. They instigated many public demonstrations, rallies, and boycotts across the United States, advised draft resisters, and met with Vietnamese women, United Nations representatives, and political officials. Arguing against the deployment of their sons as soldiers, they emphasized their identities and authority as mothers. As a component of this maternalist rhetoric, they introduced and elaborated a vocabulary of family within the larger peace movement.[52]

Among the more prominent organizations to focus Americans' attention on the pains of Vietnamese children while speaking a language of family and duty, COR was created in 1966 by a group of Boston-based doctors who visited and volunteered their expertise in Vietnam. It arranged medical attention in the United States for maimed, burned, and mutilated Vietnamese children. In an undated mission statement, COR urged all Americans to participate in their effort, "to bear their share of responsibility for innocent victims," and to redeem a U.S. government that had refused to acknowledge its culpability. The committee's work sparked widespread and largely positive coverage in the mainstream media, which printed heart-wrenching accounts and photographs of Vietnamese children with missing limbs, bloated faces, and discolored bodies. However, COR was not without its detractors. The U.S. government launched its own investigation into the medical needs and infrastructure of Vietnam. Acting on the request of President Lyndon Johnson, Dr. Howard Rusk, director of the Institute of Physical Medicine and Rehabilitation at New York University, made a one-week visit to Vietnam's hospitals and disputed COR's claims, suggesting that the group had exaggerated both injuries suffered by Vietnamese children and the limitations of Vietnamese doctors, facilities, and American support. Indeed, Rusk calculated that the United States had paid $50 million into Vietnam's health care system, an investment he interpreted as "concrete evidence of our deep concern for these unfortunate victims of war."[53] Among the savvy recipients of these monies were Tom Miller, a Stanford-trained lawyer and former staff member at the U.S. State Department, and Dr. Arthur Barsky, a plastic surgeon who had won acclaim for bringing young women disfigured by the Hiroshima bombing to the United States. Troubled by war injuries suffered by Vietnamese children, the pair established Children's Medical Relief International in 1966, and with federal assistance soon opened the Center for Plastic and Reconstructive Surgery in Saigon. Reflecting on this support, Miller explained that the "U.S. government liked this idea from a political view because they were embarrassed by the Committee of Responsibility bringing napalm burned children" out of Vietnam. However, although "we realized we were being used politically in this sense," Miller acknowledged, we "felt we needed to do something for these children."[54] In fact, Miller skillfully navigated the political waters, learning "to not be emotional" but "cool and disciplined and aware of politics and use the emotions and poignant stories of children" to assure political and financial support.[55]

Despite Rusk's challenge and the U.S. government's efforts to showcase its commitment to Vietnamese children by funding the surgery center, COR went ahead with its program to transport and treat children in the United States, arranging for foster families who provided temporary lodging and care. The decision to eventually return war victims to Vietnam reflected COR's conviction that Americans must not presume the advantages of their own culture; Vietnamese children were ultimately better off in familiar surroundings. Many of those who discovered COR's activities, however, misunderstood its vision of responsibility; they wrote the organization requesting help in the adoption of Vietnamese children, help that COR politely but emphatically refused to provide.[56] FMSVC collaborated and shared members with COR, but it embraced a broader sense of mission, one that incorporated adoption services. Led by De Hartog, a Dutch author, Quaker, and father of two adopted Korean children, the group was formed in 1966 by Quakers and like-minded individuals upset by the escalation of the conflict in Southeast Asia. Its concerns for orphaned children, in particular, prompted a partnership with Welcome House. Although its purpose and strategies did not exactly align with those of FMSVC—Welcome House paid no attention to the needs of "pure" Vietnamese orphans and did not speak as strongly against the U.S. intervention in Vietnam—FMSVC appreciated Welcome House's expertise and common commitment to children.

When seeking an adoption agency with which to partner, FMSVC found Welcome House more ideologically compatible than Holt International. In the standard literature distributed to its prospective parents, the Holt agency stated its expectation that "you will raise your child by the grace of God and in the nurture and admonition of Jesus Christ." The agency thought a Christian faith so important to a couple's preparedness for parenthood that it required them to state "what your faith is, and what Jesus Christ means to you personally." In the 1950s, the heyday of Holt's operations, many Americans declared their devotion to Christian teachings and conformed to mainstream ideals of religious practice. However, a informal consensus on domesticity, anti-Communism, and religion was breaking down by the Vietnam era, a collapse revealed in FMSVC's response to Holt's Christian bias. "As you know, Friends have a long and honorable history of social action based on religious concern," wrote Rachel Lee of FMSVC to Holt's executive director. She continued, "It would be contrary to Quaker practice to require adoptive parents to make a statement of their Christian Faith as requested in their application."[57]

With the help of Welcome House, FMSVC eventually placed twelve Vietnamese children in the homes of eager Americans. Sibbett, the California-born, World War II veteran and engineer who spent six months in Vietnam coordinating FMSVC's efforts, insisted in his 1968 letter to fellow member Margaret Watts that "such adoptions should not be politically oriented. . . . We are convinced that we are assisting individual children who can benefit from home life as well as the individual families." However, his qualification that "one does not have to 'censor' our references to the war in correspondence" and the consistently political content of inquiries about adoption received from members demonstrated how much a critique of the United States' Vietnam policy shaped the group.[58]

As an organization, FCVN did not explicitly, officially fault the U.S. government for the suffering of Vietnamese children, but they did help antiwar couples realize their political and personal aspirations to adopt a child. Organized in Denver, Colorado, in 1967 by a group of individuals worried about Vietnamese orphans including a doctor who had witnessed the devastation of regional wars firsthand, FCVN sent medicine, food, and trained personnel and arranged adoptions. Eventually it operated three separate homes for children in Vietnam and became the most active adoption agency in the period, placing 1,200 orphans with prescreened American parents by 1973.[59]

Many of the Americans sympathetic to the ideals and purposes of these organizations dedicated to aiding Vietnamese children stated their certainty that the United States had blundered in Vietnam. Invoking the tragedy of the Holocaust, one woman wrote to COR in 1967 that "my husband and I are a young couple with no children. . . . If the problem is . . . urgent . . . it is an embarrassing and degrading thing for Americans. I can at last understand why my parents and people of their generation did nothing for the tortured Jews of World War II. I do not want to be responsible for the crimes of my own generation. I don't want to ignore this."[60] A similar attitude characterized other inquiries that COR's and FMSVC's work with Vietnamese children elicited, emphasizing how adoptions offered Americans a way to articulate and act on their frustration with tragedies in Asia triggered by U.S. military action. Mrs. Donald Smith explained that her and her husband's belief that "our country is so wrong to be involved militarily in Vietnam" and their need to "ease our conscience" had motivated their decision to foster a Vietnamese child. In her letter, Mrs. Tullis Inglese did not detail her longing for a child; the age, race, or gender of the child she would prefer; or her preparedness to be a parent (facts typically included in informal requests for information about and formal petitions for adoption). Instead, she coolly analyzed and proposed adoption as a pragmatic response to Vietnam's troubling conditions. "The increasing number of refugees and homeless children, the lack of education and health facilities and the grave ills of war that are, perhaps, irreparably destroying Vietnamese culture and economic and social organizations leave little promise for a young person's future in Vietnam," she stated. "My husband and I would like to provide an environment of hope and love for a child." Other Americans expressed their grievances against the United States in even more damning language, connecting the current crisis in Vietnam to a history of misconceived foreign policy. Writing on a serene morning in snow-covered Iowa, Wanda Knight imagined a very different scene in Vietnam. "Our country is crazy and sick," she blurted, "historically I believe we would do well to compare our present situation with the Roman Empire." The question of whether the United States still had the opportunity to atone for its imperialist past and present was one she raised but could not yet answer.[61]

This politics of protest that precipitated decisions to adopt often evolved in step with civil rights and antiwar movements. In a letter to FMSVC, Ann Rayor described her own awakening as a student at Northwestern University. There, she took a seminar on Vietnam in which she learned "the moral and legal injustice of the war," an education that fueled her "disgust with the Administration's policy" as well as "despair for the population of Vietnam who are suffering . . . especially of Vietnamese children."[62] After taking a sociology course focused on Vietnam, Cherie Clark, who would not only adopt a Vietnamese girl through FCVN, but become one of the organization's most dedicated volunteers, caring for and helping to evacuate orphans, came to a similarly critical perspective. In her memoir published in 2000, she recalled that the class had "made her more knowledgeable than friends or family about the war" and crystallized her antiestablishment, pro–civil rights views. "I read everything I could, trying to make some sense of America's involvement in Vietnam," she related, but she found no clarity. Despite her despair following the assassinations of King and Robert Kennedy and her perceived helplessness as she fought "for a cause that most people didn't even care about," she "forced herself to take interest in politics," participating in demonstrations and campaigning for liberal politicians. In 1972, while reading an article in *Ebony* magazine about the plight of half-black, half-Vietnamese children, she stumbled across a seemingly more profound way to make a difference. She could "make a single, small contribution in the life of one person"; she could adopt a mixed-race child from Vietnam.[63] The decision of Pam Purdy, Clark's eventual compatriot at FCVN, to adopt was also consistent with a habit of leftist engagements and the changing politics of the period. Married to a graduate of the Yale Divinity School whose first ministerial appointment brought them to a black church in a largely black neighborhood of Chicago, Purdy pursued her journalism career at *Ebony* magazine. As the tenor of racial politics shifted in the wake of ethnic power movements, she confronted the angry looks and resentment of fellow staff members, who questioned the presence of a white woman at a black magazine. "During the turbulent sixties we had been very socially active," Purdy explained in her 1987 account of Operation Babylift, an activism that prompted the couple's adoption of one African American and one black Vietnamese child. By 1975, however, the Purdys' interracial family, born of their integrationist politics, was suspected by African Americans, suspicions the Purdys dismissed: "While we sympathized with the need for a black identity, we believed that a loving home was of primary importance."[64] Other Americans viewed the adoption of Vietnamese children as more than a challenge to or apology for misguided American actions that also fulfilled their personal principles and continued their own practice of social activism; they cheered the possibility of winning converts to the movement for peace. In 1966, Mrs. Bryan P. Michener urged FMSVC to publicize accounts of abandoned and injured Vietnamese children. By telling the story "in its plain, simple facts without preaching 'We are Torturing Innocents!' and without publishing shocking photos to which people often react by withdrawing and building walls around their previous attitudes even higher," she argued, "the average layman (or non-liberal or non-pacifist) might get a better perspective on the war in Viet Nam, might get emotionally involved." In a letter to FMSVC's Marjorie De Hartog, Wende Grant, an active supporter of the organization and a founding member of FMSVC, wondered how her women's group could "use this idea as a basis for projects to turn Hawks to Doves," speculating that "if we can get women reading letters about and seeing pictures of 'their' child[,] even if twenty women do share one child, perhaps, they will begin to care what is happening there."[65]

Despite the earlier caution from Sibbett of FMSVC that members should refrain from mixing politics and adoption, the overtures fellow FMSVC administrator Frank Ortoloff made toward Elizabeth Taylor and Richard Burton indicates how much the group accepted and acted on the advice of Michener and Grant. Having read of the famous pair's interest in adopting an African child in the *New York Post,* Ortoloff urged them to consider "another opportunity." He detailed the "thousands of homeless children" in Vietnam, many of them Amerasians who "are whole in body but they are cast-offs in a culture which shall forever reject them." Reminding Taylor and Burton "about the responsibility we all have, one way or another, to these poor victims," he also reassured them that "I cannot visualize any adverse public reaction to any of our efforts for the children. Quite the contrary."[66] In a telegram dated January 25, 1967, the couple enthusiastically responded, requesting more information. Ultimately, the pair would *not* become high-profile parents who lent credibility and glamour to the cause of Vietnamese adoptions as Ortoloff hoped (others such as Mia Farrow, Yul Brynner, and Jean Kennedy Smith would), but the search for celebrity representatives revealed the dedication of so many leftists to raising the political stakes by expanding awareness of a crisis created in part by U.S. intervention.

Convincing Americans, particularly American women, to care enough or know enough about events in Vietnam to join the opposition was a challenge activists felt confident they could conquer. Convincing the U.S. government to support their campaign, however, proved a tougher obstacle to mount. Although the government would noisily champion adoption in the last hours of the war, in the mid- and late 1960s, with the exception of congressional hearings on Southeast Asian refugees and the advocacy of a few vocal legislators, American officials remained largely silent on the matter. Even as left-leaning Americans freely used adoption to make a political point, they objected when the government appeared to do so by *not* acting on their policy proposals. In an editorial published in a January 1967 issue of the *Boston Herald*, the author expressed his support for the mission of COR and hoped that charges "that the American government's real reason for discouraging the transportation of children is of a political nature" were false. Suggesting the moral high ground on which COR rested, he concluded that "a badly injured child doesn't care which side caused the injury" and should enjoy the opportunity to get well. A rival paper, the *Boston Globe*, printed an editorial on that same date that also chastised the U.S. government for putting politics first. The writer not only found it "inconceivable that our government would turn down this great humanitarian project for propaganda reasons" but was shocked that the government had "missed the chance to improve the standing of the United States in the eyes of the world" by demonstrating its willingness to help orphans.[67]

Although activists saw adoption as a clear political opportunity that could and should be used to shape public opinion about the war, other left-leaning Americans vehemently disagreed. Their reluctance to explicitly politicize the care of Vietnamese children in part reflected new ideas about race relations, culture, and foreign affairs popularized during the social tumult of the 1960s and reinforced by the positions of prominent adoption organizations. At ISS's 1973 conference in Tokyo, Patricia Nye of the Hong Kong branch spoke about changing trends, including the growing influence of Western families desiring Asian babies and the "great feeling of ambivalence in Asia" that such influence generated. Even the more earnest and proadoption organization Frontiers in Adoption articulated an awareness of the fact that ascendant nationalism in the nonindustrialized world had a chilling effect on adoptions from Vietnam: "Developing countries view their children as their greatest natural resource. As a result only a limited number of developing countries will consent to out-of-country adoption of their children."[68]

Conceding the questionable morality and effectiveness of adoption as a solution to the problems of war, some leftists argued that the removal of young children from familiar contexts did more harm than good, continuing rather than reversing an American tradition of exploitation and falsely politicizing a fundamentally humanitarian act. Responding to the initiatives of FMSVC and COR, they espoused the position that adoption was a flawed solution to a serious problem. In a 1966 letter, a California resident and self-proclaimed Quaker described adoptive parenthood as a "delicate process" that should be "whole and complete." Mixing this "basic relationship with an overwhelming concern to do something about the Vietnam war," she asserted, "seems to me to be quite wrong. . . . I feel that no good parent-child relationship can grow out of an atmosphere of emotionally charged social concern, guilt and pity." Concluding that "parenthood has little to do with social action," she also affirmed her admiration for the general efforts of FMSVC to help children. Mary Ellen Tjossem explained in 1966 that "anything we could do to help an orphan child brought to this country for treatment would never outweigh all the mental anguish he or she would have at being taken from his homeland." She believed that the many "needy children of this country," especially blacks and American Indians, deserved priority, a ranking that challenged the relative acceptance of Asian babies by white families and revealed Tjossem's own aspiration to improve race relations at home. Wilma Brown's critique of Vietnamese adoptions similarly expressed a concern for the preservation of cultural differences consistent with racial ideologies championed by Asian nationalists. Adoption could "destroy the cultural beauty and difference of these people" by removing them from their "country and native culture." Tweaking the language of responsibility deployed during the war, she urged Americans who fostered children undergoing medical treatment in the United States to "help them preserve their autonomy, their cultural identification," thus easing their eventual reintegration into Vietnamese society.[69]

The National Association of Black Social Workers' impassioned 1972 statement condemning the adoption of black children by white families similarly complicated thinking about the cultural and political implications of adoptions from Vietnam, especially among white liberals sensitive to the sentiments of minority activists. Reflecting the influence of black nationalists, the group argued that interracial placements constituted a form of cultural assault, since white couples could not possibly appreciate or teach black children the strategies necessary for surviving in a racist society. Moreover, interracial adoptions, much like integration into white schools and neighborhoods, seemed to confirm a belief that admission into a white world assured black success.[70] Intensely debated in the media and academia, the association's declaration had as its practical and almost immediate consequence a drop in the already small number of black children matched to white families. The short but revealing accounts offered by prospective white parents about why they hesitated to adopt a part black, Vietnamese child illuminated the controversy's consequential effect on intercountry adoptions. While implying their personal comfort with interracial families, they pointed to a legal system and social climate inhospitable to such formations. In reply to a FMSVC survey that solicited views on race, gender, age, and disability, one couple wrote, "We feel we would run into problems in court if we tried to adopt a child of Negro background in this area." Similarly, Carol and James Urquhart were quick to establish their credentials as racially tolerant liberals, noting in the margins of their form, "Any race is all right with us." However, the couple asserted that "because of southern grandparents it would be better for us to have a Vietnamese or white Amerasian for our first adoption so as to bridge a necessary gap more easily." Here they acknowledged the resilience of separatist views held by whites as well as blacks, ones that they did not condone but that they felt unprepared or unwilling to challenge. Rev. Irving C. Beveridge's 1966 admission to FMSVC that he and his wife wanted a part white, Vietnamese child expressed even greater frankness about the intricacies of interracial families and black-white relations in the United States. Having already adopted four children classified by social workers as hard to place, including an American Indian and a multiracial child of European and African descent, Beveridge presented himself as more than a run-of-the-mill white racist. "Honestly and forthrightly," he maintained, "the whiter the easier for all concerned." The "Oriental racial characteristics are enough to handle all around" without the added stress of black ancestry. Indeed, as journalist Frank Chinook noted in his 1969 memoir about his adoption of a Vietnamese girl, race-based suspicions about and opposition to Vietnamese children becoming members of American families and communities inevitably confronted hopeful parents. When Chinook's wife revealed their plans to adopt a Vietnamese girl, an acquaintance responded, "Don't you know there's a war on over there, buddy? Besides, I'm not sure it's such a hell of a good idea to bring a Gook into a WASP environment."[71]

Although left-leaning couples acknowledged the pernicious power of racial and cultural differences, debts owed to Vietnamese peoples, and the difficulties of interracial families in an American society still conscious of race—ideas that encouraged some to oppose or at least agonize over adoption—many insisted on their readiness to deal with rather than avoid those distinctions and duties. In doing so, they aligned themselves with progressive ideas and practices emerging in domestic adoptions. Historian Karen Dubinsky traced the organization and extension through the United

States in the 1960s of a Canadian group, Open Door Society, whose advocacy of interracial adoptions, particularly those that brought together white parents and black children, respected the wishes and warnings of minority communities. By promoting academic research about adoption as well as teaching black history and culture to adopted children, the society sought a "politics of transracial adoption that was unifying, not colonizing." A dramatic rise in the number of American Indian children placed in non-Indian families by state welfare agencies, and the establishment of the Indian Adoption Project, a joint venture of the Bureau of Indian Affairs and the Child Welfare League of America launched in 1957, also revealed the more liberal racial views of adoptive parents even as it exposed U.S. policy makers' and social workers' construction of American Indian families as inadequate and incapable. In an article on the subject, Margaret Jacobs notes how administrators urged American couples to become agents of racial equality and integration by fostering and adopting individual American Indian children rather than aiding the youths' communities.[72]

A number of American couples seeking to adopt Vietnamese children cited previous adoptions of minority children as evidence of their open-mindedness regarding race and culture. Since Dorothy Smith's brother had adopted an American Indian boy and a Japanese American girl, she and her husband, Harvey, believed a Vietnamese child would "fit well into our larger family situation" and "internationalize the flavor of our family slightly." Alternatively, David and Leslie Leonard sought to confront the complexity of adopting a Vietnamese child in a racially divided United States by leaving the country. As soon-to-be residents of a university community in Africa, the couple proposed that such a foreign setting would "facilitate rather than complicate our raising of a Vietnamese child" because, "rather than the child alone being a racial stranger in a foreign land, our whole family will share the problem." A willingness to speak candidly about the reality of and their determination to manage cultural distinctions explained the tone and content of Paul and Amy Kaplan's inquiry to FMSVC. Rather than refute the difficulties, the couple stated that they "had thought seriously about the problems involved in raising a 'racially different child,'" and "only hope that we are capable of overcoming them." The "environments which we will be living in," they added, would at least "present the fewest obstacles possible." In their adoption statement to ISS, the Kellys emphasized similar themes. While acknowledging that the "Caucasian features and heritage" of the child they desired had precipitated her abandonment, they celebrated her "mixed culture and bloodline" as "truly attractive," and predicted "that most of this society would concur." Highlighting their sensitivity to "differences and values of Asian cultures," the Kellys promised to maintain Thu's Vietnamese heritage and "pride with her total identity." As much as personal desires, their calculations of current racial politics and ideologies shaped their approach to intercountry adoption.[73]

Marjorie Margolies, a Philadelphia-based news reporter and single woman who decided to adopt children from Southeast Asia in 1968, similarly grappled with and expressed an appreciation for the arguments against adoption, but ultimately found these assertions wanting, and made her case for a form of family reflective of the era's new gender and racial norms. In a memoir penned in 1976, Margolies explained that she became obsessed to the point of sleeplessness with finding a daughter from first Korea and then Vietnam after documenting a Holt-sponsored picnic of Asian adoptees and their new American families. Despite the initial protests of her parents, current boyfriend, fellow journalists, and select adoption agencies who urged her to observe social conventions—to marry and have a biological child—Margolies energetically pursued and eventually succeeded in adopting two daughters. The process required not only circumventing prejudices and formal restrictions against adoptions by single persons common in Southeast Asia and the United States, but also deflecting criticism about the political and cultural costs of adoption. After the adoption of a six-year-old Korean girl named Lee Heh, a former boyfriend asked Margolies whether it was "right for [the girl] to break all ties with her Korean culture and tradition," to which she replied, "It doesn't make me feel guilty at all." Much like the liberal, self-consciously political adoptive parents whose child-rearing practices reflected the era's multicultural ideals, Margolies tried to communicate some Korean traditions to Lee Heh. "We talk about Korea whenever something comes up. My father brought her a little Korean dress. . . . We've even found out how to make *kimchi*—the Korean salad—and she loves it," Margolies noted.[74] Yet, like other Korean children adopted in the United States to whose parents Margolies had spoken, Lee Heh appeared more interested in becoming and being American than in retaining Korean roots.

Having developed and refined her defense for Asian adoption in the case of Lee Heh, Margolies would defend her position against more heated challenges in the context of the Vietnam War. While simultaneously preparing a news story about and trying to adopt a Vietnamese child in 1973, Margolies secured the cautious, qualified aid of Nhu Miller—a Vietnamese-born, European-raised, and American-educated (Barnard and University of California, Berkeley) woman who had married Tom Miller and then resided in Vietnam—who told Margolies to "work with my people."[75] Nhu Miller shared Margolies's view, stating, "I'm not enthusiastic about having our children adopted and taken out of the country," preferring the traditional Vietnamese solution of care by extended family or friendly neighbors. "We have a saying in Vietnam," she informed Margolies during a conversation about the reporter's maternal ambitions: "If your father is dead, you still have an uncle. If your mother is dead, you have an aunt."[76] When Margolies asked whether mixed-race children fathered by American GIs might not "be better off coming to America," "coming to a home where they'll find love, not rejection," Miller still hesitated, observing that "Black children are discriminated in America, too." Undeterred, Margolies pushed back, telling Miller, "This is a war-torn country. It's very important to get children out of an orphanage into a family, especially in these crucial years." Miller did not disagree that war had disrupted and damaged the lives of Vietnamese children, but still recommended alternatives to adoption, namely that the United States should "take some of the money and use it to help families stay together in Vietnam, so we can take care of our children," placing many children in foster homes.[77]

Margolies, though, would have the last word, or perhaps, as Miller explained in a recent interview, Margolies's naïveté and earnestness finally convinced the Vietnamese woman to help. "I couldn't agree with you more," Margolies conceded. "But the fact is that's not the way it's happening right now, and I think we should deal with what exists. What exists is lots of kids in lots of institutions—some dying."[78] Margolies's exchange with Miller and conversations with a director filming a documentary about Vietnamese children did not sway her from her personal desire to support a Vietnamese child (she would eventually adopt a six-year-old Vietnamese American child allegedly found in a garbage can outside a U.S. Army base), but they did complicate her idea about adoption as a necessary and universal solution to the troubles of Vietnamese children. "My thinking about wholesale adoption is changing," she admitted. "Some of the children can be adopted by Vietnamese families right here. Some can be raised in foster homes. But there are some children who simply may not find a home here. I would say, get those children out."[79] In this more nuanced view, Margolies closed the distance or suggested moderate perspectives in the polarized debate about Americans' relationship with and obligations to Vietnamese children.

Single women and married couples who chose to adopt Vietnamese, especially those of mixed parentage, often accepted the view that American soldiers had contributed to if not created the problem, disrupting and

Tom and Nhu Miller, just married, 1973. Photo taken by William English Walling III. Courtesy of Tom Miller.

distressing local populations and shirking their paternal obligations. However, American men who had fathered or interacted with Vietnamese children in Vietnam objected to this characterization, revealing the complex and conflicted emotions that shaped their own engagement with the war and strengthened a call for national action on behalf of Vietnamese. Stories of American men who adopted Vietnamese children helped soften prevailing images of hardened soldiers insensitive to the people and landscapes of Vietnam, images that the U.S. military had so eagerly marketed in its defense of American intervention in Southeast Asia. Yet, in choosing to become fathers rather than part-time caregivers to Vietnamese children, removing them from the context of Vietnam and inviting them into nascent American families, they offered a version of the "gentle warrior" that undercut official representations and proposed a reimagining of gender roles and the preferred process of procreation. In his 1969 memoir, Chinook wrote fondly about Horace Muldoon, an army sergeant who fell in parental love with a young Vietnamese girl whom he found "huddled beside the dead bodies of her parents." In Chinook's telling the pair proved mutually dependent. The girl, whom Muldoon renamed Kathleen in honor of his mother, elicited an outpouring of emotions about "his doubts, his beliefs, his fears, his hopes" that the taciturn sergeant had previously repressed.[80] Despite his bachelor status, Muldoon pledged to bring Kathleen to the United States, a pledge that another GI and his wife would ultimately fulfill when Muldoon died a year later. The seemingly happy ending to a tragic tale underscored the kindness and depth of duty American men felt toward Vietnamese children. By highlighting Muldoon's affections, Chinook sought to burnish the image of soldiers and cast doubts about the U.S. intervention in Vietnam. Chinook understood Muldoon's desire to adopt a Vietnamese child as similar to his own, driven by "the way we feel about the situation there. Maybe this could be one positive act, one small saving of one small life. A grain of sand, I know, but it's something we individuals can do."[81] Chinook believed that this saving of one small life had a larger effect on the war. In the memoir's conclusion, he described the favorable reaction of an army colonel to the sight of him, his wife, Jan, and adoptive daughter, Kim, dining at a local restaurant. "'She's very beautiful,' the colonel noted, 'I wish my son could see her now, a part of your family, so happy. Maybe it would help him to—justify himself why he's over there. Thank you for giving me a—a better dream. Maybe something good can come out of it all. God knows, I hope so.'"[82]

Although Chinook emphasized his wife's willingness to become a mother to Kim, his longing for and discovery of a Vietnamese child overshadowed her parental ambitions. It was he who made the journey abroad, felt transformed by Vietnam, searched for and chose a child, and eventually brought the little one back to the United States. It was also Frank who spoke so romantically, even passionately, about the girl whom he found while touring the Duc Anh orphanage in Saigon: "And suddenly I knew. At that precise second, I knew. I knew—and could hardly restrain myself from reaching out and touching her head. But I guessed that if I did, like a butterfly she would flit away. It was enough to look. One from so many. . . . After all the searching, in one instant and at last, I knew."[83] In this drama of family creation, father and daughter take center stage while a presumably patient American mother waits for her cue to enter. Chinook portrayed that entry as effortless, suggesting that Jan and Kim formed an instant and intense attachment the moment they met at an American airport. If he had sidelined his wife and assumed a typically maternal role of bringing a child into being, Jan and the nuclear family appeared to recover their authority once Kim reached the United States.

Ken Armstrong, an army medic who defied social conventions and jumped bureaucratic hurdles to adopt a Vietnamese boy, was another American man who complicated gendered tropes about service and care. ABC News correspondent George Allen met Armstrong in 1967 and published the soldier's story in 1978, hoping to "celebrate Americans who did humane and heroic work during an unfortunate war." Armstrong expressed his misgivings about the conflict by selecting a specialization that would "best help people rather than shoot people who shouldn't be our enemy."[84] Assigned to the Vietnamese ward of an American field hospital, Armstrong cared for Vietnamese civilian casualties. Although he would develop a general appreciation and affection for the Vietnamese people whom he served, recognizing how closely their hopes and dreams resembled those of Americans, he formed a more focused fondness for a young, charismatic Cambodian amputee named Ri who entered the hospital after the death of his parents and siblings in 1967. In a letter written to his parents, Armstrong confessed that as much as the boy needed him, "this is a lonely place and I've become very attached to him."[85] Armstrong promised the boy that he would find him a family and a new leg, a promise he doggedly pursued even after Vietnamese working on the military base declined his request to adopt Ri and American friends dismissed his efforts as misguided. As he searched for alternatives, Armstrong attempted to host Ri on base, an unusual but not unheard of event; American soldiers in Korea and Vietnam cultivated local children as "mascots," young boys who wielded their charms and performed simple chores in exchange for food and shelter.[86] However, when Armstrong's superior officer refused to permit Ri in the barracks, Armstrong began a tour of orphanages that revealed the problems of institutional care in such a poor country. "A lot of the kids were dressed in old raggedly clothes and some looked as if they didn't get much to eat," Armstrong related. The discovery of and publicity about such conditions had persuaded many other Americans of the necessity of adoption. Armstrong did not make such a sweeping generalization—his current and later work with Southeast Asian children fostered an awareness of the challenges to and complexities of Vietnamese family relationships—but he decided he "wanted Ri. I didn't want to give

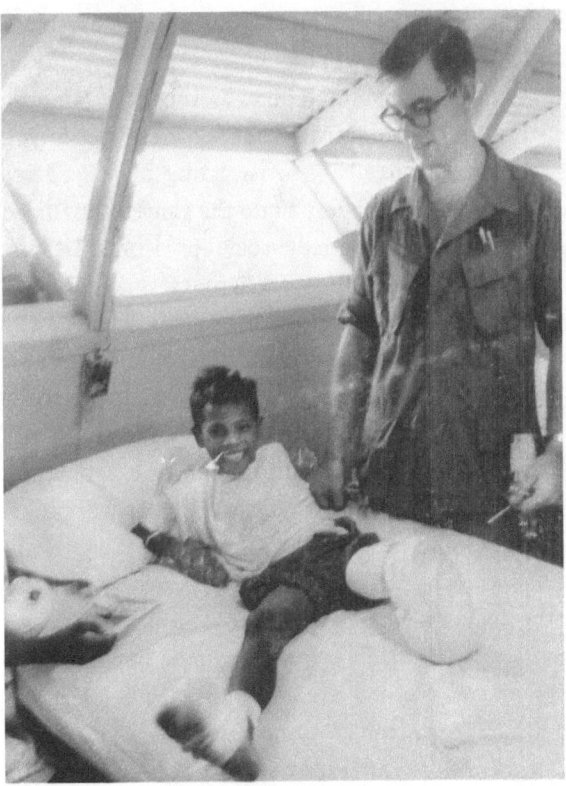

Ri and Ken Armstrong at field hospital in Vietnam, 1969.
Courtesy of Karen Armstrong.

him up. I had gotten to be a lot tighter with the little monkey than I had realized."[87]

Armstrong's decision to adopt Ri demonstrated the depth of his commitment, the transformative effects of Vietnam on soldiers, and the rigidity of American ideals about family. Armstrong realized that his status as a young, unmarried, white man might preclude his becoming Ri's father. His ingenious solution—to convince his parents to formally adopt Ri while he practically fathered the boy—revealed how attachments to Vietnamese children conjured conceptions of family at odds with still prevalent preferences for the nuclear type. In addition to the legal prohibitions against adoption by single Americans that had confounded the family ambitions of Margolies and others, Armstrong would have to anticipate sociocultural barriers, his friend Ralph reminded him. "Could you and your parents deal with neighbors who might not like having a dark child on the block?"

Ralph asked, and added that "it's a heck of a burden for a single person to try to bring up a child. Will the girl you'll want to marry some day be interested in a package deal that makes her an immediate mother? . . . Suppose he [Ri] has a delayed reaction to the traumas he has suffered? Could you give him the emotional support he needs?"[88] Armstrong dismissed his friend's cautions (and Allen invited his readers to do the same), convinced of his and his parents' ability to weather possible social pressures. Despite his resolve, Armstrong suffered the opposition of Vietnamese and American officials that only ended after years of repeated pleas and the advocacy of Wayne McKinney, an American doctor with World Vision who cared for children at Vietnamese orphanages. Armstrong stated, "I learned in three weeks that Wayne was an adoption nut: he believed that children should not live in orphanages. Every child was entitled to parents," a conviction that informed McKinney's status as "a real wheeler-dealer on adoption" who broke "laws left and right" and persuaded "all kinds of people who didn't care about adoptions to do things for him." Such creative circumventions of laws and protocols included arranging for Protestant and Jewish families to adopt Vietnamese children prior to Catholic baptisms and stealing blank birth certificates on which a compromised official would forge the names of children.[89] Armstrong's sympathetic portrait of McKinney's sometimes extralegal actions reflected how grateful he felt for the doctor's help securing Ri's exit visa as well as his work on behalf of Vietnamese children in orphanages.

As the most telling evidence of Armstrong's kindness and the capacity of American soldiers for redemption and a gentle form of paternal citizenship, Armstrong chose to linger in Vietnam and assume McKinney's medical responsibilities even after Ri flew to the United States to meet Armstrong's parents. "Wayne knew damn well that when I had fought so hard to save one kid, I couldn't walk away from all those others at An Lac, and Viet Hoa, and the two or three other orphanages," he explained.[90] At the close of Allen's account, Armstrong and Ri were finally reunited in Colorado, where the pair hunted, fished, and laughed. During Armstrong's absence, Ri had so quickly won the devotion of Armstrong's parents and five siblings that he chose to reside in their bustling household and regularly visit Armstrong and his fiancée, Patricia.

ISS officials doubted the verity or at least the universality of such happy endings to adoption stories, puncturing holes in the romantic image of American paternity and recovery. Elsie Hower observed that American soldiers became attached to children in orphanages who were often not orphans but "separated from families in this very fluid war." "The GI's emotions overcome him," she continued. "Almost impulsively he decides to adopt an appealing child." She conceded that the adoption might work out, but questioned what would happen if, "upon returning home with child, he finds his family rejects the foreign youngster whom they have never seen." "Or," she asked, "suppose he later finds out the child is retarded, emotionally disturbed or suffering a congenital defect? He and his wife now assume a tremendous financial and psychological burden" that might lead them to say, "We don't want the child. Take him away."[91]

Rather than speculative or alarmist, her concerns rested on specific cases of attempted or realized adoptions that frayed marriages. In one instance, an American GI adopted a Korean girl even though the girl's mother was alive. At age thirteen, the girl began corresponding with her birth mother and felt torn between two worlds. Exhausted by her behavior, the serviceman's wife threatened to leave him.[92] Another case featured a U.S. Air Force sergeant who won the initial support of his American wife and children to adopt a fourteen-month-old Vietnamese girl, Phan Thi My Le. According to an ISS worker, the Vietnamese mother felt "pleased to release her daughter because she is poor, she cannot support her and she is very young and she wants to get married." However, when Mrs. Scallion discovered that her husband had fathered Phan Thi My Le, she expressed reservations about her husband's ongoing relationship with the Vietnamese mother and fears that "the child will be his child and not a shared child." Taking seriously the woman's worries and evidence of broader marital tensions, ISS halted the adoption process.[93]

Despite the cautions of ISS officials, as the war dragged on and antiwar sentiment spread, a growing number of U.S. elected officials came to champion the cause of Vietnamese children, especially those of mixed race. Their advocacy suggested how completely the subject of adoption politics had become characterized by national recrimination by the early 1970s. No longer were politicians making exuberant speeches about the importance of liberalized adoption laws to the containment of Communism and the conversion of innocent children to the side of freedom (as had the likes of Senator Richard Neuberger when he defended the adoption program of Holt in the 1950s). In more chastened, if still dramatic, terms, they spoke about taking responsibility and burnishing the nation's dulled image in the world.[94]

In 1971, the Pearl S. Buck Foundation cheered the introduction of new laws intended to help Amerasian children, particularly a bill sponsored by Senator Frank Moss of Utah. The legislation would provide for the care, housing, education, training, and even adoption of orphaned children of Vietnam, giving special consideration to the sons and daughters of American soldiers. The timing of Moss's proposal and his impassioned defense of the bill mattered; mainstream political representatives now embraced views about the war and American obligations to Vietnamese children that they had long ignored or rejected. Moss noted that because mixed-race children of Vietnam were "as much a consequence of the United States' participation in the war in Vietnam as an American soldier who has been killed or wounded, or a peasant who has been shot or a group of villagers whose village has been destroyed," and since the United States had accepted responsibility for these soldiers and peasants, "it is a matter of conscience that the United States should likewise accept the responsibility of these orphaned children."[95]

Such official confessions of guilt and promises to make amends also shaped the policy recommendations issued by a special congressional subcommittee on refugees led by Senators Edward Kennedy, Harold Hughes, and Harrison Williams. After touring Vietnam in the summer of 1973, the committee reported that there were nearly 880,000 orphans or half orphans in Vietnam (a figure many experts deemed exaggerated) and recommended that the U.S. government act more assertively to address the crisis. "We look forward," Kennedy announced to President Johnson and fellow senators, "to working with you and members of your Administration in helping to heal the wounds of war within our society and among the people of Indochina."[96]

In lobbying for a proposed bill to facilitate the adoption of Vietnamese American orphans and resettled Vietnamese refugees that he had coauthored with Representative Howard Robison of Wisconsin, Representative William Steiger of New York echoed Kennedy's language of contrition and possible reconciliation. "We have a moral obligation to the thousands of Vietnamese children with an American parent who are left to fend for themselves," Steiger asserted. He then articulated a broader, more historical understanding of the problem, drawing clear lines of connection between repeated U.S. interventions in Asia since World War II and recurring generations of orphaned or displaced children. "This is a haunting reminder of the thousands of Japanese-American and Korean American children also left behind after the troops departed."[97] One might expect liberals to have celebrated the conversion of public officials to their way of thinking. However, in a sign of how adversarial the political climate had become, and how diminished were American expectations about the ability of its government to do good work in the world, many expressed only suspicion and distrust.

They questioned the authenticity and practical implications of official statements of responsibility. In 1971 Tom Tiede of the *Union* reminded Americans that "whether or not the Vietnam War is winding down, the social consequences of U.S. involvement there are assuredly winding up." Indeed, Buck insisted that the nation had reached a critical juncture, explaining that "there is nothing more important for our nation right now, for our image in Asia, than for our government and people to respond to these helpless babies and say, We recognize our responsibilities."[98] In 1973, as the United States dramatically drew down its troop levels, the media questioned the government's stated commitment to Vietnamese children. James Reston of *Providence Journal* chastised the Department of Defense for its failure to track the number of illegitimate children fathered by Americans or implement a program of care that offered citizenship and educational assistance akin to one designed by the French in 1954. Meanwhile Lawrence O'Rourke of the *Philadelphia Evening Bulletin* accused the nation, in its rush "to forget the Vietnam War," of "ignoring the tragic legacy of tens of thousands of orphaned children left behind." The children "survived the war," he added, but, "despite official denials from Saigon," "they are dying in the peace."[99]

As the United States escalated its commitments in Southeast Asia, Americans increased their commitments to the region's children, often choosing adoption because they believed in the power of the family to remake political wrongs and realize ideals of racial and gender fairness championed by the era's civil rights movements. Yet, rather than settle disputes and satisfy questions about the United States' place in the world and its obligations to Vietnamese, the migration of Vietnamese children exacerbated conflicts and intensified doubts about the nation's future. A botched airlift of children and its aftermath would further spotlight Vietnamese children, their tangled ties to Vietnamese kin, and the complex, unresolved outcomes of U.S. intrusions in Asia.

2 After the Airlifts

While debates about Vietnamese children had permitted Americans to openly negotiate their positions on race relations, foreign policy, and national identity, the conclusion of the conflict forced a hasty and ultimately failed effort to bring those negotiations to a close. In 1974, while Richard Nixon resigned and Gerald Ford assumed the presidency, Le Duan, Ho Chi Minh's successor and the first secretary of North Vietnam's Communist Party, met with army leaders and devised plans to win control over South Vietnam and reunify the country. A year later, the North Vietnamese Army attacked the Central Highlands, prompting a strategic retreat by the Army of the Republic of Vietnam (ARVN) and the migration of thousands of South Vietnamese civilians seeking surer ground. Yet, Communist troops pursued, winning control of coastal cities and Da Nang. When they eventually entered Saigon, President Ford accused the DRV of violating the 1973 Paris Peace Accords,[1] appealed to China and the USSR to help enforce compliance, and begged the U.S. Congress to authorize additional economic assistance for South Vietnam. Such measures failed to correct the course of defeat; President Nguyen Thieu, whom the United States had propped up since 1965 despite popular disapproval, widespread corruption, and internal divisions, fled the country and an overwhelmed ARVN surrendered. As Saigon collapsed, the U.S. government hurried to remove remaining American personnel and their South Vietnamese allies. Pushing against the desperate crowd, dodging bullets, and gripping the edges of military planes and helicopters, thousands found their way to safety. However, in the chaos of April 1975, most South Vietnamese first escaped not by air but by sea, a route of exodus that would define the mechanism and iconography of their migrations throughout the 1970s. In fishing boats, sampans, and rafts, they floated toward American and South Vietnamese vessels in the South China Sea.

Amid the confusion and as part of its targeted evacuation efforts, the U.S. government, in collaboration with social welfare and adoption agencies such as Holt International, Welcome House, United Catholic Relief Services, Friends for All Children (FFAC), and FCVN, also arranged for military and commercial planes to transport Vietnamese children to the United States.

In theory, the airlifts simply facilitated adoption proceedings already in motion; children selected for the airlifts had already been paired with appropriate American families, who impatiently awaited their arrival. However, in its rushed execution, the program resulted in confusion and tragedy. One of the first official flights, carrying an estimated 300 children and adult caregivers, exploded in midair. Christine D. Leivermann, who survived the crash of the C-5A Galaxy, remembered that "some part of the plane broke off, and started on fire." When she glanced to her left, she noticed "a hole worn in the side of the place, and I saw some of the rice paddy through that hole."[2] Although the craft's skilled pilot managed to land eventually, only half of the flight's passengers survived.

Rather than derail the evacuations, however, the horrific accident only strengthened the resolve of organizers to get children out of Vietnam. While expressing sorrow for the victims of the crash, President Ford insisted that "our mission of mercy must continue. . . . This tragedy must not deter us but offer new hope for the living."[3] In prioritizing the plight of Vietnamese children after years of relative inattention, the U.S. government adopted the rhetoric of responsibility long articulated by left-leaning Americans. Admitting the nation's culpability in the destruction and dissolution of Vietnamese families, officials sought not simply to atone for American sins and relieve the suffering of Vietnamese children but to control the peace. The war had gone poorly, they acknowledged, but they could still salvage the nation's reputation by arranging an honorable departure from Vietnam; saving more than 2,000 orphans from the clutches of Communists would be the perfect exiting maneuver. As historian Jeffrey Olick has noted, traumatic events such as the Vietnam War problematize the stories individuals and collectives tell to create a sense of national cohesion. What does a nation do with elements of its past, even a past that has not quite passed, that it wishes to forget? The government-backed Operation Babylift proposed a politics of regret, a preemptive attempt to manage the memory of the Vietnam War and thus the narrative of U.S. history by fulfilling an obligation to Vietnamese children. In expressing and acting on this obligation, American officials hoped to legitimize the U.S. government and unify the nation.

Thus politicians such as State Senator Paul Tsongas of Massachusetts defended the airlift, stating, "Very simplistically, it is better to live in elitism in the United States than to be dead in Viet Nam," a perspective echoed by presidential adviser, former air force brigadier general, and medical doctor Theodore C. Marrs. He praised the "basic decency of the American people," who were determined to help "when they see a child in trouble."[4] President

Among volunteers and military personnel who gathered at San Francisco's Presidio, President Gerald R. Ford carries a Vietnamese baby from Clipper 1742, one of the planes that transported South Vietnamese children from Saigon, April 5, 1975.

Ford agreed and seized the political moment, greeting one planeful of orphans at San Francisco International Airport on April 5, 1975. The deliberately choreographed and widely circulated photograph of the president holding a Vietnamese baby encapsulated the message the administration most hoped the public would accept: that the U.S. government was a fundamentally benevolent and trustworthy actor capable of correcting its mistakes.

Yet Vietnamese would disrupt these efforts and dispute this message, reappearing as refugees who sought familial reunion and re-creation within the United States. They fled the devastating consequences of decades of war. U.S.-led bombing campaigns between 1965 and 1972 in North Vietnam had destroyed factories, damns, bridges, schools, hospitals, villages, and even cities, precipitating a wave of migrants who looked for sanctuary in the south. Chemicals designed to strip away foliage and increase visibility for American troops not only poisoned Vietnam's air, soil, and water but caused sickness and birth defects. Overall, fighting between 1954 and 1975 had left 3.1 million Vietnamese (1.1 million military and 2 million civilians) dead.[5] Seeking to preserve life amid unfathomable loss, death, and ruin,

Vietnamese mothers, fathers, aunts, uncles, cousins, and grandparents had strategically chosen Operation Babylift as a means of assuring the safety of their young relations, with whom they intended to reconnect when or if they migrated to the United States. Thus, rather than orphans abandoned or relinquished, many of the children airlifted from Vietnam appeared to have family members who hoped to reclaim them. Vietnamese had embraced the evacuation as a necessary, if desperate, step in a larger process of migration and survival that could mitigate or manage their grief and disorientation. Those fortunate enough to reach the United States and initiate their plans of reconciliation, however, confronted the contrary ambitions of American families, agencies, and government officials who viewed adoption and the assimilation of Vietnamese children as both an apology for the nation's wrongs and an affirmation of its material and moral worth. In arguing for their parental rights and introducing Americans to the forms and obligations of the extended Vietnamese family, these refugees rejected American interpretations of the war in favor of their own, interpretations that challenged misconceptions of Vietnamese women as either helpless victims or scheming enemies, and shaped how they settled in the United States, sustained ties to Vietnam, and influenced foreign policy.

In the early, hectic days of Operation Babylift, most Americans endorsed the government's evacuation efforts, cheering media accounts of first encounters between parents and Vietnamese orphans. Writing that "not since the return of the prisoner of war two years ago has there been a news story out of Viet Nam with which the average American could so readily identify, one in which individuals seemed able to atone, even in the most tentative way for the collective sins of government," *Time* magazine suggested the event's importance to many American onlookers and participants, who were seeking a happy ending to the tragic tale of Vietnam.[6]

However, the initial exuberance and unqualified support American citizens and the mass media expressed in response to Operation Babylift soon turned to dismay and doubt. A flurry of editorials and news stories bitterly criticized the motives and conduct of the Ford administration, the Thieu regime, aspiring parents of Vietnamese children, adoption agencies, and volunteers. It was as if the floodgates of disappointment and frustration about the course of conflict had suddenly opened. On the brink of peace as well as during the war, adoption offered a medium through which Americans debated changing views of nation, family, and race relations. In 1975, the persistence, even escalation, of controversy about responsibilities to Vietnamese children and their increasingly visible and vocal families, mourning the loss of homeland and kin while building lives in the United States, anticipated the war's continued relevance to American society long after its formal end.

Observers challenged the humanitarian claims of Operation Babylift, highlighting its political motives. Disagreeing with the premise that one could "ferry freedom to children," or "ferry freedom at all," a lesson that she believed the United States should have learned after its "twenty-year involvement in Vietnam," Shana Alexander of *Newsweek* depicted the airlifts as an "abhorrent" government policy designed "to snatch honor from the jaws of dishonor." She reserved her strongest condemnation for the U.S. ambassador of Saigon, Graham Martin, whose "cynicism and stupidity" encouraged him to wonder if Operation Babylift would "help create a shift in American public opinion in favor of South Vietnam."[7] Awareness of this widely circulated comment prompted *Ms.* magazine's Grace Paley to come to the harsh conclusion that the "orphan airlift was a cynical political game played by the government in the hope that drama and sentiment would persuade Americans to give military aid to Saigon and continue the war."[8] In more qualified language, the *Christian Century* similarly doubted the purity of the U.S. government's motives. "Even as we rejoice in the happiness of those American families who have received Vietnamese children," the writer suggested, "we must once again look at the larger picture and consider that our government has acted in a manner that leaves it open to the charge of manipulation for public relations purposes."[9]

Rather than a new injury inflicted on the Vietnamese people, many journalists portrayed Operation Babylift as a continuation of a pattern of abuse, one that exposed the fundamental arrogance that had guided U.S. foreign policy for decades. Stating that "the final indignity for the Vietnamese is that, after we have bombed, strafed, napalmed and maimed half the population, we now take their children from under them," Desmond Smith, also a reporter for CBS, concluded in the *Nation* that these adoptions constituted a "traffic in used babies" that government officials should stop. Judith Coburn of the *Village Voice* agreed, arguing that despite its best intentions, the United States had once again "wreaked havoc on Vietnam's innocent," reflecting the same "kind of wrongheaded thinking that led to our involvement in Vietnam in the first place." This notion that the United States was a repeat offender who resisted reformation explained the intensity of the media attacks.[10]

The media targeted American citizens as often as it did the U.S. government in its critiques of Operation Babylift. Smith pointed an accusatory finger at infertile middle-class Americans with parental aspirations. Instead of selecting "the children of American ghettos, thousands of whom cannot find even foster homes," these couples followed fickle trends and Orientalist views, Smith argued, choosing to adopt Vietnamese children. Gloria Emerson represented adoptive parents in similarly unflattering terms. Barely disguising her contempt, she described the "middle-class women" who tearfully greeted their new "dark-eyed children" while "telling their reporters that their new names would be Phyllis and Wendy and David." Although they may have waited for years to adopt these children, Emerson acknowledged, "it is more than clear that the children are filling their needs as the Vietnamese have been doing for Americans for so very long." That these parents would suppress rather than nurture Vietnamese culture, as in the case of one woman who expected her Vietnamese daughter to light Hanukah candles and accept Judaism, was further evidence, Emerson claimed, of the selfishness and injustice of the airlift. Others accused those adopting of more than cultural insensitivity. According to an official statement issued by the ACLU, Americans were practicing the "same racism that permeated the war itself"; they mistakenly assumed that "growing up in a good American home is the best of all possible solutions for the children." What would happen to these "non-white children in white homes," queried Susan Abrams in an article published in *Commonweal*, when they inevitably began to "question their identity, to confront racism," but lacked the guidance and preparation presumably only minority parents could offer? The "affluence, status, upward mobility and Americanism" that an earlier generation of Americans had accepted as fitting and even preferable substitutes for native families and cultures were rejected by Abrams as against the "best interests" of the child.[11]

The concerns raised by African American newspapers and social service agencies shaped the highly critical position of the mainstream press. Alfred Herbert, director of the Black Child Development Institute's Adoption Project, objected to the practice of matching the majority of part black children airlifted from Vietnam with white couples. "The best placement for the black Vietnamese orphans is with black families," he insisted, because "there the children can best survive the racism in America and achieve a healthy identity through adoption by black families." An article published in the June 1975 issue of *Ebony* magazine challenged the racial implications of the airlift on different grounds. In speaking "for a good number of black Americans," it objected not to the evacuations per se but to the failure of the United States to make similarly heroic efforts on behalf of black orphans in domestic institutions. "The federal government is doing almost nothing about an adoption problem that is much larger and of longer standing than the Vietnam War problem," the author argued, and thus it should initiate "a domestic babylift," permitting "homeless black American children to find a sanctuary." In these and other responses to Operation Babylift, there resurfaced the same suspicions expressed by many minorities and white liberals during the war about the viability of interracial families in a society conscious of persistent ethnoracial hierarchies and determined to protect cultural differences.[12]

Vietnamese immigrants and South Vietnamese officials joined African Americans and white liberals in their condemnation of the airlift. According to Coburn, "Some antiwar Vietnamese legislators believe the Babylift is an effort by the U.S. to strip their country of future generations," and most Vietnamese social workers recommended that the United States invest money in Vietnam's child welfare system rather than evacuation programs. Coburn also reported that the Union of Vietnamese in America depicted the airlift as a "kidnapping" that demonstrated a lack of concern for the "millions of children and other Vietnamese left in the South." If Americans truly cared about Vietnamese children, they should persuade their government to end "the kind of political interference that created these orphans in the first place," a spokesperson of the organization argued during a press conference.[13] The most damning attacks from Vietnamese, however, were excerpted in Emerson's piece for the *New York Times*. She quoted both a Vietnamese immigrant who accused the United States "of killing us with your kindness for twenty years" and a South Vietnamese lieutenant who, soon after the crash of the C-5A plane, sardonically remarked, "It is nice to see you Americans taking home souvenirs of our country as you leave—china elephants and orphans. Too bad some of them broke today, but we have plenty more." Such bitter and frustrated expressions from Vietnamese only reinforced the angry, accusatory mood of many Americans.[14]

Vietnamese families, some of whom participated in a class action lawsuit instigated by the Center for Constitutional Rights (CCR) on behalf of their Vietnamese children removed during Operation Babylift, offered the most compelling criticism of the evacuation and revealed the complexities of Vietnamese migrations, family reformation, and gendered notions of nation in the wake of the war. The lawsuit and controversy originated at the Presidio, the largest of the reception centers quickly mobilized to tend and process children airlifted from Vietnam. Here, under the operation name Support of Vietnamese Orphans, an ad hoc planning committee of local political and business leaders called Orphans Airlift, volunteers, and military officials provided communication services, shelter, food, security, and medical assistance. Among those who answered the call for volunteers, specifically those fluent in Vietnamese, were Muoi McConnell, a Vietnamese nurse married to a former U.S. serviceman; Nhu Miller; and Mai Chaplin, a homemaker of Vietnamese descent. While caring and conversing with children at the Presidio, the trio expressed surprise that some of the youth did not appear to be orphans: they stated confusion about their whereabouts and a longing for living Vietnamese parents and kin. McConnell asserted that of the twenty-three children whose names she recorded, three reported having two living parents in Vietnam, fourteen asked about their mothers, and two described grandparents residing in the United States.[15] Chaplin recalled her exchange with two sisters who claimed their parents were alive and well in Qui Nhon. Reportedly, they had placed their daughters—two of their nine children—in a Catholic orphanage whose director agreed to send the girls to the United States to live until they could safely return to Vietnam.[16]

Dismayed and determined to resolve the seeming problem of the nonorphans, McConnell and Miller approached U.S. officials, whom they claimed promptly ignored their appeals for help. However, attorneys in the region active against the war, including Miller's husband, Tom, listened to the women's concerns, formed a committee, and immediately filed an action, *Nguyen Da Yen et al. v. Kissinger et al.*, in the U.S. District Court, Northern District of California, charging Secretary of State Henry Kissinger, former secretary of defense James Schlesinger, Attorney General Edward Levi, and seven adoption agencies with bringing children to the United States who were not orphans properly released for immigration. The plaintiffs argued that "some Vietnamese children are being held in the U.S. in violation of their right to liberty, separated from their natural parents and prevented from leaving the country to restore their natural ties." They deemed the children a unique group of aliens detained without the resources or awareness to challenge their condition. Plaintiffs demanded "the accumulation of defendant's records to determine each child's adoptive status and enable any living parents to be located," a process predicated on halting the adoption proceedings of American families, whom they conceded may be "concerned and loving" but "no substitute for biological parents."[17]

Indeed, while expressing sympathy for adoptive families and eschewing political motives, the plaintiffs emphasized the superiority of Vietnamese families and the harm done to displaced Vietnamese children, and suggested the U.S. government's fundamental flaws. In their motion for preliminary injunction, lawyers asserted that they did not intend to challenge the wisdom of admitting children during the last days of war, a clarification that seemed to remove the question of child custody from the context of controversy about the war's closure. However, over the course of the trial, they struggled to maintain an apolitical stance and refrain from a broader commentary about the perceived injustice of the war and the ignorance of American couples. In their complaint for declaratory and injunctive relief, the plaintiffs' attorneys aired their grievances, accusing the government of orchestrating Operation Babylift "to create a climate of opinion favorable to the continuation of unconstitutional and illegal U.S. involvement in the war in South Vietnam to the end of securing from the United States Congress authorization and appropriation of additional funds to militarily support the war, and to provide a cover for United States military intervention." In other documents, the plaintiffs found fault with adoptive parents as well as the officials and agencies who enabled their efforts. "It is not difficult to imagine the pain and suffering the plaintiff children have already undergone, living their entire lives in a country torn by war, ripped from their families and home, brought thousands of miles away, held on military bases to be placed with families, no matter how well intentioned, of an alien culture with whom they are unable to communicate," insisted lead attorney for the plaintiffs, Nancy Stearns, in a court memo. As support for this interpretation, she offered the testimony of Joyce Ladner, a sociologist and civil rights activist who studied transracial adoption. Although Ladner acknowledged that "Asians may not experience as much hostility in the predominantly white American society" as African Americans, she believed that "they do experience subtler forms of discrimination." Moreover, she predicted that Vietnamese adoptees in particular would "face additional hostility as a result of feelings of anger in many Americans regarding the Vietnam war" and would suffer "a racial identity crisis comparable to that in black children." Claiming the virtues of Vietnamese families, she concluded that "even if the circumstances to which they return are less economically secure than the American homes they are presently in, emotional security must not be traded for a middle class life style where racial and cultural gaps are so broad and so often ignored."[18] Her portrait of Americans as a group whose false faith in material advantages blinded them to the problems of transracial families exposed a broader, leftist opposition to capitalism that had served as the foundation for the antiwar movement and informed the plaintiff's case, but that members of the CCR strategically preferred to understate.

In her April 1975 affidavit, Miller further elaborated these points. She noted that Americans misunderstood the structure and strength of Vietnamese families, creating an unnecessary and self-serving crisis. Vietnamese practiced an extended system of family in which "if you lost your father, you still have your uncle. If you lose your mother, your aunt will still nurse you." Rather than asylums, she explained, orphanages were used as places for boarding children during times of economic or political crisis. She stated, "Foreign adoption is an alien and repugnant notion to the Vietnamese." Miller countered a picture of neglectful or absent Vietnamese mothers, chastising "foreigners, who see only orphanages and assume the Vietnamese don't care for their children, do not hear about mothers struggling alone to care for ten children or women caring for children left in their care permanently who would never consider putting them in an orphanage."[19] Miller's portrait of maternal struggle and adaptation disrupted prevailing images of Vietnamese women that had shaped U.S. assertions in South Vietnam. Perpetuating a habit of feminizing Asian nations and casting Asian women as victims or vixens, U.S. media, soldiers, and policy makers alternatively imagined themselves as protecting and punishing a vulnerable, if sometimes treacherous, South Vietnam. Lost within these gendered constructions and justifications of military action were the real Vietnamese women whom Miller depicted: individuals making tough but deliberate choices amid arduous circumstances.[20] So confident was Miller in her conception of caregiving customs and the will of Vietnamese mothers that she and her husband long resisted assuming fuller responsibility for Oktober, the son of a Vietnamese woman, A., who had pleaded for their help.[21] Miller's mother, BachLan, had first supported the boy, but when she died, Miller felt compelled to help A. "take care of her own child." Miller removed Oktober from the orphanage where he spent some of his days, after determining that its operators "were essentially selling the children." And when she finally agreed to A.'s pleas "to take care of him" more permanently and bring him to the United States, Miller made certain Oktober sustained a relationship with his Vietnamese mother.[22]

The cases of Vietnamese families who endured separations and sought reunions in the United States seemed to underscore Miller's picture of caring Vietnamese kin and Americans' propensity to sin. Le Thi Hang, whose work as an interpreter in a U.S. hospital in Vietnam familiarized her with

American personnel and regulations, placed two of her five children, Phuong and Holly, with Catholic charities, and begged the organization "to get them out" before conditions deteriorated further in 1975. As she said her farewells, Le Thi Hang pressed into their hands a photo inscribed with a message intended to reassure and inspire: "My wish is for you to grow up free. We would rather be away from this country and live in freedom than be together under Communism." When Le Thi Hang and her remaining children arrived in the United States four months later, she began hunting for Phuong and Holly. Despite the reluctance of an Oregon-based foster family to release their charges, the adoption papers they had filed were not yet processed, and Le Thi Hang recovered her children with the help of a Catholic priest. During a 2011 interview, she recalled the joy of the trio's meeting. Her antipathy to Communism animated not only her plans of dividing, migrating, and eventually reuniting her family, but also her service to other Vietnamese refugees. After settling and opening a successful restaurant in Decatur, Georgia, during the 1980s, the Le family would sponsor as many as 150 Vietnamese families.[23]

Reclaiming her children within a context of virulent anti-Communism and diaspora, Le Thi Hang confirmed an American narrative about the downfall and doom of Vietnam. However, her assertion of maternal rights as a refugee sheltered by the United States also underscored the failure of modernization and militarization in South Vietnam; rather than being rescued or reprimanded under the discipline of American masculine power—fantasies that had propelled American policy in Southeast Asia—Vietnamese women surfaced as independent forces seeking a place and power as parents within their new nation. Despite the trauma of dislocation and migration, experiences that many refugees have sublimated with silence, these women spoke out. Their declarations repurposed Vietnamese social norms and cultural types. Vietnamese society had valued women's reproductive and motherly talents. The war both intensified the importance of and imperiled their duty to protect and prepare the next generation. While men's contributions to the nation were typically connected with their military service and camaraderie, Vietnamese women demonstrated service by enduring separations from their adult children, especially enlisted sons, and waiting for peace. These gendered interpretations persisted in postwar Vietnam. Women were honored for surrendering and mourning their lost sons, a form of reverence that elided the less passive and broader roles they had played in combat and in daily life by managing households, businesses, farms, and family.[24]

Like the Les, many refugees replayed and refined Vietnamese constructions of gender and family within the United States, using the lawsuit spearheaded by CCR to reunite with their dependent relatives. After the death of one son and one daughter in 1968, Nguyen Thi Phuc feared for the future of her remaining children. "If I don't let [my sons] go out, then when they grow up the boy have to go military, had to go fighting. They die. I know that," she stated during court testimony. Resisting the trope of sacrificial mother and risking retribution for being disloyal to the Socialist Republic of Vietnam (SRV), Nguyen Thi Phuc sent her boys to the United States in 1972, and two years later, as she heard "the bomb and rocket shoot very close to Saigon," she placed her daughters in the care of a Mr. Jacobs, who agreed to bring the pair safely to the United States. Nguyen Thi Phuc insisted that she had never signed relinquishment papers, and she had secured the promise of Mr. Jacobs that "if I stay in my country, later where I stay I be safe, he return my children to me." However, eighteen months later, when she arrived at Fort Chafee, Arkansas—the domestic military base that processed more Southeast Asian refugees than its counterparts, Camp Pendleton in California, Eglin in Florida, and Indiantown Gap in Pennsylvania—and attempted to recover her four children, she met significant hurdles. Her sons' foster parents wished to adopt rather than surrender the boys, and despite her queries to immigration officials, the United States Catholic Conference, and local press, she could not determine her daughters' whereabouts.[25] Dang Thi Hao showed similar resolve and met similar obstacles as she solicited assistance in winning back her two-year-old daughter—whom a Catholic organization had brought to the United States—from Camp Pendleton officials. Fear, not neglect, had prompted Dang Thi Hao to yield the girl, she pleaded, but her pleas fell on deaf ears. Reportedly, one authority even urged her "to have another child," a deeply disrespectful, even if not premeditated, remark that betrayed an insensitivity to the histories and individuality of Vietnamese refugees. Dang Thi Hao told Tom Miller that "there were other women seeking the return of their children, but they were being intimidated by the military and voluntary agencies."[26] Char Thi Lan also portrayed American bureaucrats, specifically those employed at the California Department of Health and INS, as anything but helpful. Despite her appeals, she had failed to recover her four-month-old niece, whose mother had not consented to the airlift.[27] In these three cases and many others, Vietnamese women not only found fault with the American government and demanded reflection on its responsibilities to refugees, but configured their authority and relationship to the United States in parental terms. They drew on a respect for mothers in Vietnamese culture while criticizing a war and regime that had compromised their ability to fulfill that function. Rather than shore up SRV by gifting their children, these women had dispatched the youth to the United States, where they now expected to retrieve them and enact their maternal powers.

In another instance illuminating the confusion of Vietnamese migrations, their flexible notions of kinship, and their dedication to family renewal and reassertion in the United States, San Shie admitted that she had accepted the evacuation of a female cousin and surrogate daughter, San Nang-Hien, to ensure the girl's survival, but never intended the girl to be adopted by a U.S. State Department official. According to San Shie's biological daughter, her mother, who "raised San Nang-Hien as her own," as "is common in Vietnamese families that are very close knit," had entrusted the two-year-old to the temporary care of a United States Agency for International Development (USAID) employee with the expectation that San Shie would reclaim the baby when she eventually reached the United States. Much to San Shie's stated surprise, San Nang-Hien had been given up for adoption to Marie Dehner, a State Department official whom San Shie claimed "refuses to speak with me or my family on the telephone," a refusal that caused the Vietnamese refugee "great personal stress and anguish." When a friend and advocate of San Shie finally managed to contact Dehner, the American allegedly explained that she could not return the baby because "she would not have time to complete the adoption proceedings before her next assignment," and "she had already suffered the sharp disappointment of having to return another child." Dehner flexed her powers as a white American, a government employee, and a woman who longed to parent, but her rival countered by demonstrating persistence, emphasizing the value of kin, and communicating her anguish as a victim of war. Finally resolved in favor of San Shie, the custody battle displayed a muddied process of adoption, the tangled webs of Vietnamese familial relations, and the divided streams of Vietnamese migration that sought confluence.[28]

From the perspective of Vietnamese families, whose stories of separation and attempted recovery bolstered the plaintiffs' assertions, adoption agencies were as much to blame as the U.S. government. "My son, Tung, is not an orphan, but was brought here under false documentation by the adoption agency. I never signed a release for his adoption and never intended that he be released for adoption," wrote one Vietnamese woman in a letter to the acting district director of INS. Making clear her maternal affections and dedication, she stated that she had tried to locate her son "ever since coming to the United States as a refugee" and "loved him dearly and am able to provide him with a good home." She expressed gratitude for those who "helped bring my son to safety when there was danger in Saigon," but wished that "the same kindness will be shown in returning my son to me now that the danger is over."[29] Hoang Van Thanh, a Vietnamese refugee wishing to locate his nephew and niece, similarly portrayed the agency as recalcitrant. When he contacted Holt International, Helen Miller, supervisor of social Services, acknowledged the placement of his one-year-old niece, Quy, with an American family, but flatly dismissed the possibility of the girl's return. Instead, she asked the uncle to "tell us more about her parents, and other relatives," since "this sort of information is very helpful to the adoptive parents when she begins to inquire about her Vietnamese heritage." Revealing the assertive maternalism and Christian confidence emblematic of many adoption agencies, Miller urged Hoang Van Thanh to focus on "getting adjusted to living in the United States" while his niece was "getting adjusted to her new family."[30] However, Hoang Van Thanh refused Miller's advice to redirect his energies and abrogate a promise he had made to his sister, who, reassured by his pledge to find her two eldest children, had "felt alright to stay behind in Vietnam to take care of her two other children." In a letter to Nhu Miller, whose help he implored, he described the Holt agent's advice as "too cruel," and the source of heartbreak for him and his wife. "We wished our nephew and niece be dead rather than living on this American soil and being unable to see us," he exclaimed, suggesting the intensity of his commitment to repairing his family and repudiating the offered wisdom of adoption agents.[31]

Cases of Vietnamese families searching for lost children in Vietnam, presumably unaware that their kin had reached the United States and resided with Americans, not only raised questions about the clarity of the adoption process, but made visible the reach and endurance of Vietnamese families. *Tin Sang*, a private, Catholic newspaper based in Saigon, published the photos and physical descriptions of missing children. Examples of its brief postings included "Uncle Nguyen Van De seeking nephew, Locung Vann, 8 years old," "Ding Van, 4 years old. Last seen wearing blue pants and yellow cotton shirt," and "Seeking Nguyen Ngoc Chau, 4 years old, Hair parted, Round Head. Last seen at the stone bridge in Nha Trang. . . . If anyone has seen or is taking him, would you please come to 99 Pham Nguy Lao."[32] Certainly, reasons other than emigration and adoption may have explained the disappearance of these children—death or alternate homes within

Vietnam—but their numbers and age and the timing of the appeals suggested the possibility that they now resided within the United States. From both within and outside Vietnam, Vietnamese demanded reunions, and made vows that disputed American efforts to contain the legacies of the war.

While evidence of Vietnamese families attempting restoration shed doubt on the intentions and consequences of the airlift, adoptive parents and agencies represented by the defense countered that these children were legitimately abandoned, suffering, and available; that agencies had followed proper protocols; and that "the lawsuit was politically motivated and had nothing to do with the children."[33] In speaking in defense of the mass evacuations and adoptions, they represented themselves as voices of responsibility and reason who had sometimes risked their lives and definitely invested their time on behalf of Vietnamese children. If American soldiers had hoped to substitute or at least soften their image as strong warriors fighting the enemy with images of father figures caring for the innocent casualties of war, many women wished to maintain their politically influential positions as the protectors of national values and creators of American families. Such constructions, however, often positioned them against diasporic Vietnamese families, and especially Vietnamese women, who just as actively deployed gendered ideas of care and belonging to claim space and command in their adopted home. In an affidavit describing the procedures by which South Vietnamese children came into the custody of FFAC, Rosemary Taylor insisted that agencies operated "devoid of political associations" and helped children who were confirmed as orphans within institutions recognized by the Ministry of Vietnam. Her longtime collaborator, registered nurse and airlift participant Susan McDonald, agreed and expressed incredulity, when asked about the lawsuit during an interview in 1990, that "back in America," their actions were questioned and "some people were saying that the children we brought out were kidnapped." She countered this skepticism, stating, "[I had] seen how orphanages were" and "how many orphans were left in Vietnam."[34]

When approached by INS about the legality of bringing Vietnamese children to the United States, former activist and FCVN member Pam Purdy also defended the operations of agencies by emphasizing the chaotic conditions in Vietnam and opportunities in the United States. She exclaimed, "What's legal about war anyway! Sure, some mothers might have panicked and rushed their children onto planes. But what would there be for Hoang Stephen [the Vietnamese boy whom she had adopted] if he were returned—half-American and half-Vietnamese in a Communist country?"[35] Cherie

Clark, the adoptive parent and admitted leftist whose admiration for American volunteers in Vietnam had changed her mind about the virtue of allowing political principles to motivate adoption, agreed.[36] As overseas director of FCVN, Clark maintained the integrity of agency protocols and challenged the plaintiffs' negative representation of its work with Vietnamese children. The organization provided "primarily life support" and "secondarily facilitated the adoption" of "hopelessly and undeniably abandoned children."[37] She noted that FFAC had never had reason to distrust the actions of orphanages, nor had mothers or their relations contacted the agency seeking the return of such children.[38]

In fact Clark and other workers consistently held that they discouraged Vietnamese from giving up their children, but those who did so felt at peace with the choice. "[Duong Bich] Van called me on the telephone and I talked to her for a long time about Tuan. Van stated that she was pleased he was doing well," Clark reported of a conversation with one Vietnamese woman whose child now resided with American parents. When Clark told Duong Bich Van that Tuan "loved his adoptive father very much," the woman replied that "he always wanted a father." According to Clark, although tearful and touched with great emotion, Duong Bich Van expressed no doubts about the placement, saying, "I'm glad he is happy," and she never suggested she wanted the boy back.[39] Clark's depiction proposed the possibility for real empathy and understanding between Vietnamese and American women, despite gendered iconography to the contrary: in the minds of American soldiers and policy makers, white, middle-class women and Vietnamese women were antagonistically constituted.

Clark shared another tale of contented relinquishment, one that emphasized the methodical, emotional, and collective process by which large Vietnamese families plotted plans for their survival. Clark related that after escaping from Pleiku province with their extended family, Nguyen Hun and his wife, Lam Hoang Phuong, "were pleading and begging" her to accept three of their children, Tuyen, Yen, and Vuong, for adoption because "they wanted so many things for their children that were not possible under communism." Yet, she had initially refused their appeals and urged them to reflect. Lam Hoang Phuong's aunt, who served as an associate director of FCVN, reported that her family did not waver in its belief that the children were better off in the United States because "we won't have freedom to live our lives, the way we wished, to raise our children in a good way and they won't be able to have a good life." Tuyen, Yen, and Vuong's great-aunt, Le Thi Nga, echoed these views and further illuminated how adoption emerged after conference among extended kin. In her affidavit she explained, "We made a plan to evacuate the children. . . . So, it was the best solution for our young and innocent children out of a war-torn country under Communism. . . . It was a heart-broken decision that we all faced. I know it very clear because those meetings and discussion was happening at my house [in my] presence most of the time."[40]

After similarly wrenching, inclusive conversations and displays of persistence, other Vietnamese families would persuade Clark (and presumably other agency workers) to facilitate the adoption of their relations. Nguyen Khanh Lien remembered her aunt and uncle's earnest discussions with their sisters, brothers, and twelve children about the love, care, education, and freedom that only Americans could provide. Clark explained that when she consented to help Khanh Lien, the mother put her arms around Clark and cried, "Camon Ba Cherie" (Thank you, Cherie), while the father "held my hand and said Thank you." Their gratitude and commitment did not fade, Clark asserted, even as they "expressed sorrow because they loved their children *very much*." These testimonies portrayed Vietnamese as caring pragmatists who so believed in the advantages of American society and the dangers of Communism that they agonized over, but ultimately advocated, family division. They also displayed American women as the confidantes and enablers of Vietnamese, those who could best translate and transfer the powers of family formation.[41]

While echoing her colleagues' defenses of agency activities and sensitivity toward Vietnamese families, Wende Grant also attempted to unmask what she viewed as the unstated intentions of the plaintiffs.[42] In a letter to adoptive parents of FFAC notifying them of the class action suit, she wrote, "I believe the motivation of these people who brought the suit is political and that the children are being used as an instrument without real regard for the best interests of the children as a group or as individuals." Expressing a sense of outrage and injury that captured the likely sentiment of her audience, she explained that "I am filled with anger that the role of the agencies in Vietnam has been maligned, at least by inference, after years of work with the children in Vietnam. Those who worked with the thousands of abandoned, orphaned, sick, malnourished, handicapped, retarded and psychotic children in Vietnam are being accused of stealing healthy children."[43] Responding to Paley's article in *Ms.* condemning the airlift, Suzanne Dash, the adoptive mother of four Vietnamese children and a former staff member in an adoption agency, reiterated that "most of the women were not attempting to save the children from Communists, offer them

Christianity, salve their guilt about the war, steal the babies from their mother's arms, or deprive a country of its future generations," as the plaintiffs and leftists contended, but to give Vietnamese children "a chance at life—the promise of a mother and father instead of a no one."[44]

On learning of the lawsuit, adoptive parents—once convinced their actions were just, even praiseworthy—struggled to comprehend its origins and consequences. Some adopters, including John DeCamp, a Nebraska state senator, Vietnam veteran, and once avid proponent of the airlifts, accepted the pleas of Vietnamese parents and voluntarily surrendered airlifted children.[45] Less public figures also prepared to give up children whom they had begun to make their own. After six months of bonding with her new Vietnamese daughter, My Hang, her adoptive mother, Lisa Brodyaga, became convinced that the girl was not an orphan. Brodyaga claimed that rather than facilitate an investigation, adoption agencies and social workers pressured her to file for adoption, accept My Hang as her child, and think "less about the possibility that she might be returned to Viet Nam." She also faulted INS, whose investigation, pursuant to a court order, she described as "highly superficial," because the agent had made no attempt to speak with My Hang directly or through an interpreter.[46] Despite this resistance, Brodyaga continued to seek details of My Hang's migration and offered a broader, leftist critique of the airlift and its aftermath. "I don't think we can say that My Hang was abandoned at all. I think her status would be questionable both morally and legally, even if we had a signed release for her. It seems the Americans were involved in spreading the belief that children of mixed parentage . . . would be killed by Communists."[47] In a December 1975 letter to Congress, she sustained her criticism and proposed a new approach to U.S.-Vietnam relations. Americans could best fulfill what she deemed the "compelling moral mandate to reunite these children with their families" by normalizing relations with Vietnam and then assisting Vietnamese "in the arduous task of rebuilding their homeland and healing the wounds left by the war. The American people deserve an opportunity to demonstrate that their concern is genuine." Anticipating the appearance of My Hang's mother and the rightful claim she would make for the child, Brodyaga struggled to maintain My Hang's knowledge of her native language and "awareness of her mother, and family as far as possible." Yet she feared that "the longer she is away, the more entangled her family becomes in fantasy, and the less urgent her demands to return." The girl still collected "treasures for her mother, Dzui, and her baby sister, Tu Oanh," Brodyaga noted, but had begun talking about bringing her family to the United States rather than returning to Vietnam, a sign that her expectations had shifted away from repatriation. To "well meaning Americans" who presumed Vietnamese children were worse off under Communism, she countered that "I cannot convince myself that kidnapping is an appropriate response to ideological differences," and argued that it would not satisfy the ultimate curiosity of children who wondered, "Who am I and how did I get here?" By arguing that Vietnamese children best belonged with their native families and culture despite traces of assimilation or the affection and material prosperity Americans could offer, Brodyaga expressed an opposition to the consequences of war, anti-Communist beliefs, and American perceptions of Vietnamese culture emblematic of the Left and the politicized discourse of adoption.[48]

Unlike Brodyaga and State Senator DeCamp, many other new American parents refused even to consider relinquishment; they doubted the legitimacy of the Vietnamese parents' claims, expressed their deep attachments to Vietnamese children, and highlighted the greater comforts and security U.S. society could offer. Some acted collaboratively in newly created parents' groups such as the Council for Rights of Adoptive Families in Cupertino, California, to protect their interests.[49] Others protested the charges and implications of the lawsuit independently. Joan Thompson, an adoptive mother and one of the most vocal defenders of the airlifts, argued that "we think this is the best country possible—the kids have a much better chance to grow up here, to be what they want."[50] Katherine and Dale Strand agreed, noting that although they had no intention of encouraging their adoptive Vietnamese daughters and son "to disassociate themselves from their family or existence in Vietnam, their overriding concern was (and is) to provide a warm, loving, safe environment for three beautiful but very sickly children who arrived at our home just a little over a year ago."[51] According to a home study completed by the Department of Social Work, the couple occupied a "large, clean house" in a cosmopolitan neighborhood that hosted a chapter of the Open Door Society, were "outgoing" and "friendly," and had proved through their successful adoption of a Korean girl years earlier that "they can accept and parent a child different from themselves."[52] Katherine acknowledged that Rebekah, Rachel, and Aron (aka Tuyen, Yen, and Vuong, the same three Vietnamese siblings discussed above) had learned English and American customs slowly, but insisted that the children soon felt very comfortable, secure, and determined to fulfill their Vietnamese mother's wish that they "go to America to live and be happy."[53] "In the months which have passed since the three children have come into our family, my wife and I and our four other children have grown to love them and the converse is true as well," Dale elaborated in his affidavit, expressing an affection that he and other adoptive parents offered as evidence that it was in the "best interest" of the children to stay with their American families.[54] Whenever possible, the adoptive parents emphasized that migration and adoption realized the will of Vietnamese families to obtain better lives for their children.

Committed to maintaining custody and incredulous of charges raised by select Vietnamese families, some Americans moved to mitigate their risk. Although adopted in 1975 by an American professor of music, Sandra, who was informed that her daughter's Vietnamese mother had died and relatives disappeared, a four-year-old Merrie Li knew differently. She remembered her grandmother promising that aunts and uncles who had resettled in California would assume care for her and her younger brother, Tony, while her mother labored to leave Vietnam. "From what they knew I was an orphan," Merrie Li recalled of Sandra and her American sisters, "yet they couldn't understand how I knew the things that I knew, things like I could set a table with multiple silverwares, like I was expecting a five-course meal. They didn't understand how I knew how to do that stuff, but that was actually how we were raised." If Sandra did not realize the circumstances of Merrie Li's upbringing or the existence and specific intentions of her Vietnamese family, she still worried enough to send the girl away from their home outside Andrews University, a Seventh-Day Adventist institution in Berrien County, Michigan, to a private high school in a small Tennessee town. According to Merrie Li, while working with immigration authorities to clarify her daughter's citizenship status (as a single mother barred from adoption, Sandra had used a proxy in 1975, an act that raised legal complexities), Sandra learned that Vietnamese "trying to locate their families and trying to take them back because they felt that it was the duty of the family to take care of the children" were searching most diligently in locations where the Seventh-Day Adventist Church, which had handled Merrie Li's adoption, had a strong presence.[55]

Although sympathetic to the accounts of adoptive parents and agencies, Judge Spencer Williams felt sufficiently swayed by the arguments of the plaintiffs to order an investigation of adoptive cases, a decision that immediately prompted objections by the defense about invasions of privacy and the possible harassment of children. Not trusting the integrity of the INS review process—the plaintiffs charged that investigators failed to use Vietnamese interpreters, ruled children eligible despite incomplete or falsified documentation, and generally bent to federal pressure to favor American parents—the government and plaintiffs' attorneys chose experts, Mas Yonemura and Ta Van Tai, respectively, to read a sample consisting of 500 of the 2,242 case files on behalf of the court. Independently, Yonemura and Tai arrived at the conclusion that 30 percent of the children were *not* validly released for adoption, a figure that differed dramatically from INS's 10 percent.[56] Although higher than the INS's calculation, plaintiffs' attorneys believed the experts' figures still undercounted ineligible children. After reviewing *all* the records and applying a broader standard, they had excluded almost 68% of cases: 246 files of children who were in the process of being adopted or released but lacked documentation, 715 cases missing parental releases, and 553 instances in which family had signed releases under duress during the final months of the Vietnam War.[57]

Confronted by these conflicting reports and divisive testimonies, the judge ruled that "the case was not properly a class action suit" because "each child's situation [proved] so individual that common questions did not predominate over individual issues." He represented the cases as so complex and dizzyingly unique as to defy the kind of generalization the plaintiffs desired. While acknowledging the confusion and occasional duplicity that had shaped the removal of Vietnamese children, he expressed skepticism about the plaintiffs' broad advocacy of reunification: "While beyond the scope of this court's inquiry in this litigation, it is possible, in the individual circumstances peculiar to certain children, that the best interest of the children would not be a return to biological parents. It is not necessary to ruminate too extensively to imagine many situations where, for emotional, psychological, medical or other reasons, a child would be better off remaining with the adoptive parents." He also raised doubts about the process of tracking down and restoring parental rights to Vietnamese relatives who had not initiated searches, a process Tom Miller and cohorts had attempted to instigate by placing newspaper advertisements and writing letters that invited action in Vietnam. "If the parents of the children did not want them to remain in Vietnam, such contact as could be directly made might awake guilt feelings and prompt a desire for the return of the children which might in turn be an illusory desire," and thus the minors, whose interests the court had a duty to protect, "might not be in a satisfactory situation," Williams noted.[58]

This assertion echoed the views of McConnell, the Vietnamese nurse named guardian ad litem in the suit, and suggested that in stretching their discovery efforts to Vietnam, the plaintiffs may have overreached. In a letter to Judge Williams dated September 17, 1976, McConnell traced the path to her disenchantment. "As a mother, I had strong feelings for these children.

I could imagine how distressed I would be if my children were lost in another country and no one helped reunite the family," she offered as explanation for her participation early in the case. However, over time she "[went] along with the position of the lawyers," even though, "generally, I thought the interests of the children and their family were being lost in the ambiguities of legal matters." Her willingness to accept the strategic choices of the plaintiffs ended when they allegedly altered a letter sent to Vietnamese parents that she had translated. According to McConnell, "The entire tone and content of the letter sent was not the same as the draft I approved."[59] The doctored version portrayed Vietnamese children in preadoptive homes as mistreated, a portrait likely intended to rouse Vietnamese families to rescue their youths. Such seeming manipulation of her words and circumstances prompted McConnell to withdrawal from the case, telling the judge, "I do not wish any further involvement with people who seem to be using me and my feelings as a mother to further their political ambitions."[60] The plaintiffs regretted McConnell's defection and the court's ruling, which sidelined their political critique of American actions in Vietnam and minimized the likelihood that children would reconnect with their Vietnamese kin, who would now have to initiate their custody battles independently in state courts.[61]

Disappointed, but not dissuaded, select Vietnamese families did exactly that—sometimes with the aid of CCR, which reached out to Vietnamese refugees in the United States and pressed the State Department to locate families in Vietnam seeking lost relatives—and thus perpetuated disputes about cultural autonomy, responsibility, belonging, and imperialism that had surfaced during the class action suit and the war itself. Moreover, these exhausting fights over children's best interests and parents' rights revealed the efforts of Vietnamese to repair and re-create their extended families across and within national borders despite the disruptions of war, the expectations of assimilation, and the contrary ambitions of Americans to manage the war's legacies and the terms of migration. In 1975, Phuong Thi Musick initiated an independent action to assume custody of her nieces, Kim Ly, Mai Ly, and Khanh Ly, until they might enjoy reunion with their biological parents. In establishing her case, she submitted a letter to the court from her brother, Nguyen Dang Tuc, explaining the dire circumstances that precipitated the relinquishment and his hopes for the future. "Try to talk to the Catholic Association in order to bring these three children to your house so that they can be together otherwise they must be miserable," he urged his sister. Then, presumably seeking the sympathy of the court and the Catholic Association as advised by counsel, he wrote, "Because of past panic in

Vietnam we lost our three children and our family was scattered," but now "we agree to give the right to take care and raise our three children to my blood sister, Nguyen Thi Phuong (Phuong Thi Musick) who presently is in the United States. I hope that in the future we may have a chance to meet our children and family again."[62] Musick expressed her willingness to fulfill her brother's wishes and her shared belief in the obligations of family, the value of its repair, and possibilities for recovery and reinvention in the United States.

Huynh Thi Anh's attempts to assume custody of her four grandchildren also conveyed this expansive idea of family and the aspirations of refugees to remake their lives in the United States. The grandmother asserted that she had arranged for their evacuation by giving them to a caregiver who then delivered them to the Hoa Binh Orphanage in 1975. At the appeal of a representative from the Agency for International Adoption, the director signed releases for forty of the orphanage's residents to the Michigan Department of Social Services. After Huynh Thi Anh and her son, Dao Thanh Linh, left Vietnam and were detained in Guam and then Camp Pendleton, they sought to reconnect with the four boys, only to discover that the Michigan Department of Social Services had taken, separated, and placed their kin with two different foster couples, each of whom acted promptly to adopt. Huynh Thi Anh charged that she had neither intentionally abandoned nor released her grandchildren and claimed that, having raised them in the absence of their mother or father, she enjoyed parental rights. In pursuing her interests in federal court, her attorneys argued for the priority of Vietnamese law, the existence of racial discrimination, the duty of INS to guarantee the boys' reunification with relatives, and the failure of Michigan adoption proceedings to ensure due process. Ultimately, the court refuted these points and dismissed the case, making clear the complexity of and sometimes reluctance to rule on individual custody conflicts.[63]

In a number of other cases that reached trial, though, Vietnamese families proved victorious and succeeded in pressing their rights as refugees. Duong Bich Van convinced a Michigan judge that the son whom she had surrendered at a moment of crisis belonged with her despite the protests and virtues of the Pedersons, the heteronormative American family who now claimed him. Born in 1971, Duong Quoc Tuan, renamed Matthew David by the Pedersons, migrated to the United States as a young child. Under the direction of FCVN and under the authority of INS,[64] Duong Quoc Tuan was placed with the Pedersons, who then filed to adopt the boy. Based on Duong Bich Van's testimony, other evidence, and in defiance of Clark's representation of Duong Bich Van's desires and FCVN's actions,[65] the judge accepted that she had *not* abandoned her son and expressed admiration for her courage: "Tuan's mother did not reject her responsibility with respect to Tuan, but rather exercised the highest type of responsibility toward him trapped in dangerous circumstances over which she had no control. She was ready and willing if necessary, to make the ultimate sacrifice of final separation to insure protection and safety of her child." After arriving at this conclusion, the judge interpreted the "best interests of the child" by referencing the relevant Michigan state statute. On key measures, including "love, affection," "capacity and disposition . . . to provide the child with food, clothing, medical care," and "mental and physical health," he deemed the competing parties equally qualified. He expressed respect for the Pedersons, whom he described as a "fine Christian family . . . of the highest type without question," but concluded "that in the long run and because of his personality and because of his nationality the best interest would be to be with the natural mother." A preference for the biological mother, recognition of the perils of the Vietnam War, the absence of a formal release document, and the relative brevity of Tuan's stay with the Pedersons convinced the court to grant custody to Duong Bich Van in June 1976, an outcome that repaired a Vietnamese family and reinforced the value of kin relations in professing and making one's place within the United States.[66]

The reformation of Vietnamese families through bruising court battles sustained rather than concluded painful discussions about how to manage, minimize, and remember the consequences of war. When Doan Thi Hoang Anh attempted to recover her four-year-old son, Ben, the boy's adoptive parents, Bonnie and John Nelson, resisted. During the court proceedings, Bonnie Nelson described Ben as disinterested in his biological mother—"If he reacted to her in a loving way, if he knew her and ran to her, we would know she was someone whom he could accept and love, but Ben barely looked up from his coloring book"—a disinterest she offered as proof that she and her husband should retain Ben. She presented herself and her husband as conventional and thus rightful parents, whom Ben had chosen rather than suffered; the court should respect and protect the boy's detachment from his single Vietnamese mother and his difficult past. Yet, the Iowa Supreme Court ruled in favor of Doan Thi Hoang Anh, who had released her seven children to FCVN during the final days of the Saigon regime and after the death of her husband. Doan requested the youths be taken to safety without formally consenting to adoption, obtained the Denver address of the organization, and dedicated herself to tracing and reclaiming her children as soon as she reached the United States. "There is no way, even in my own language, to express the way I feel when I see my boy," the elated mother told journalists of the *San Francisco Chronicle* when she learned of the verdict. Swayed by Doan Thi Hoang Anh's resolve, a version of family that privileged cultural origins, and possible regrets about the Vietnam War, the court made room for Vietnamese refugees. Yet, the resolution disrupted as much as it settled tensions. The photo of Ben wearing a blue denim suit and white cowboy hat featured in the *Chronicle* suggested his fast attachment to American culture and the loss borne by the Nelsons, who reportedly cried as they waved good-bye.[67]

Indeed, the custody conflicts typically pitted the material comforts, nuclear form, and economic advantages of American couples against the cultural, historical, and natural claims of Vietnamese families seeking restoration. In another custody case that followed the dismissal of *Nguyen v. Kissinger*, a Vietnamese mother tried to win back her son's affections despite her poverty and his reported acclimation to American conveniences. Amid the chaos of 1975 Saigon and with the expectation that she would never escape, Le Thi Sang arranged for a civilian helicopter pilot, William Knight, to transport and care for her son, Tuan. When Le Thi Sang achieved the unexpected—migration to the United States—within hours of her son's departure, she sought to recover him. However, the Knights had grown so attached to Tuan, renamed Dean, and he seemingly so enamored with his playthings, baseball team, and pets, that they refused. William Knight asserted that Tuan "doesn't want to speak any Vietnamese," had "made a fantastic adjustment," and felt "proud of being an American boy."[68] The dispute moved to the Superior Court, where Judge Bill Dozier ordered a three-month trial period during which Tuan would reside with his biological mother and then choose his preferred parents. Reportedly, Tuan left the Knights' home reluctantly, and Le Thi Sang fretted over how to win his favor. Although she bought him "clothes and toys," the Vietnamese refugee, employed as a hotel maid, could not compete with the abundance and nuclear structure of the Knight household. Thus she deployed a maternal strategy that emphasized common history and culture. She explained that she gave him "Vietnamese and Chinese food so that he will remember," took him fishing, and told "Tuan that I love him." Ultimately, the time and tactics succeeded; at the close of the three months, Tuan decided to live with his mother, a saddening decision for the Knights.[69] The conclusions of these emotional custody battles validated Vietnamese kinship ties and offered reconciliation and resolution to distraught refugees. However, they also called into question American faith in the aptitude of their largely heterosexual, Christian, and prosperous families—even those who had questioned and wished to absolve American actions in Vietnam—to absorb and transform newcomers.

Perhaps the most compelling case that pitted Vietnamese attempts at reconcilement against American efforts of retention and revision featured Hoa Thi (known as Lon) Popp, a Vietnamese mother and refugee, who endeavored to reconnect with her three sons with the aid of her American husband, William (Bill) Popp, a former pilot of the Flying Tigers. In a letter reflecting on the past and deciphering Lon's repeated intimacies with foreign men stationed in Vietnam, Bill described Lon as a woman whose poverty and instability made her marvel at the freedom and ease of outsiders. Lon had fallen in love with an American pilot with whom she bore her first child, Vo Huy Khan. Soon afterward, Lon met an Australian civilian, "a good guy," Bill noted, who fathered her second child, Vo Anh Tuan. In both cases, the men "tried to take [Lon] and the boys out with them" when ordered to return to their respective countries, Bill explained, "but she had promised her mom she would always take care of her baby sister." Later, Lon would partner with a poor, young American GI and give birth to a third son, Le Thanh Tung,[70] aka "Larry." Bill related that once again, when the soldier relocated, familial love and obligation—rather than the transitory and superficial nature of the interracial relationship, as many Vietnamese and Americans assumed—shaped Lon's decision to remain in Vietnam.[71] As the setting worsened and tales of Communist retaliations against multiracial Vietnamese circulated, Lon, like so many other Vietnamese mothers and their kin, made arrangements for the security of her children that involved separation, migrations, and hopes for eventual reunion. In accentuating the vengeful intentions of Communists—a refrain of testimony offered by Vietnamese—she also aligned herself with dominant American political ideals and underscored the worth of refugees. On April 15, 1975, Lon placed her two older two sons with FFAC. In what she would depict as conditions of duress, Lon signed formal papers of relinquishment that FFAC interpreted as permission to give up the boys for adoption to oil executive and Connecticut resident Richard Lucas.[72] Meanwhile, a friend delivered Lon's youngest, Larry, to a Catholic priest who promised to bring the infant to the United States; soon after Larry's arrival, he was handed over to Bob and Joan Zenk, who planned to formally adopt him.

Not only did Lon arrange the evacuation of her children, but she managed the more difficult feat of getting herself out of Vietnam, a timely migration that would have assured the speedy reformation of her family if not for the competing expectations of the Americans seeking to assimilate the boys as their own. To aid her search, Lon contacted William Popp, whom she had met briefly during his detail in Vietnam and who felt so drawn to the woman and her story that he offered his phone number. Together the pair made inquiries to INS and the Red Cross that led them to the Zenks and Lucas. Reclaiming the boys from their new homes, however, would require five years of anguish, uncertainty, and frustration. During the process, Lon and William married and established a household in California from which they waged their two-front battle. A conference with the Zenk family arranged by County Social Services and mediated by social worker Betty Davis—who described Lon "as a determined young woman" who in her short time in the country "had become 'self-supporting and independent'"[73]—ended without resolution. The Zenks noted that the boy did not recognize his mother and felt comfortable in his new home, perpetuating a narrative of belonging that had guided the pronouncements of other American couples seeking to establish their merit. Lon called their assertions cruel distortions of facts. "They say mother mean *nothing*. Nothing. I want my son! They try to make me crazy. They say I don't have a husband, they say why don't I come for my son sooner, but I don't know [who] has him. I have no money," she exclaimed to a *Los Angeles Times* reporter after the conference. As further evidence of her despair and determination to find her boys, Lon noted that despite access to "enough food, more than I want," she could not eat and had lost twenty pounds.[74]

During the court case that followed, competing depictions of historical events, parental intent, and child desires invited a broader discussion of the justness of removing and adopting children from Vietnam. The Zenks argued that Lon not only had wished to be free of her children but had mistreated them, offering the report of one doctor who documented the children's bad teeth, sores, listlessness, and ear infections. Buttressed by the comments of a Vietnamese social worker who testified about the "lasting and devastating effects of removing this child from the Zenks," they further contended that Larry best suited them. Lon and her lawyers successfully challenged this characterization of her actions and the interests of her son. They attributed Larry's poor health to limited medical care in Vietnam, established Lon's compassion, and tracked the alacrity of her search for Larry. In his decision granting custody to Lon, Judge James Delaney wrote that the court had a responsibility to consider "the preservation of the family and the protection of parental rights," and stated that "the Zenks in the parlance of the law are strangers to the child." While ruling in her favor, Delaney also took the opportunity to chastise adoption agencies and cast doubt on the mass removal of Vietnamese children. "I find it distressing that when the problem here was recognized, the tragic impasse that had been reached by the placement of the child who was not properly cleared for placement, the only thing that happened was to tell Mrs. Popp to go and get an attorney and get legal advice," he noted of FFAC's action, stating that he viewed the organization as "derelict in their duty." Although acknowledging possible differences in the circumstances of other Vietnamese children's removal, he concluded that if their "status is as tenuous as the child in this case, I think there's a serious question as to whether these adoptions are really valid."[75]

Relieved by the retrieval of her youngest son, Lon still fought to prove her maternal competence against the paternal claims of Lucas, a fight that invited even more national conversation about the place and powers of Vietnamese refugees in American society, ideas about forms of family, and the meanings of wars in Southeast Asia. Increasingly frustrated by Lucas's refusals and what Bill would later describe as the "lies, deceit . . . and complicity of the government and agencies," Lon and Bill chose to take matters into their own hands. On June 2, 1976 (almost a year before the formal end of the first custody trial), the couple intercepted the boys (now known as Mark and Paul) while they were waiting for their school bus and flew the boys back to California. In making the plan, Bill had investigated state abduction laws and discovered that charges could not be brought against natural parents. Despite this interpretation, a federal grand jury issued indictments and the state of Connecticut issued arrest warrants for the couple, charging them with kidnapping. In their defense, Lon cried out, "How can I kidnap my own children?" while Bill more quietly explained, "We had run out of options. What could we do?"[76]

Undeterred by the charges and order to surrender the boys to Lucas, Lon filed a motion for their immediate return. In this custody dispute, the trial court proved less sympathetic to the refugee's account of her unwavering parental affection. The judge took seriously the form she had signed relinquishing the boys to FFAC and expressed doubt about her ability to provide a stable home environment.[77] However, the Connecticut Supreme Court overturned the lower court's ruling; Judge Joseph Bogdanski argued that despite the document, "the plaintiff has a constitutional right to preserve her parental rights in the absence of a powerful countervailing state interest." After fighting for five years, Lon had restored her Vietnamese family and showcased the resilience of a refugee determined to rebuild her family and life in the United Sates. Yet, the length of the confrontation, challenges to her character, and intensity of media scrutiny would leave her and Bill still pained and suspicious decades later. Indeed, whether winners or losers in these custody cases, both sides expressed feelings of hurt and a readiness to blame the U.S. government for mismanaging the war's closure in ways that reenergized rather than relaxed conflicts between Vietnamese and Americans.

The end of the Vietnam War, the U.S. District Court's dismissal of the class action suit, and the formalization of Vietnamese adoptions dulled the intensity of hard-fought battles about the legitimacy of the airlifts and global commitments made in the name of anti-Communism. In debating the practicality and morality of adopting Vietnamese orphans, Americans had engaged with, if not resolved, larger questions about the nation's responsibilities to third-world peoples, the prospects for racial equality and integration in an era of heightened consciousness about cultural difference, and the role of family as a site for social and political change. Their rhetoric and practices of adoption interrupted a pattern of thinking about race relations, foreign policy, and parenthood that had originated in the early Cold War. Rather than represent adoption as a realization and extension of American democracy consistent with Christian ideals and conventional domesticity, many Americans of the Vietnam era used adoption to unsettle social conventions and establish political priorities. In taking care of Vietnamese children, they challenged and attempted to make amends for the perceived mistakes of the nation, assuming responsibility not for the abstract and inevitable consequences of war but for the specific and preventable effects of a war the United States had worsened, if not created.

Yet Vietnamese deflected and rejected these designs; whether as residents of Vietnam or refugees in the United States, they strove to repair familial ties worn away by war, claiming their children and shaping the outcomes and remembrance of recent events. Many had employed a high-risk but carefully conceived strategy of migration, choosing separation as a necessary prelude to reconnection. As time passed and the Vietnam War became a memory to invoke rather than a conflict to fight, Vietnamese children who were reunited with their biological kin, adopted by American families, or belatedly invited to immigrate as young Amerasians would mature and become actors as well as emblems in discussions about the legacies of the war, the construction of ethnoracial communities, and patterns of assimilation.

3 Amerasians' Families and Hopes of Homecoming

More than a decade after the last American troops withdrew and hundreds of Vietnamese children were airlifted from Vietnam, Americans rhetorically and practically returned to helping Vietnamese children, specifically those who could prove through documentation, testimony, or simply physical appearance that they had American fathers. These young men and women—described as the "dust of life" because their multiracial backgrounds, absent fathers, and impoverished mothers typically placed them on the fringes of Vietnamese society—could have been, but were not, adopted as infants or young children by American families in the 1970s, Americans would reason. The rediscovery of these offspring and the revival of familiar arguments about the nation's responsibility to the unwanted children of Vietnam offered during and immediately after the war suggested a hoped for but still unreached resolution about the conflict itself. By finally admitting and taking on the duties of national paternity, Americans believed they could heal old wounds and improve relations with Vietnam. Moreover, in portraying itself as a refuge from the anti-American and racist attitudes of Vietnamese society, the United States sought to highlight the gains of civil rights struggles and the sway of cosmopolitan ideals.

While Americans continued to think about Vietnamese children and the consequences of its imperialist ventures in Southeast Asia after 1975 and the severance of diplomatic and economic relations, Vietnam struggled to reconcile, recover, and rebuild. The newly configured SRV confronted challenges of political reunification and economic reconstruction. Its forceful restrictions on speech generated political distrust while its awkward attempts to knit together long divided, regional economies produced shortages, disruptions, and suffering. Wishing to purge the south of neocolonialist and feudalist influences, the SRV removed to reeducation camps or denied food rations, education, and employment to hundreds of thousands of individuals with suspected ties to the defeated RVN or the U.S. government. Its energetic economic plans, which included confiscating private property, collectivizing agriculture, and relocating residents of urban areas to new economic zones in the countryside, inspired more hostility than productivity.

Meanwhile, international rivalries and U.S. animosity complicated the nation's position. In 1979, the United States gathered its European allies into even stricter trade and aid embargos, banning commercial and financial transactions, prohibiting foreign investment, and freezing Vietnam's assets in the United States. As a result, Vietnam could not participate in the world's largest markets or secure multilateral bank loans. That same year, provoked by the Khmer Rouge's oppression of Vietnamese residents and its violation of Vietnamese borders,[1] the SRV sent troops to topple Pol Pot and establish a more sympathetic regime. The costs of this advance, however, proved substantial: the expense of occupation; condemnation and isolation by the international community; China's invasion of North Vietnam. In response to these dire political and economic circumstances, hundreds of thousands of Vietnamese fled; first, Saigon sympathizers, and then ethnic Chinese whose loyalty was questioned and property seized.[2]

Similar frustrations and aspirations motivated Amerasians to vacate Vietnam. From their perspective, migration offered economic opportunities and political stability for themselves and their Vietnamese kin, the possibility of social acceptance, and the prospect of reconnecting with Vietnamese family and American fathers. However, controversy about the arrival of their "fake" relatives (unrelated Vietnamese who pretended kinship to win entry), the difficulty and rarity of father-child reunions, the retraction of social programs and multicultural ideals in the Reagan era, and the challenges of feeling comfortable in a country that was still foreign despite having an American parent, compromised their integration, sustained doubts about the legacies of the Vietnam War, and underscored the creative and varied interpretations of family enacted by Vietnamese immigrants and enabled by U.S. immigration laws.

Although the passage of the Indochina Migration and Refugees Assistance Act in 1975 had established a precedent and pattern of accepting Vietnamese refugees, the conviction that Amerasians were fundamentally American children "coming home" to the land of their fathers rather than foreigners who, like other immigrants, would struggle to find jobs, learn English, understand American customs, and feel a sense of belonging made possible the passage of favorable legislation in the early 1980s and the subsequent migration of Amerasians.[3] Such beliefs also prompted the prediction that Amerasians would rapidly, readily assimilate, a prediction as problematic as Amerasians' own hopes of sudden prosperity and acceptance. What distinguished Amerasians from other Vietnamese refugees and earlier populations of immigrants was the relative difficulty, rather than ease, with which they would become American. Social workers noted that the Amerasians' romantic beliefs about happy reunions with their American fathers and probable job opportunities ill prepared them for the rigors of entering American society. Their limited education, poverty, and experiences of trauma added to their exertions. Moreover, because Amerasians sought to distance themselves from other Vietnamese immigrants, who typically treated them as inhospitably in the United States as they had in Vietnam, they could not draw on the resources and guidance of an emerging ethnic community. Nor did many enjoy the support of the pretended family members with whom they parted ways when they reached American soil.

Although awareness of and debates about preferred American policies toward Amerasians faded in the years immediately following the airlifts, a collection of concerned parents, politicians, journalists, foundations, and religious leaders would redirect public attention to the young adults, largely by scripting Amerasians as American children worthy of better lives in the United States, and ultimately precipitate the Amerasian Homecoming Act in 1987. One vocal group of parents—Americans who had adopted Vietnamese children—spoke in favor of policy revisions, but in ways that could diminish or elide the presence of Vietnamese parents. Among them was actress Julie Andrews, who adopted two Vietnamese girls, Amelia Leigh and Joanna Lynn, with her second husband, Blake Edwards, in the mid-1970s. Andrews first won acclaim for her appearances in Broadway productions during the 1950s, but her performances in *Mary Poppins* (1964) and *The Sound of Music* (1965) assured her celebrity and expressed her affinity for roles about surrogate motherhood. In both films, she plays nannies whose good cheer, compassion, and resistance to authoritarian regimes bring joy to gloomy children. Whether swooping in by umbrella or dancing to the door with her carpetbag swung high, she substitutes for distant fathers and distracted or missing mothers. She not only rescues her charges but offers a more harmonious, free-spirited, and emotional rendering of parenthood expressive of the counterculture and likely the source of her popularity among audiences.[4] Most likely, Andrews's choice of parts and the strength of her portrayals (so associated was she with her characters, Mary Poppins and Maria, that she struggled to find more diverse roles in the late 1960s and 1970s) anticipated and informed her adoptions. Her membership in COR, her close friendships with Mia Farrow and Yul Brynner—adoptive parents of Vietnamese children—and the timing of her search likely directed her to Vietnam.[5]

Julie Andrews interacting with two Vietnamese children. Committee of Responsibility Records, Swarthmore College Peace Collection, Swarthmore, Pa.

During a visit to Southeast Asia in 1982 on behalf of Operation California, a three-year-old relief agency focused on the troubles of the region, Andrews expressed her determination to "keep politics out of her statements about what she has seen." She told reporters she "wants them [Americans] to pressure the government to make room for Amerasian children and their families. She wants to see the State department relax its politics about development aid." To strengthen and personalize her policy recommendations, Andrews linked the present problem of Amerasians to yesterday's solution of American adoption, confessing, "I had always wanted to be able to talk to my daughters about their country. And when I went—I never thought I would be able to love them more than I did already as my own children. But somehow, having seen what would have happened to them—it made me want to hold them so tightly."[6] The implication of her expression of maternal affection and gratitude—that Americans had not done enough to help Vietnamese children at the close of the war and should now assume responsibility for the consequences—became a prevailing theme for advocates of Amerasians. Linking the two populations of children raised the profile of American parents in discussions of foreign policy and family but risked displacing Vietnamese women. Indeed, most steered clear of conversations about the painful circumstances that had brought Vietnamese women into intimate, often coercive contact with American men. During the late 1960s, an economy organized around sex and service developed in South Vietnamese cities as American troop levels rose, the ARVN drafted more men, and South Vietnamese women departed the devastated countryside and assumed work as hostesses, bar girls, business owners, factory workers, secretaries, prostitutes, and maids. Although genuine compassion and connection sometimes marked encounters between American men and Vietnamese women, U.S. militarization still cast its shadow.[7]

Americans were encouraged to envision abandoned, infant orphans rather than consider the complexities of adult Amerasians with Vietnamese mothers and mature family ties. In his testimony before the Subcommittee of Immigration and Refugee Policy of the Senate Committee on the Judiciary, Walter Martindale, a U.S. State Department official and father of two adopted Vietnamese children, similarly structured the Amerasian issue. He explained that in 1973 he had accepted two children from a pleading Vietnamese woman who had feared for their safety. Presuming to speak for and professing a shared perspective with this Vietnamese mother, Martindale insisted that "she further believed, as I do, that these children and children like them would have a happier, more equitable opportunity to achieve their potential in a multiracial society such as the United States." "They should not be made to bear the burden of our policies nor be denied the rights of their American heritage," he then concluded. "They are our obligation. . . . We must bring our American-Asian children home to America." Importantly, he depicted Vietnamese society as averse to racial difference, Vietnamese women as in agreement with his views, and Amerasians as individuals without family obligations and attachments, presumably characteristics that would simplify the process of their immigration and settlement.[8]

Americans portrayed Amerasians as mistreated and marginalized, a portrait informed by the testimonies of Amerasians and the observations of Americans in Saigon. Angelina Memon remembered suffering the torment of her Vietnamese classmates in the late 1970s. They called her a "half-breed with twelve assholes," kicked her, pushed her, and placed lice in her hair she remembered. Jimmy Miller (Nhat Tung) shared similar experiences of discrimination, recalling that Vietnamese peers shouted, "American, go back to your country," and called him "bad names." Although some Amerasians "just walk away without saying anything" and "don't give them the chance to use that against us even more," others chose to "fight back, and we talk back, and there would be a fight." Exhausted by the constant conflict, many Amerasians left formal schooling and sought refuge with their families. In Jimmy's case, his mother, Kim, arranged for a tutor to visit his home, but few Amerasians had that opportunity.[9]

Accounts of mixed-race individuals denied education, work opportunities, and basic rights exposed the real difficulties many Amerasians confronted, but they also supported an emerging thesis about the intolerance of Vietnamese and the relative acceptance of Americans in the aftermath of wrenching civil rights movements. These representations revived ideas about the cruelty of a Communist Vietnam and the kindness of a democratic United States that had dominated the discourse about Vietnamese children during the Vietnam War. The media consistently depicted Amerasians as unrelentingly miserable, suffering the jeers and hostility of peers, strangers, and even relatives troubled not only by their multiracial heritage but also by the presumed indiscretion of their Vietnamese mothers (mischaracterized as promiscuous and treacherous) and American fathers (identified as young and undisciplined). Many appeared to barely eke out an existence, sleeping in the streets, begging for money, selling cigarettes, and digging through piles of garbage in search of food. Amerasians, journalists suggested, felt an innate loyalty to and deserved a reprieve in the United States. "He has been forced to sit each day through two hours of indoctrination," wrote one journalist of an Amerasian youth, "in which the United States was blamed for all of Vietnam's ills." The thirteen-year-old boy resented the classes and conveyed his American affections, explaining, "I couldn't stand hearing how bad the U.S. is. My father is American."[10] In a *Nightline* broadcast aired in 1982, Ted Koppel echoed this theme of troubled children who would do better in a more accepting, American culture. "They are the children of American fathers and Asian mothers, and in Asia, few of them are treated with anything but contempt," he stated, but "in America attitudes are different, so different that to bring these children here is to give them a new lease on life."[11]

The journalists helped popularize a solution for these multiracial outcasts—bringing them to the United States—that the Pearl S. Buck Foundation, one of the first and noisiest champions of Amerasians, had recommended for decades. A monograph about Amerasians published in 1980 by Buck Foundation director John Shade emphasized the large numbers of Amerasians who were denied jobs, schooling, and basic rights throughout Asia. These representations influenced and were repeated by policy makers, including Senator Jeremiah Denton, who in 1982 cosponsored the first immigration reform targeting Amerasians. He argued that Amerasians were subject to "unremitting social discrimination because the Asian cultures resist assimilating children of mixed parentage," but expressed confidence that "we all feel compassion for the Amerasians partly because of the discrimination to which they are subjected."[12]

Complicating this portrait of lone and lonely Amerasians were their Vietnamese mothers, who dreamed of immigrating to the United States. Like Vietnamese refugees who had labored to recover children and repair families shattered by violence during excruciating custody battles after 1975, these mothers struggled to ease the aches of war and its aftermath by arranging for their and their kin's exodus. They advocated for special immigration status, submitting exit applications that quickly covered the desks of American Orderly Departure Program (ODP) officials. Created in 1979 under the auspices of the United Nations High Commissioner for Refugees to manage the mass exodus of Vietnamese, particularly ethnic Chinese, the program initially treated Amerasians no differently from other Vietnamese seeking immigration to the United States. However, as the Bangkok office's director, Don Colin, and other officials took notice of the mothers' pleas and paperwork, they began to argue that Amerasians be reclassified and receive preference as those "people closely associated with the U.S. presence in Vietnam." Vietnamese mothers also revealed themselves and their interests in congressional debates about immigration and refugee policy. In a translated note attached to an application for admission submitted as evidence in congressional hearings held in 1982, a Vietnamese woman wrote, "We are Vietnamese women and we have an American halfbreed children. . . . . We hope you don't forgetting We children orphans right now living VN, and come to live in USA That is why, we write and send you this application about circumstances."

The quickness with which Vietnamese mothers responded to the first formalized program to aid Amerasians in 1983 not only revealed the intensity of their desire to depart but defied suppositions about their acquiescence that had shaped American actions during and after the war. After hearing about the prospect that Amerasians could immigrate to the United States, Memon's mother immediately sold the family's house, filed an application, and readied to leave.[13] Truc Tran's mother demonstrated similar resolve and alacrity. Concerned that Truc Tran's American appearance and her own past associations with Americans placed them both in grave danger, she collaborated with friends and family to gather the necessary funds and paperwork.[14]

Oftentimes, years passed before these purposeful mothers realized their objectives. Jimmy Miller's mother, Kim, submitted an application as early as 1983. Uncertain of the outcome, though, she hedged her bets. She "tried to buy a boat and escape by boat," Miller recalled, attributing her determination to her opposition to Communists and explaining, "She desperate, she want to get out of the country, you know, for freedom." Unfortunately, a police officer discovered her efforts and "sent her to jail for five years."[15] Eventually, Kim won her freedom, secured and passed an interview with American officials, and left Vietnam with Jimmy and his siblings in 1987.

Americans who had long worked with and had intimate knowledge of Amerasians tried to make clear the presence and power of their Vietnamese mothers, countering images of maternal neglect or resignation and readily adoptable American children without family ties. Father Alfred Keane, a Maryknoll missionary and the director of Amerasian Affairs for International Aid, told members of the Senate Judiciary Committee that unlike Americans, who defined adoption "as a way to take care of children born out of wedlock," in Vietnam, "adoption of someone who is not your family or clan is a very foreign idea and is basically culturally unacceptable." He speculated that if Amerasians had been adopted by Americans at a young age, "the problem could possibly be resolved," but "requiring adoption as a condition of immigration to the United States fails to take into consideration the natural ties that have been established between mother and child."[16]

Despite these efforts to educate Americans about the forms and traditions of Vietnamese families that had structured the lives of Amerasians, the first major amendment to the Immigration and Nationality Act designed to facilitate their entry treated them as independent individuals. The Amerasian Immigration Act of 1982 allowed the children of American fathers born in Vietnam, Cambodia, Thailand, and Laos after 1950 to apply for permanent resident visas.[17] The chairman of the House Committee on the Judiciary cheered the legislation as a "long overdue" and "effective" response to "a most difficult humanitarian problem" that recognized "the moral responsibility that we have to these children who have been fathered by Americans abroad."[18] Since the legislation did not require their fathers to file petitions claiming them, Amerasians could prove paternity by introducing a range of materials such as birth and baptismal records, photographs, letters, or witness testimony. Processing officials would also consider physical appearance. The Amerasian had to secure an American sponsor of "good moral character" who would assume financial responsibility and, in the case of Amerasians under the age of eighteen, legal custody. Acknowledging (without apology or justification) the forced separation of Vietnamese mothers from their children, the Justice Department noted that Public Law 97-359 "was not intended as adoption law." Although mothers or guardians of Amerasians younger than eighteen years of age had to sign an irrevocable release permitting the minor's emigration, this did not constitute a legal relinquishment of parental rights. Immigration officials predicted that after lengthy placements in the homes of their American sponsors, Amerasians "might assume the role of permanent family member," but encouraged these sponsors to support "the youth's desire for an on-going relationship with his or her natural mother." Thus, the immigration law and those tasked to enforce it admitted the existence of, and even expressed respect for, Vietnamese mothers, but they readily and conveniently accepted the indefinite estrangement of those mothers from their sons and daughters.[19] In doing so, they reprised a familiar, gendered script in which Vietnamese women suffered, surrendered, and faded away.

Ronald Reagan's support for the act and advocacy of Amerasians reflected a highly selective embrace of refugees in the 1980s consistent with his conservative ideas of family, opposition to Communism, and rebranding of the Vietnam War as a conflict the United States could and should have won if not for the weakness of his presidential predecessors. Indeed, during a speech before the Veterans of Foreign Wars convention in 1980, he debuted a Cold War defense of American intervention in the region—North Vietnam's aggressions precipitated war rather than civil or revolutionary conflict; other Communist powers were fully invested; the antiwar movement, media, and dissenting politicians undercut tactics that would have assured American victory—that conservatives have since championed. The duration of the refugee crisis in Southeast Asia through the 1980s had prompted calls for reform, specifically the substitution of a comprehensive, consistent system for the ad hoc, parole-based measures. The resulting Refugee Act of 1980 allowed for the annual entry of more than 50,000 refugees from all over the world and elevated human rights principles over anti-Communism in fulfilling this quota. Yet, Reagan implemented the act in ways that realized his primary foreign-policy goal: the restoration of the United States' position vis-à-vis the Soviet Union through a muscular military buildup and support for anti-Communist, American-friendly regimes in Asia and especially Central America. Throughout the 1980s, Africa, South and Central America, and the Middle East were assigned the smallest refugee quotas (a few thousand per region annually), and Eastern Europe, the Soviet Union, and Southeast Asia the largest. In 1982, Southeast Asia secured 96,000 spaces, compared with the 11,000 won by Eastern Europeans, and 20,000 granted to residents of the Soviet Union.[20] Despite their large share of the total refugee population admitted to the United States, many Southeast Asians objected that after Reagan became president in 1981, INS had begun to slow the process by distinguishing between those deemed "real" victims of political persecution and those merely of "special concern" to the United States.

During his public signing of the 1982 Amerasian Immigration Act, Reagan enacted his political principles and cultural values, valorizing American soldiers, male-headed households, and needy Vietnamese. He also reinforced the core assumption that Amerasians were solitary figures, unmoored to Vietnamese society and culture, who would quickly become part of American households with present fathers rather than Vietnamese units led by single mothers. After highlighting the service of American men who had fought "to prevent aggression and protect the vital interests of our country" in Southeast Asia, Reagan casually, and without discussion of origins and paternal responsibilities, noted the birth of a "number of Amerasian children." Unfortunately, when the fathers returned to the United States, "far too often innocent children were left without parents or without country," he continued. The proposed bill—"a good and humane law"—would recognize "the rightful claim of Amerasian children to American citizenship and permit their entry into our country." While conservatives had fretted over and faulted social movements of the 1960s and 1970s for unraveling traditional forms of family and authority—weakening men's sources of power while widening women's responsibilities and autonomy—the recovery of Amerasians offered an antidote: recentering American men as fathers. Reagan would also stress the importance of the sponsoring families and private organizations in the United States for the integration of Amerasians, deemphasizing the role and resources of government. Notably, he made no mention of the roots and relationships that might keep Amerasians in Vietnam, an omission that underscored the finality of their migration and the power of the normative, heterosexual American family to absorb and transform a "lost" relation.[21]

Media coverage of the first Amerasians who capitalized on the bill emphasized the compassion of their American fathers and the indifference or disappearance of their Vietnamese mothers, thus sustaining the notion that they would readily assimilate into American families and communities. Spotlighting the first eleven Amerasians bound for a "world of things [they] have never known before from English to E.T., Safeways to sodas, burgers to baseball—and fathers," Bob Sector, like other American journalists, stressed the opportunities and excitement of their migrations. Although Sector drew attention to the sadness of one Amerasian, Nguyen Quoc Viet, on bidding farewell to her family, he noted how quickly the novelty and luxuries of the airplane distracted the young woman. Another Amerasian featured in the article seemed as ready to embrace her American life, which she equated with consumer abundance and "happiness." She noted that "you have lots of clothes and anywhere you go, you can go in an automobile."[22]

Credited as the first and only American to have traveled to Ho Chi Minh City "to bring his child home," Gary Tanous shared his trials and joys with journalists. His confessions helped counter prevailing constructions of dispassionate and irresponsible American soldiers, which had energized critiques of American interference in Vietnam. While a civilian communications adviser in Vietnam, he had met and married a Vietnamese woman in 1966 and had a daughter, Jean Marie. The threesome had come to the United States, but according to Tanous, his wife grew dissatisfied with American life, returning to Vietnam within a year, just before the Communist takeover in 1975. Leaving their daughter in the care of her mother, Tanous's wife fled. Tanous and reporters, though, chose not to expand on the causes and outcomes of her flight, perhaps because an explanation would distract from the central, preferred story about a father-daughter reunion.[23] Tanous lost contact with Jean Marie, but in the early 1980s initiated a search. He spent nearly two years and $30,000 arranging for the young woman's emigration. Although she had voluntarily made the decision to join Tanous in the United States, accompanied by her Vietnamese grandmother, Jean Marie still expressed what Tanous described as "a tremendous amount of animosity built up towards me because she thought I had abandoned her," feelings Tanous cautioned other American fathers to prepare to confront. Jean Marie had also struggled to adapt to the new language, climate, and food. Yet Tanous suggested those difficulties had passed, depicting his daughter as an ordinary American teenager, obsessed with cosmetics and the music of Willie Nelson. When her Vietnamese grandmother decided to move from Tanous's hometown of Portland to San Francisco, Jean Marie had elected to remain. Most telling, "she was coming to accept me as her father," Tanous proudly remarked, explaining that she had withheld her love until "she knew I loved her." Having loosened ties to Vietnamese kin in favor of her American friends and father, Jean Marie seemed to have made the choice intended and assumed by the Amerasian Immigration Act, reassuring the American public of their own good deeds.[24]

Among the most dramatic and documented cases of reunions between American fathers and their Amerasian children was that featuring Barry Huntoon, a Vietnam veteran who believed he had recognized his daughter on a magazine cover. As presented by the press, his efforts corroborated the validity of the Amerasian Immigration Act and the morality of American fathers. In a televised interview with Hugh Downes on the ABC program 20/20, Huntoon confessed that he had unexpectedly fallen in love with a Vietnamese woman, Tuyet Nyung, during his tour in Vietnam. When he received orders to return to the United States in 1972, he tried desperately, and unsuccessfully, to bring a then nine-months-pregnant Tuyet Nyung with him. Huntoon recovered slowly from his loss. He explained, "It was very, very hard. I found myself unable to have a normal relationship with anybody for years and years. The memory of what happened I couldn't forget."[25] He eventually started a new family in the United States, but in 1985 a *Life* magazine story about Amerasians, which featured a young woman named Tuyet Mai, would lead him back to Vietnam and his past. Convinced by her appearance, age, and brief biographical sketch that she was his daughter, Huntoon sought to meet and "adopt her." He detailed his exhaustive and exhausting battles with U.S. and Vietnamese officials to secure Tuyet Mai's immigration, insisting that he and at least 200 other Vietnamese veterans wished to find their lost children.[26] In referencing other veterans, Huntoon and the American journalists publicizing his story highlighted the eagerness of Amerasians' fathers, an eagerness that seemed to confirm ideas about "coming home" and reaffirm masculine authority through the acceptance of fatherhood.

Yet Huntoon made clear that helping Amerasians was a desire and duty not simply of the American fathers but of all Americans who wished to feel good about their nation again. Although he began with a highly personal reflection, "When I went into the service, I was proud of my country. My country meant a lot to me. I was patriotic. I lost that in Vietnam," Huntoon then framed his concerns more broadly, noting that "there are 15,000 children in Vietnam without families. They are getting older day by day. Some right now in their 20s. How long can we turn our back? I mean, how long—how long can we?" The implicit prescription for the renewal of his and the nation's patriotism was further support for Amerasians.[27]

Huntoon's question in part inspired the creation of the Amerasian Registry in 1986, a collaboration of Vietnam veterans and Vietnamese immigrants that defined its mission of reuniting children and fathers as "an important part of that national healing process," echoing Huntoon's call for a shared investment. Given the organization's youth, the souring of U.S.-Vietnamese relations that forced a temporary suspension of the Amerasian program in 1986,[28] and Amerasians' lack of identifying data about their fathers, founders and Vietnam veterans Bruce Burns and Jim Barker acknowledged their slow progress. In addition to assisting Huntoon, the Amerasian Registry had connected only one other veteran, Peter Newcomer, with his Vietnamese daughter, Nhung Nguyen. Yet the pair evaluated their success not by the number of matches but in "each new query by a veteran," which they argued was "a step forward in a national assumption of responsibility." While recognizing the role of individual men, they stressed a communal concern for their children.[29]

This willingness to forgive veterans and enable them to assume their parental obligations suggested how much their reputations had recovered since 1975 and how much the Amerasian issue remained entangled in American ambivalence about the Vietnam War. When asked during a 1987 interview with ABC News correspondent Koppel, "Is this a national problem that we ought to confront as a nation, or does it really have to wait for each of these individual fathers to come forward?," Father Keane, who had figured so prominently in the discussions leading up to the Amerasian Immigration Act, responded that "certainly the government that sent these fathers into these countries has a responsibility. And you know when you look at some of these treaties . . . the father's actual responsibility is in some ways kind of protected. He can act irresponsible and walk away." Without exonerating American fathers, Ellen Goodman similarly argued for a more collective sense of accountability, one that embraced new sexual and gender norms. In a 1982 editorial, Goodman celebrated the arrival of seven Amerasian boys and four Amerasian girls who "carried a story headed for a happy ending. Along with their names, most of them had an American father who cared." Yet the appearance of these few, fortunate individuals led her to contemplate the fates of the "thousands of children, our Vietnam legacy," still in Vietnam. "It's hard to judge these young, young men sent to war," she argued. "But it's easy to wonder about the culture that taught them to accept one responsibility and allowed them to slough off another. What was true in Vietnam under wartime conditions is true in America at peace." Despite the wished-for gains of the sexual revolution, Goodman complained that "in our lopsided ethics, we used to blame men for getting women pregnant, now we insist that it is basically the woman's fault, the woman's mistake, the woman's problem. . . . We tell our young women today how to get birth control and how to say no. But few young men are told what we want them to know: be caring, be responsible." Thus the necessity and accomplishment, Goodman concluded, of the just-passed legislation, in which "we did something that most of the men in Vietnam did not do. . . . We admitted a national paternity."[30]

Although Americans seemed willing to make such an admission, they reluctantly conceived of Amerasians as other than conventional orphans in need of American parents. In rare instances, Amerasians sought foster or adoptive arrangements with American families. Such was the case of My Phuong, an eighteen-year-old woman who had no information or recollection of her birth parents and had been raised since infancy by a series of Vietnamese kin. According to her foster father, Joseph Cerquone, after migrating to the United States, My Phuong felt pressure to live independently or with other Vietnamese, but she believed the company of an American family would best ensure her survival. Cerquone described his experience as challenging and rewarding: "I am on a path headed away from the abstract endlessly shifting realm of policy and towards the world where everything is fixed, where everything is single, unavoidable question—how much do I care?"[31]

However, Americans who thought the Amerasian Homecoming Act would offer a similar opportunity for parenting and self-discovery were disappointed. A February 1989 article in *American Legion* magazine, "We'll Accept Them All," precipitated letters of inquiry from prospective host families directed to the Lutheran Immigrant and Refugee Service (LIRS), one of the organizations involved in coordinating resettlement. The piece accurately explained the origins and structure of the Amerasian Homecoming Act, detailing the opportunities for Amerasians and their close family to relocate to the United States. However its featured photograph of a sixteen-year-old boy, who appeared much younger than his age, sitting across the desk from an earnest, white teacher with no Vietnamese relative in sight created the impression that the youth was alone.[32] Responding to this image and associated text, Pastor Howard Killingbeck expressed his and his wife's wish "to adopt an orphan child, or two siblings," because "our hearts reach out in Christian love to their situation." He noted that they had attempted to do so several years before, but unexplained obstacles had barred their path. In the concluding sentence of his letter, he demonstrated a wider awareness of the Amerasian program, offering to help in the resettlement, but only if he could *not* adopt or foster a child.[33] As an American married to a Vietnamese man who had resided in the United States for nearly thirteen years, Lina Le stated their interest "in children that do not have families or relatives and need the love, support, and direction that we can offer to them in their efforts to establish a new life and adjust to their new environment," believing that their mixed marriage and experience "dealing with the every-day problems and prejudices of our society" prepared them to help "these children whom have been shunned and been looked upon as outcasts by the Vietnamese government."[34] Her appeal conveyed an admirable sensitivity to the cultural and racial challenges Amerasians would likely confront in the United States, but an insensitivity to how their maturity and familial bonds would define their migration and integration. Marta Brenden, director of LIRS, likely answered the queries of the Killinbecks and Les as she did that of the Wilsons, who had called about the prospect of adopting an Amerasian: "Most Amerasians are part of a family, including their mother and brothers and sisters and other relatives." What these immigrants, who averaged nineteen years old in age, most needed, she declared, were "friends—Americans who value their bi-racial, bi-national, bi-cultural heritage," not parents.[35]

Despite all the congratulations and expectations among Americans about the consequences of the Immigration Bill, relatively few Amerasians actually took advantage of its provisions. Only an estimated 4,500 Amerasians and 7,000 of their relatives had actually immigrated to the United States (the family members had emigrated as undifferentiated refugees through the ODP) in the six years after its passage.[36] Although the Vietnamese government, if not actively resistant, was reluctant to cooperate because it objected to the formal classification of Amerasians as refugees—a classification that suggested political persecution and the failures of the SRV—Amerasians' unwillingness to leave their mothers and close kin behind best explained the low numbers. The Center for International Policy, a self-described nonprofit education and research organization concerned with U.S. foreign policy toward developing nations, including Indochina, observed in March 1983 that "the great majority of Amerasian children in Vietnam are, after all, not orphans, but adolescents with close emotional ties to the mothers, grandparents and brothers and sisters with whom they have grown up."[37] By 1987 a series of senators had already proposed various amendments, noting that the early iteration of the bill had proved less effective and inclusive than intended. In addition to lightening the requirements on sponsoring organizations and individuals, a version supported by Stewart McKinney promised to make eligible all Amerasians regardless of their date of birth; add Japan, Taiwan, and the Philippines to the list of sending countries; and, most important, permit their mothers to accompany them.[38]

Ultimately, the final bill—commonly called the Amerasian Resettlement Act or Amerasian Homecoming Act of 1987—sponsored by congressmen and veterans of the Vietnam War, including Thomas Ridge, Robert Mrazek, and John McCain, provided for the admission of Amerasians and close kin. Although set to expire in two years, it was extended. Defending its special protections and more inclusive understanding of Amerasians' familial connections, the act pointed out not only that "Amerasian children are ineligible for ration cards and often beg in the streets, peddle black market wares, or prostitute themselves," but that their mothers were "not eligible for government jobs or employment in government enterprise and many are estranged from their families and destitute." Thus, their desperate circumstances and "undisputed ties to the United States" justified more favorable terms of immigration. The maintenance of "family unity" was defined as a humanitarian concern, but the law betrayed Americans' unwillingness to draw the circle of family too widely. Although the mothers of single Amerasians could readily secure an exit visa, they could not do so if those sons and daughters were married. Amerasians' spouses or children received preference, but the act made no mention of cousins, aunts, or uncles, despite the expansive Vietnamese concept of family. Moreover, the act seemed to anticipate and seek to circumvent a problem of Vietnamese stretching the bonds of family, requiring that an immigration officer first determine if an aspiring immigrant had a "bona fide relationship with the principal alien [the Amerasian] similar to that which exists between close family members." To ensure the compliance of the Vietnamese government, which objected to the classification of Amerasians as refugees, the act had massaged the question of identification, relabeling them as a unique category of immigrants with refugee benefits.[39]

The process of implementing the legislation demanded the patience of its prospective beneficiaries and significant coordination between U.S. and Vietnamese governments. Amerasians and their families first applied to the Vietnamese ministry for inclusion in a list of eligible persons to be interviewed by the ODP, which drew its staff from the U.S. State Department and the International Catholic Migration Commission located in Bangkok. After receiving the approved list, the ODP interviewers would compile a caseload of applicants to investigate during their monthly visit to Ho Chi Minh City. Early on, most cases won approval without requests for additional documentation or exploration, and applicants proceeded with required medical exams. With a list of persons authorized by U.S. officials, Vietnamese authorities prepared a flight manifesto so that Amerasians and family could travel to the Philippines, where they would have access to six months of cultural orientation and language courses. Eventually, the immigrants flew to the United States (expected to repay their transportation costs at a later date), and enjoyed limited resettlement assistance through private agencies.[40]

The Amerasian Homecoming Act had the desired effect of bringing thousands more Amerasians to the United States, but the process of identifying, approving, and facilitating the migration of their Vietnamese relatives would raise concerns about what constituted a "family" and the nation's commitment to family as a privileged category of immigration. In supporting the 1987 reforms, Americans selectively recognized Amerasians' close Vietnamese kin, but did not expect and were quick to criticize the strategic, opportunistic relationships that Amerasians and Vietnamese sometimes pretended for mutual benefit. As Amerasians, their mothers, siblings, and spouses learned about and sought to participate in the Amerasian program, they often discovered that a desire to emigrate and proof of American paternity were insufficient. To grease the wheels of a Vietnamese bureaucracy described as corrupt, they had to pay bribes they often could not afford. At the same time, Vietnamese with resources but no ties to Amerasians courted these offspring with the hope of securing their own place in the United States.[41]

Some Amerasians resented and refused these solicitations, unnerved by the dramatic turn in their social value from worthless to worthy. While awaiting the processing of his exit application in Amerasian Park, Tuan Den, a black Amerasian whose biological mother had disappeared soon after his birth and who had stories of discrimination and unfair imprisonment similar to those of other Amerasians, was approached by a Vietnamese woman holding a picture. "Now that she met me, she said she wanted me to come home and live with her," Tuan Den related, "but I said you didn't take care of me as a child, so I don't go with you now. Many women come and try to tell Amerasians that they are their mothers, to try to go to America, so I was suspicious about that." Vu, an Amerasian residing in Saigon, also rejected Vietnamese who promised rewards. "But I feel very angry," he explained, describing his response to a woman who approached him. "I knew at that time she needed me, but when she would be finished with her dream, she wouldn't care . . . she would throw me out. I don't want anybody to look down on me. I am a human being." Years later, while recalling her efforts to escape Vietnam, Memon expressed similar anger and noted a pattern of manipulation. "It was an outrage, unspeakable and an injustice for Amerasians to be victimized" and " robbed of their rights," as unrelated Vietnamese "were threatening, cheating, and persuading Americans to claim them as relative or husbands or wives."[42]

Although Amerasians' suspicions were often confirmed, some accepted the requests of strangers to fake a family relationship in exchange for money and a better chance to leave Vietnam. Fearful that her six Amerasian children would suffer under a Communist regime, Thanh Thi Nguyen[43] planned to leave Vietnam in 1975. Although she used the local orphanage to ease the labor of caring for her large family, dropping off her two youngest, sickliest children in the morning and retrieving them in the evening, an unnamed official believed it safer to place Trista and Jeffrey with a Vietnamese foster family before their migration to and adoption in the United States. Convinced the pair had safely arrived in the United States, Thanh Thi Nguyen arranged for passage on the first flight of Operation Babylift. According to Trista, with whom she would reunite decades later, Thanh Thi Nguyen panicked, failed to board that flight, and remained in Vietnam. As she labored to support and protect her four remaining children, she longed to leave Vietnam and leaped at the opportunity offered by the Amerasian Homecoming Act. Her daughter Cuc agreed to marry a wealthy Vietnamese man who wished to emigrate. He eagerly paid all application fees and bribes, assuring the family's approval for departure in 1991. As soon as the U.S. government resettled the mature children and Thanh Thi Nguyen in Lansing, Michigan, Cuc and her husband of convenience separated.[44] As black Amerasians, the siblings Loan, Be, and Dung were eligible for immigration under the Amerasian Homecoming Act, but officials denied their visa application in 1984. Eager to depart, they accepted the proposals of wealthy strangers to claim them as their spouses. "We didn't know these people, they are not relation to us," Be explained in a 1995 interview, "but we did what he said. He must have paid the necessary bribes, because after that, we left Vietnam quickly."[45]

By 1992, a year before the expected end of the Amerasian program, U.S. officials had become more conscious and concerned about fraudulent cases that complicated the approval process and compromised the intentions of the program. Select U.S. government officials and voluntary agencies estimated that fake families accounted for almost half of the more than 50,000 Vietnamese relatives of Amerasians who had resettled in the United States since 1989.[46] One dissenting U.S. official involved in the program viewed such statistics as "an inevitable consequences of a program conceived in emotionalism," and called for its reassessment, perhaps even cancellation. Others, including one of the program's champions, Mrazek, proposed a careful review in order to better serve the population.[47] In the U.S. Government Accountability Office (GAO) report he solicited, Assistant Comptroller General Eleanor Chelimsky chronicled the different forms and motives of manufactured families. While "Amerasians may be forced to join with a family," others often "may join willingly" to "achieve success in reaching the United States," she related. In addition, ODP officials had reported instances in which Vietnamese individuals changed their physical appearance to more closely resemble Amerasians, sometimes resorting to mild cosmetic surgery that whitened their skin, widened their noses, and rounded their eyes.[48] Rather than accept such misrepresentation as an unfortunate or unintended consequence of successful legislation and an expression of the depth of Vietnamese desires for emigration, U.S. officials dedicated themselves to more aggressive tactics of surveillance reminiscent of those deployed by immigration inspectors tasked with distinguishing the true from the "paper" relatives of Chinese immigrants at the turn of the twentieth century, tactics that reflected and perpetuated the construction of Asian immigrants as dangerous and forever foreign. Agents explained the difficulty of authenticating family relationships given the scarcity of birth, population, and marriage records in Vietnam. Despite these limitations, they had escalated their efforts by demanding more documentation and asking more probing questions of applicants. However, language and cultural barriers created opportunities for misinterpretation. As a result, the rejection rate had dramatically increased from 20 percent in 1991 to 80 percent in 1992, a development that precipitated despair among legitimate Amerasians and invited more fraud and misunderstanding as Vietnamese interpreters present during the interview allegedly coached applicants, even those with nothing to hide or misrepresent, for a fee.[49] Fears of dismissal prompted Amerasians to distort their testimonies in ways that harmed rather than helped their cases. Pearl, whose Vietnamese mother spoke fondly of his American father, who had returned to Texas soon after Pearl's birth, acted on a rumor that unaccompanied Amerasians received priority in admission to the United States. So, despite his affection for his mother, he had described himself as an orphan. When he attempted to correct this information during his interviews with U.S. officials, they refused to believe him, issuing him, but not his mother, a visa.[50] Among those most at risk of rejection, noted the GAO report, were Amerasians who did not have "clear physical features that would distinguish them as Amerasian, or who have distinguishing features that could be mimicked by a non-Amerasian Vietnamese (such as 'Afro hair')."[51]

Fabricating families not only bothered U.S. officials in principle and practice but proved disruptive for Amerasians and their actual families. By substituting pretend spouses for their real marital partners, siblings Loan, Be, and Dung assured their departure from Vietnam and separation from loved ones. The siblings hoped to sponsor their husbands and wives once they resettled in the United States, but the likelihood of successful reunion was uncertain.[52] Moreover, greater scrutiny amid uncertain information resulted in more rejections of real Amerasians such as Hoang Thi Thanh, who implored the U.S. Consular Office to reconsider its decision. Seeking to immigrate with her husband, younger sister, and daughter, Hoang Thi Thanh had surrendered documentation and completed an interview only to be told she had not clearly established her identity. "I am real Amerasian," she insisted. "When my mother were still alive she told me about the name, age, rank, unit of my father. I only know my father is an American [with black skin] who was in the U.S. Military Forces."[53] Cau and his much younger wife, Trang, also fretted over an official's verdict. Despite paperwork proving the legitimacy of their marriage, the wide gap between the couple's age—he was forty-six and she twenty-four at the time of their application—raised suspicions. When Katie Kelly—a former NBC news and entertainment reporter who published a memoir in 1992 chronicling her yearlong experience teaching and helping Amerasians in Saigon—tried to support the couple's case, explaining to an ODP worker that she had visited their home, met their mother, and knew their child—he countered by acknowledging that cases sometimes proved so confusing that caprice and randomness guided the resolution.[54]

However, an even greater, more disorienting challenge confronted Amerasians with pretend families who successfully fooled officials (especially before 1992). Amerasians, as well as the professionals and volunteers who sought to educate and assist them at the Philippines Refugee Processing Center (PRPC) and various voluntary resettlement agencies in the United States, observed how quickly relations between pretend family members dissolved.[55] A twenty-four-year-old Amerasian related that his pretend family treated him kindly during the interview stage, but once they reached the PRPC, "they insult me, berate me, and the daughters even have attacked me. They loved the Amerasian when they needed to leave Vietnam, but now they despise me."[56] Loan, Be, and Dung, who had agreed to present three strangers as their respective spouses, shared a similar account of tensions that surfaced in the camps. Soon after their arrival, "these three look down on us and treat us like dirt," Be stated, prompting her to wish she and her brother and sister could travel without their marital partners to the United States. A 1991 report of overseas activities by the American Council for Voluntary International Action (aka InterAction)—a collection of nongovernmental agencies that services refugees—stated that negotiations to return four Vietnamese families falsely claiming Amerasian relatives had begun after reports of physical and emotional abuse.[57]

Sometimes these families survived the processing center but fell apart in the United States. "As soon as we got to California," Loc confessed of his supposed relatives, "they turned on me and threw me out. I feel like I am in hell."[58] Peter Daniels, coordinator of St. Anselm's Cross-Cultural Community Center Amerasian program in Garden Grove, California—one of the sixty such programs created by the Amerasian Homecoming Act, serving one of the largest concentrations of Amerasians in the United States—reported that 70 percent of their counseling cases involved Amerasians suffering the repercussions of separation from fake families.[59] Without homes, jobs, or their federal benefits, they had nowhere else to turn, Daniels posited. In one extreme case illustrative of how destructive the dissolution of even invented families could be, a young Amerasian, Kiem Van Do, stabbed to death a Vietnamese woman, Hang Thi Thay Dinh, with whom he had pretended kinship, telling police during his arrest that he was angry and wished to return to Vietnam. Kiem Van Do said that he and Hang Thi Thay Dinh had intended to marry, until her parents withdrew their alleged consent. Kiem Van Do cried, "I wouldn't have come here if she didn't promise to be together. . . . Her mother knew that. She agreed to let us marry."[60] The striking case suggested the intricacies of these created families. Clearly, genuine affections developed between members that mimicked or substituted for the bonds of their real kin, again challenging the standards of family conceived by lawmakers. An equally unintended and tragic, if less deadly, consequence of Amerasians' deception was their disappointing realization that despite their "strongest desire to bring their real families to the United States," explained a GAO report, "by joining a fake family they have disqualified themselves under U.S. law from sponsoring their real family later." Thus, Amerasians who had envisioned their ties to fake relations as a temporary and necessary means of securing opportunities for their actual family in the United States were frustrated and foiled.[61]

For all the attention paid to Vietnamese "cheating" their way into the United States by building utilitarian family units, and then grieving the effects of dislocation, the legislation also offered an opportunity to strengthen extended families and protect their wishes for better lives. Truc Tran and her mother reconnected and resided with relatives who had resettled in Salt Lake City during the early 1980s. Although their "help is limited because they had five kids of their own," Tran explained, her cousin helped her apply "to a technical college in hope that I can go in to get more skill."[62] Lieu Nguyen had borne two boys and one girl with an American civilian who unapologetically and abruptly left Vietnam in the early 1970s. Reportedly terrified by rumors that a victorious Viet Cong would seek vengeance on her multiracial offspring—echoing a theme that had dominated the testimonies of Vietnamese women during court battles to recover their children—Lieu convinced members of a Seventh-Day Adventist church to take two of her three children, Than Van Thi (renamed Merrie Li) and Tony, to the United States. Wrapped up "like mummies," the pair were presented as burn victims (presumably to ease their exit) and then placed with American families. During a 2013 interview, Merrie Li, who was four years old at the time of her migration, recalled the harrowing flight out of Vietnam: "And as we were taking off there were bombs that were being dropped all over the airport. There were people hanging onto the plane and onto the wings, and as the plane is taking off, if you were to look out the window, you would see these people just hanging onto anything and everything."[63] Meanwhile, Lieu and her eldest Amerasian son, Tung, prepared for their own departure. When their expected plane, perhaps diverted or destroyed, never arrived, Lieu remained and raised Tung in Vietnam.[64] She remarried, bore two additional boys, who died before reaching the age of five, and struggled to farm a one-acre, hillside plot whose steep slope limited its output. Despite Lieu's pleas, local schools refused to admit Tung, he recalled in a 2013 interview. He remembered "looking in, and wishing I was on the inside going to school just like the rest of them." Instead he spent his days "basically just wandering in the street all day in the sun, no food, no water, just wandering around."[65]

Lieu also struggled and longed for her and Tung to join her other children, "dreaming that she was in the States . . . and then waking up in tears, realizing that we were still in Vietnam, with not enough to eat."[66] When Lieu learned of the Amerasian program, she applied immediately and, aided by her relative English fluency, secured her migration and that of Tung and a nephew (Hai). As proved the case for so many Southeast Asians seeking solutions to regional violence and instability, the decision of who, when, and how to migrate was made after careful analysis of the relative costs and benefits for the extended family. Although family members discouraged the migration of Lieu's husband, whose drug problems they worried would worsen in the United States, they promoted the migration of Hai, whom they expected would prosper outside Vietnam. Using the birth certificate of one of Lieu's deceased sons, Hai passed as Tung's brother. Rather than a mercenary act that maligned the meanings of affective family embedded in the Amerasian Homecoming Act and U.S. immigration policy generally, the impersonation expressed the endurance and breadth of family ties. After time spent within the PRPC, the trio—Lieu, Tung, and Hai—resettled in Rochester, New York.[67]

In 1985, after one year of residence in the United States and with the help of a Vietnamese aunt who lived in California, Lieu had tracked down her son and daughter. Adopted into two different families, the Camps and the Andersons, Merrie Li and Tony had grown up separately and rarely communicated. Yet when they overheard a conversation between Sandra Camp and M. Anderson about the prospect of reuniting with their Vietnamese mother and siblings, they pressed their reluctant American parents to act. Merrie Li remembered that immediately before the arranged meeting, Sandra "broke down and started crying," prompting Merrie Li to reassure her, "It's not that big of a deal. We need to know who they are." She credited Sandra's emotions to the woman's fears that Merrie Li would become less attached.[68] Thus, when the two American families met with the Vietnamese kin in Rochester, expectations for restoration and reflection were high. Tung described the emotional and unsettling encounter. "We sat there for a while, and then this big van pulled up, and the two of them walked out. I looked at them, and I said, 'That's my sister, that's my brother,' and they looked at me and did the same thing. I mean, we knew instantly, as soon as they walked out of the van. My mom cried all day long, everybody cried." Recalling that reunion in 2014, Tung related that "we just want to hang out with each other. We didn't talk much. We just running around and play together as like kids, without even asking about each other's feelings, how we feel about one another." Merrie Li remembered less certainty about the identity of her Vietnamese family and greater confusion about the mechanisms and meanings of their interactions. "There was a little bit of hesitation there because we had been told for so long that our family was dead," she explained, and Sandra seemed determined to shed doubt, saying, "Joe [Tung] doesn't look anything like you" and "There's no proof that this was your family." Despite these early misgivings, Merrie Li and Tony "knew in our hearts it felt right," and felt warmed by the gold, heart-shaped necklaces Lieu had brought with the inscription "I love you."[69]

After more than a decade of separation, Lieu may not have intended to resume custody of her children. Tung believed that she wished "to know that her kids are well taken care of" and help Merrie Li and Tony understand "the circumstances that they were given away" and that "she loved them so much that she had to let them go to save their lives." Merrie Li concurred that Lieu wished not "to rip us away from the family that loved and cared for us and raised us," and "did not expect us to come live with her," even though she left "that as an option that we had, but that was not something that she tried to force on us."[70] Although Merrie Li and Tony would not sever ties with their adoptive parents, they, Tung, Lieu, and Marie (Lieu's youngest daughter, born in Rochester) would remain in intermittent contact for the next three decades. Merrie Li even invested in learning Vietnamese to ease communication with her mother, who had difficulty articulating her thoughts in English, especially as she aged. These commitments to remain connected across time and territory exposed the elaborate strategies of survival and revision practiced by Vietnamese families and made possible by immigration laws that favored refugees and the selective reunification of kin.

Dai Nguyen's mother also bent the boundaries of family to open up opportunities, extending patriarchal expectations embedded in Vietnamese culture about women as caretakers, but also challenging American assumptions about their docility and disappearance. Although she wanted to accompany her Amerasian son to the United States, she could not afford the journey. So she initiated contacts with Vietnamese who would pay for the privilege of claiming him as their own. While practicing for interviews with Vietnamese officials, Dai Nguyen reported that his sham relatives screamed at him. His mother implored him to bear their unkindness, because "she said I must come to the United States, that I didn't have a future in Vietnam." Once settled in Orange County with the family whom he lamented "did not like me anymore" and told him he should go, Dai Nguyen noted that he missed his mother more than ever and wished to bring her to the United States. Similarly, Thu-Ha Le's mother had given a Vietnamese man permission to pose as her daughter's husband so that the young woman could reach the United States and find her father. "She says that finding my father will mean I have a better future," Thu-Ha Le told reporters, but she seemed less interested in finding her dad and verifying the proclaimed purpose of the Homecoming Act than in bringing her mom to the United States.[71]

Even Vietnamese mothers who did not collaborate with Vietnamese strangers to secure their family's passage to the United States often accepted division—marking the irregular patterns of Vietnamese migrations—but

Merrie Li holding baby sister, Marie; brother, Brandon (*front*); Tony (*back left*); Tung (*back right*) and their mother, Lieu (*left*). Courtesy of Merrie Li Camp.

aspired to togetherness. A Vietnamese woman, Nguyet, made the painful choice to remain behind with one of her Amerasian daughters, Roan-na, whose application for immigration inspectors had initially declined, while her other daughter, Kim, left Vietnam and reunited with her American father. Almost a year later, Nguyet's risk and patience were rewarded when she and Roan-na finally won permission to immigrate. "I was so happy to see my mother and sister again," Kim gushed during a phone call to reporter Kelly. "I got off the plane, I cried, she cried."[72]

To satisfy its promise to welcome Amerasians as a special group of immigrants straddling the line between stranger and family member, the United States offered resettlement services at fifty-two sites spread across the United States for the nearly two-thirds of Amerasians who did not have Vietnamese relatives ready to receive them after their tenure at the PRPC, among the busiest of camps housed on U.S. military bases to contain and prepare Southeast Asian refugees since the mid-1970s (others were located in Guam; Thailand; Wake Island; Camp Pendleton, California; Eglin Air Force Base, Florida; Fort Indiantown Gap, Pennsylvania; and Fort Chaffee,

Arkansas). Amerasians rode the edge of a larger wave of more than a million refugees who received temporary asylum in Southeast Asia between 1970 and 1988 before being resettled in twenty countries, including the United States, which accepted 56 percent of the total.[73] As early as 1989, veterans groups and other interested parties complained about the inability of Amerasians and their families to come directly to the United States, arguing that time spent at the PRPC promoted misperceptions and unnecessarily delayed the integration of people who were not conventional refugees. Some teachers at the camps remarked on a perceived difference between the deference of earlier refugees and the insolence of the Amerasians, comments that highlighted strains at the camp and the construction of Amerasians as a distinct group expected to demonstrate gratitude and subservience.[74] Complaints about the PRPC's work with Amerasians compounded those made by Vietnamese and their advocates who had doubted its educational and cultural efforts for over a decade and spotlighted the tension between the privileged position of entry enjoyed by refugees and the reality of their internment in camps operated by the U.S. military. Although refugees fashioned forms of family and community life within these barren spaces of detainment and countered ideas of U.S. benevolence, they still grieved their dislocation and chafed under their restrictions. The United States may have insisted that humanitarian rather than political or military priorities motivated its evacuation of Vietnamese, but many Vietnamese leaders and members of a repatriation movement centered in Guam charged that the United States' efforts were a thinly veiled attempt to continue to meddle in Vietnam's affairs.[75]

After approximately six months, most Amerasians and their relatives were released from the military camp and relocated to cities chosen by the Department of Health and Human Services because of their supposed abundance of resources: affordable housing, relevant jobs, and a core of previously resettled Vietnamese. Voluntary agencies ("volags")—nongovernmental organizations authorized by the federal government—coordinated food, clothes, shelter, counseling, and sponsors.[76] Some Amerasians remembered appreciating such offerings, struck by the contrast between conditions in Vietnam and the United States. United States Catholic Charities, one of the most active volags, gave Jimmy Miller, his mother, and his siblings a furnished apartment with a fully stocked kitchen, where, he recalled, they had "enough for us to get by. And after that we have the money, we can buy more stuff what we need. But they provide the basics." Tung Nguyen agreed that despite "the strange country, strange sounds, sights," and cold of Rochester, he and his mother felt warmed by having a "house and a mattress on the floor, and a couple boxes of food to eat," because "it was more than what we had before."[77] In addition to material support, volags held orientation sessions where they brought together public schools, employers, refugee assistance organizations, Vietnam veterans groups, police, and churches to ease the acclimation of Amerasians. Although architects of the resettlement such as Marta Brenden of LIRS emphasized the advantage of clustering Amerasians for purposes of "mutual support," critics then and since have suggested that the dispersion of Amerasians and other Vietnamese realized a government ambition to limit the visibility of and potential opposition to the refugees, a thesis supported by the absence of cluster sites in California, the state where more Vietnamese would ultimately reside than any other in the country. As much as concern for the well-being of Vietnamese refugees, political and racial instincts shaped the resettlement. Americans aided Vietnamese because such outreach authenticated their faith in the freedom and fundamental goodness of the United States. Moreover, many intended Vietnamese generally, and Amerasians especially, to rapidly assimilate and reinforce their antipathy to Communism. The construction of certain immigrants as refugees has always conferred greater privileges and imposed greater obligations—Americans have supported their special treatment not only because they care, but also because they *expect*. In the case of Vietnamese Amerasians, the intensity of emotion and divisiveness of thought about the U.S. involvement in Southeast Asia elevated those expectations. Ultimately, the refugees would navigate the limits and opportunities of the U.S. resettlement program and their own tangled memories of war and dislocation, at times performing their prescribed role as fans of free markets and speech, but also countering official efforts by remigrating, growing more concentrated Vietnamese communities, and expressing feelings of trauma alongside hope.[78]

Those tasked with aiding Amerasians formed a profile of the population that shaped their endeavors. They noted their limited education, family support, and job skills, which distinguished them from Americans and even other Vietnamese refugees. Amerasians also appeared more likely to experience depression and alcoholism than their counterparts.[79] The majority of Amerasians arrived with two or three other family members, and 75 percent traveled with their mothers, whose backgrounds proved more varied than conventional wisdom suggested. Of them, 31 percent had worked in nightclubs, 25 percent as vendors, and 13 percent as housekeepers. The distribution of Amerasians' ages—4 percent were older than twenty-two years, 72 percent were between the ages of seventeen and twenty-two, and 24 percent fell within the range of fourteen to sixteen years—highlighted their relative maturity.[80] Experts also observed and expressed misgivings about Amerasians' common eagerness to build new lives and find fathers in the United States. A World Vision pamphlet detailing its new mentor program described Amerasians as young people with "unrealistic expectations about life in America" whose "fantasies might have sustained" them in Vietnam "while growing up under harsh conditions" but did not serve them in the United States.[81] Dave Anderson, coordinator of the Amerasian resettlement program for Catholic Charities of Los Angeles, similarly depicted Amerasian hopes. "There's a lot of disillusionment once they arrive and discover that they don't belong here either," he noted, "almost like a Cinderella story without a happy ending."[82]

Fairy-tale endings seemed especially unlikely for black Amerasians whose hardships in Vietnam and the United States prompted race- and culture-specific educational efforts. Perhaps because Americans had represented the United States as a more cosmopolitan and tolerant society due to its promotion of Amerasian immigration, workers for and defenders of resettlement seemed especially determined to ease the integration of black Amerasians, whom World Vision estimated composed one-third of the total Amerasian population, and prove the rhetoric right.[83] Of the 20,000 Amerasians who had arrived in the United States between 1982 and 1993, approximately 5,000 were identified as of African heritage. Government studies indicated that black Amerasians had higher rates of unemployment and seemed at greater risk for school failure given their lower scores in math and reading tests, a difference attributed to the intense discrimination that had restricted black Amerasians' school attendance in Vietnam.[84]

Believing that black Amerasians should or would have to confront the legacies of slavery, segregation, violence, and activism that defined black experiences in the United States, they sought to teach them African American history and culture. At a national conference that brought resettlement workers and scholars together to discuss how best to serve the Amerasian population, Ruben Conner of the Black Evangelistic Enterprise, who had spent time at the PRPC, recommended an increase in African American professionals working with the young adults, more educational opportunities to enhance awareness of their African heritage, and additional multicultural celebrations and events. "Afro-Amerasians are often mistaken as American," an error that he argued "continues the confusion of the individual."[85] Linda Ralph Kern, a black social worker who also resided and labored at the PRPC, agreed, advocating classes that taught a sensitivity to racial, ethnic, and cultural differences to black Amerasians, who, "because of rejection and discrimination, see little value in themselves and who may internalize negative stereotypes and perceptions that exist in the wider world."[86]

Some black Amerasians seemed to embrace an American black identity and the company of African Americans, appreciating a context and community absent in Vietnam. Conner shared the story of Thi Toan Tran, who had approached him at the PRPC. "Thi seemed to have a real need to be sponsored by persons of her own color. She needed to affirm her worth as a Black person, she needed to see that Black people like other people are achievers, significant, caring hospitable and above all, godly," a need that he predicted animated "many, many others."[87] Experts cautioned that the discovery of a black identity could cause problems as Amerasians confronted prejudice and discrimination in the United States, but still stressed the value of this engagement. Le, who attended Martin Luther King High School in New York's Bronx neighborhood, explained that "at the beginning I was surprised to see so many people with the same color skin," but his surprise turned to comfort as he became more acquainted with his black classmates and felt "I belong to this society."[88] When seventeen-year-old Khanh Milton finally met his African American father and saw hundreds of other black people in Los Angeles, he told reporters that "he felt at home."[89]

Tina Trent also displayed an emerging respect for African American experiences, offering an impassioned description of black history and its relevance to the present in *Amerasian Update*, the publication instigated by InterAction to strengthen community spirit among Amerasians. "What does it mean to be a black person in America?" she queried. "All Americans are worried about the relations between black and whites today. . . . We must begin by understanding the history of slavery, racism and repression that shaped black people's lives in America." Trent then highlighted commonalities between Africans and Southeast Asians intended to further contextualize her own life and invite solidarity rather than division between the groups. "Like modern-day refugees, the captured Africans were permanently separated from their families and their native lands. At the end of the Civil War, the troubles of black ex-slaves were similar to the troubles experienced by the South Vietnamese after the Vietnam War. Blacks could not return to Africa and America was a hostile, repressive place for them to call home." She concluded her lesson on an admiring note, stating that hard work "had made these ex-slaves brave and strong for the trials that were yet to come."[90]

Others resisted associations with blackness, including two black Amerasians placed with a black foster family outside Philadelphia—a choice informed by the prevailing preference to racially match minority children. Within days of their residence, however, the pair asked to be removed from their new home, citing their discomfort with the family's racial background. Such strong and surprising reactions, some social workers concluded, expressed the virulence of racial prejudice in Vietnam, where Amerasians and their mothers had been pushed to the margins of society. Another black Amerasian girl, whom volunteers had purposely assigned to a black foster family, responded with rage and disappointment. When questioned, the girl explained that "she had promised her mother never to let a black man touch her like her father had touched her mother."[91]

Among the most stirring, unique, and discussed challenges of the Amerasian resettlement was the search for their fathers, a seemingly necessary, if rarely realized, step along their path of assimilation. Advocates of the homecoming had spoken in broad and confident terms about the father-child reunions that would finally put to rest unsettled ideas about the war and reinstall a benevolent version of American manhood, which had been troubled by images of soldiers' violence and indiscipline. However, few had envisioned the practicalities and probabilities of a successful search. Amerasians looking for their fathers could expect limited help from the American Red Cross, the Department of State's Bureau for Refugee Programs, the Pearl S. Buck Foundation, the Veterans Administration, and the Amerasian Registry. Too often, the scarcity of clues about a father's identity halted efforts before they began. Proposals for the U.S. government to create a centralized registry of men seeking offspring were initially dismissed as useless; too few prospective fathers had come forward.[92]

If reunions proved unlikely—some estimated that fewer than 5 percent of Amerasians would actually succeed in locating their fathers[93]—this did not dissuade many Amerasians from trying or prevent resettlement workers from agonizing over the meaning of those attempts and how they might assist in them. In a 1991 essay titled "The Dream of Meeting with the Blood Father," published in *Amerasian Update*, Nguyen Huynh Tuyet expressed the intense, conflicting emotions that defined the quests of so many Amerasians. "He is always the most holy—beautiful imagination in my life. I had the dreams of meeting my FATHER, MR. DAVID. . . . But will that FATHER accept me as his daughter? I do not want to meet HIM. . . . I write these words from the depth of my heart, I pray to GOD to send my thoughts to Mr. David, my beloved FATHER."[94] Indeed, even if they found their American fathers, many were not welcomed and had to manage that disappointment. With the help of his Vietnamese aunt, Tung Nguyen located his father, who had worked for a Vietnamese-based company during the war, but the man expressed indifference to a reunion with his son. Tung accepted this decision, explaining that "in my mind he's not my father. My father was the one that was still in Vietnam [Tung's Vietnamese stepfather].... That's the one that I care about. That's the one that I was attached to." Thus, he concluded that not connecting to his birth father "was perfectly fine. I don't feel loss whatsoever."[95]

In contrast, Jimmy Miller's and Angelina Memon's searches ended in reconciliation and the revision rather than the rupture of family possibilities. As depicted in interviews, their meetings with their respective fathers represented the rare realization of sentimental reunions so often imagined by Amerasians, policy makers, and the general public. Telephoned in 1994 by James, his North Carolina–based father, who had found Jimmy as a result of his sister Trinh's investigations, Jimmy at first doubted his father's identity. Eventually, James assuaged these fears, arranged for the pair to meet in Spokane, Washington, and, as Jimmy described it, "we just give each other a hug. We just hold each other, not say anything. You know? We not saying anything. Not a single word." James would visit for more than a month on the occasion of his grandson's birth and remain in regular contact with the family till he died a year later. Finding his father also introduced Jimmy to his American-born stepsiblings, who soon overcame their surprise and displeasure about their father's concealment (he had not previously disclosed Jimmy's or his mother's existence) and developed a friendship with their Amerasian brother. Memon also spoke fondly, even effusively, of seeing her father in 1990 after an eighteen-year separation. "The father I dreamed of really did exist," she stated, and came to regularly rely on his support and care. Memon felt so strongly in her attachment to her American father and invested in an Americanized identity that she took his last name; the Vietnamese woman born Pham Ngoc Anh became Angelina Wentz.[96]

Although Amerasians seemed the most vested in pursuing their American fathers, their mothers typically played integral roles, instigating the investigations, offering stories, providing photos and letters as clues, and layering their own hopes for recovering the past on those of their children. Their collaboration displayed a commitment to reweaving frayed strands of family and flouted popular perceptions about Vietnamese women as abandoned by and indifferent to American men. Volunteers in Houston

Left to right: Jimmy Miller; his father, James; son; and father-in-law, Charlie. Courtesy of Jimmy Miller.

reported the story of Sang, an Amerasian who had grown weary of his mother's "tireless" talk about his father. He complained that "she shows everybody her little diamond ring, an old coat, and a dozen old pictures of herself with Sang" taken more than twenty years ago. Dejection over a failure to find his father rather than disinterest in the discovery seemed the source of his displeasure with his mother.[97] For her daughter Thuy's sake rather than her own, Nguyen Thi Phuong also wished to find her former lover. "One thing I hope: I hope Thuy can see her father some day," a hope she sought to realize by approaching United States Catholic Charities. When the organization informed her that Thuy's father had a wife and other children, she responded, "[I] don't care for myself," having spent nineteen years alone, but would encourage Thuy to contact him.[98]

Often a Vietnamese mother's reception of her American husband or lover proved important to Amerasians' own story of reconciliation and acceptance in the United States. Memon organized a meeting between her mother and her American father, whom neither Memon nor her mother had seen in almost two decades. In her memoir, Memon described the encounter between her parents as affectionate. "Their conversation became a little awkward, like they had knots in their throats. They became shy and hesi-

Angelina Memon and her father. Courtesy of Angelina Memon.

tant. I hadn't seen my mother so charming and lovely like that evening." Stripped of years and a heaviness of heart, "she was the mother I used to remember in the past," Memon wrote.[99] Jimmy Miller recalled a reunion of parents just as filled with possibility. When his American father, James, located him and his mother in 1994, the Vietnam veteran felt so relieved and drawn to his former Vietnamese lover, Kim, that he proposed divorcing his current wife, Nancy, and marrying her. Kim declined the offer, not because she no longer loved James, but because she decided, as Jimmy explained, "if now she go back and she already sad in the past, she accept it. Now if she do that for herself, she would make Nancy sad." In a tragic inversion of the popular musical *Miss Saigon*, in which a heartbroken Vietnamese woman kills herself after her American lover departs Vietnam, James returned home to North Carolina so saddened by Kim's refusal that he stopped taking his medication and died of a heart attack.[100]

Counselors typically described the search for one's father as an expression of an Amerasian's desire for certainty and inclusion in a life marred by rejection and instability. Officials cautioned workers to manage the expectations of their Amerasian clients, honor paternal privacy, and maintain objectivity. David Brigham of the Veterans Assistance Service Program urged staff at the LIRS who contacted veterans to proceed with "extreme caution and sensitivity" and prepare Amerasians for the news that "some veterans will not desire this contact and their rights should be respected."[101] Representatives of the United States Catholic Conference echoed this advice, explaining that "the desire of the child to know his/her origins must be balanced" not only by the complicated emotional and psychological dimensions of his or her "discovery," but by "the need to maintain the alleged father's privacy and confidentiality."[102] Current and later critics would contend that the officials overvalued the rights of fathers and undervalued the interests of their offspring.[103]

Acknowledging the continued salience of competing positions and strong emotions about the Vietnam War, Julie MacDonald, a leader of LIRS's children's services, encouraged staff "to deal with our own guilt about the rejection of these children in their native land" without "insisting that the father counteract that rejection with unreal acceptance," an insistence she believed would do more harm than good to Amerasians and their mothers.[104] MacDonald also cautioned against the prevailing belief that a longing for one's American father meant a rejection of one's Vietnamese mother and culture, a belief that had supported an exceptionalist vision of Amerasian migration and resettlement. "These young people are as much Vietnamese as any other Vietnamese national that we serve. When we try to protect Amerasians by denying their Vietnamese cultural heritage, it leaves them doubly rejected, this time as Vietnamese," she explained.[105] Indeed, experts strove to contextualize the father search by uncovering as much as possible about an Amerasian's background, especially his or her relationship with the mother. One psychologist coached counselors to "discover fantasies of the father communicated by the mother" and proposed that anger as much as affection may drive the Amerasian.[106] MacDonald also stressed the influence of mothers, arguing that "the stronger the mother's positive feeling toward the father, the stronger their child's comfort with an American identity is likely to be."[107] Bringing Vietnamese mothers into the conversation about paternity may have been standard practice among psychologists, but it also effectively diluted the power of fathers and made clear that Amerasians' past and current relations with mothers and other kin shaped their assimilation.

In creative recognition of how American veterans' struggles to reintegrate and manage memories of the Vietnam War resembled those of Amerasians, some veterans introduced the two populations. Noting the uniqueness of Amerasians' resettlement challenges, David Hall of the Organization of Vietnam Veterans in Binghamton, New York, announced a program in which local veterans who were "no strangers themselves to living in a hostile America" would mentor Amerasian children. Spending time with veterans in educational and recreational settings—the vets played sports as well as taught English to their mentees—the Amerasians reportedly bonded with their new friends, a connection Hall hoped would "positively influence other Americans."[108] In Sacramento, Don Truitt founded Friends of Amerasians, a collection of veterans helping their fellows find Amerasian children. Truitt hoped that by bringing the two groups together he could correct the misperceptions and bad feelings that had lingered since the war's end.[109] The president of Vietnam Veterans of America (VNVA), Gary Vancena, similarly imagined the coming together of veterans and Amerasians as a mutually restorative act. Discouraging resettlement workers from asking VNVA members to collectively engage with Vietnamese people "because of feelings of resentment that stem from the Viet Nam War," he recommended approaching individuals and requesting a limited commitment. "Amerasians are often very pleased to work with veterans," Vancena noted, "because the veterans may serve as father figures for them." He predicted that as veterans became more involved, "they can serve as advocates for Amerasian issues," suggesting that familiarity bred comfort and understanding.[110] Thus, if Amerasians did not always find their actual fathers, friendships with American men familiar with Vietnam offered both parties the opportunity to reinterpret and ruminate about the past.

On reflection, government officials, journalists, and the general public arrived at the conclusion that despite all their protestations about the unique adaptability of Amerasians and the speed with which they would become part of the American family, the group closely resembled other immigrants. Kelly, the retired reporter who taught and befriended Amerasians, wrote pessimistically about their chances for acceptance in the United States on the eve of their migration. "Despite their very American features, despite their hard work at establishing and then defiantly celebrating their American selves, by this late date these kids were simply American wannabes.

And, for a terrible time at least, they would not fit in anywhere. Not into mainstream America, nor into any established Vietnamese community."[111] Kelly speculated that Amerasians would be considered "Vietnamese who do not speak English," rather than "Americans born in Vietnam," as they desired. In considering the sources of their false hopes and troubled paths of integration, Kelly blamed herself and other Americans who projected their own expectations and needs onto the young adults. "Americans—like me, like those veterans I met—came over and fussed over these young Amerasians. We were overwhelmed by our encounters with these kids because in a sense they were all our children. . . . For these were our special, spiritual children haunting us by holding our past up to us, reminding us where we'd been, what we had done."[112] She recognized what so few Americans would admit: that Amerasians mattered for what they seemed to represent—the unsettled but powerful legacies of the Vietnam War—as much as who they were. Her assessment also underscored a broader truth about Vietnamese refugees: that Americans extended acceptance on the condition of the refugees' easy assimilation and professions of gratitude.

Thomas Bass's *Vietnamerica*, published amid the wave of Vietnam-focused memoirs, films, and literature that washed over its American audience in the early 1990s, offered a similarly emotional and recriminating portrait of the status of Amerasians in America. During a visit to the Mohawk Valley Resource Center in Utica, New York,[113] he detailed the frustrations and despair of underserviced Amerasians who appear destined for lives of poverty and criminality. "Amerasians have to settle for four months of 'survival' English and a minimum-wage job. Refugee Agencies called this 'successful integration into American life,' but Amerasians call it 'a lack of love,'" Bass explained. In Bass's account, unrequited love led Amerasians to prostitution, violence, self-mutilation, and attempted suicide. Those employed earned low wages at unskilled retail and factory jobs with few benefits and no security. Welcome Home House, a project conceived as a selective substitute for the PRPC, had closed after only one year. Bass blamed patronage, nepotism, and incompetence for the quick end. Supposedly, the 375 Amerasians and family members placed in the project graduated with the same levels of anxiety and depression, exposure to sexual coercion, and "feelings of being alien creatures dropped on the back side of the moon" found among those who passed through the PRPC.[114] The testimonies of Amerasians underlined Bass's central thesis that despite legislation and programs intended to welcome and ease the entry of Amerasians, Americans had not embraced them. Le Ha, an Amerasian whose mother Bass depicted as abusive, voiced the author's explanation of why not: "We remind people of all the things they want to forget—the war, the bombs, the killing and suffering.... Here in America, we remind people of the soldiers who went to Asia and never came back. Le Ha means 'river of tears.' My life is too much like my name."[115] Bass's account honestly revealed the difficulties faced by many Amerasians in the United States, but its unrelenting focus on their problems rather than their possibilities and achievements typecast the population and served his political point about the unresolved issues of war in Southeast Asia.

Government investigators and resettlement workers offered less impassioned but equally strong censures of American efforts to help Amerasians. A 1994 congressional report assessing the outcomes of resettlement noted that "as past experience has shown the process of moving to a new country creates its own difficulties. It separates immigrants from their families ... as well as from their language and culture," and in the case of Amerasians that separation had created difficulties not overcome by special attempts at assistance.[116] The report speculated that Amerasians might have adjusted more readily if they had immigrated earlier, but "were brought to the United States too late to grow up American and thereby become mainstream Americans," a timeline that one could interpret as partial recrimination for delayed action.[117] Volunteers and paid officials of resettlement agencies challenged American optimism about the fate of Amerasians while complimenting their desire to help. "It is a generous sentiment reflecting the sense of responsibility and spirit of welcome that many Americans feel toward Amerasians. But Amerasians are not 'our kids' and they are not 'coming home,'" Douglas Gilzow and Donald Ranard of the Refugee Service Center insisted, with a deliberate use of language that had also dominated justifications of the 1987 law. "In their adjustment to a new and very different culture, Amerasians will experience many of the same problems that other refugees and immigrants have faced. Their biological heritage will not spare them the ambivalence that most newcomers feel, as exhilaration and high expectations are gradually tempered by a sense of loss."[118] The realization that biology would not assure belonging undermined the fundamental belief that had driven the Homecoming Act: that Amerasians were essentially Americans and would quickly adjust to their new environment, thus permitting Americans to congratulate themselves on the fulfillment of neglected obligations. The seeming failure of Amerasians to feel at home in the United States conveniently delayed closure on the subjects of the Vietnam War and American obligations to its newest immigrants.

Amerasians may have confronted the same challenges as other refugees and immigrants, but they typically did so without the cultural and economic resources provided by a common ethnic community, making their adjustment more complex. Hoa Bui, refugee coordinator of the Don Basco Center in Kansas City, confessed in 1991 that "it would have been better if the Amerasian children could have come here 10 years ago rather than now," because "our culture is strict, and though the children are innocent, they're never accepted. They're seen as coming from a bad mother."[119] Of Amerasians asked whether they considered themselves Vietnamese, American, or "other" as part of a congressional study in 1994, only 44 percent said Vietnamese, a choice that highlighted their detachment from the ethnic community, in part because they "continued to be rejected by many of the Vietnamese living in the United States," the authors concluded.[120] The celebrated example of Vietnamese refugees helping Amerasians in Washington, D.C., highlighted the rarity of such connections. Designed to bring attention to the problem of disconnection and encourage similar outreach, the *Amerasian Update* reprinted an article first published in the *New York Times* that featured a black Amerasian employed and mentored by three Vietnamese at a mechanic's shop. One of the owners of Tune Up Kit explained that self-interest should lead Vietnamese to help Amerasians. "If the Vietnamese community doesn't do something and the government doesn't do something to help young people, it will haunt them," he insisted, "You'll always have a gun in your house."[121] His call to help betrayed the active prejudices that discouraged so many Vietnamese from lending a hand; they too often assumed that Amerasians would remain or become criminals.

Despite the reluctance of many Vietnamese to embrace Amerasians, and the dreary conclusion drawn by government officials and media in the mid-1990s that the program had fallen short, many Amerasians and their family members would enjoy relative successes in the United States. After settling in Spokane rather than Seattle—a choice shaped by his conviction that a city with a smaller Vietnamese population offered more opportunities—Jimmy Miller took an exhausting and chilly but well-paid job on a crab boat. With greater experience, education, and continued dedication, he eventually secured a position as a mechanic and advanced through the ranks at the Boeing Corporation. Meanwhile, his sister studied dutifully, graduated from the University of Washington with a degree in food science, and was hired by the Food and Drug Administration. Tung Nguyen's story also underlined the possibility of integration and socioeconomic mobility despite the difficulties of dislocation and prevailing perceptions of Amerasians' failings. After researching microelectronics at a university in New York, Tung joined and made a rewarding career in the U.S. military. Memon depicted the relative ease of her adjustment. Although disarmed initially by certain American customs such as looking elders directly in the eye during conversations, she appreciated the food, the friendliness, and the candor of her Philadelphia neighbors. Determined to help others "because through my experience and difficult life and I understand how the children have to go through being abandoned and nobody care for them and I want to be the guidance and try to help them and support them,"[122] she eventually obtained a bachelor's degree and enjoyed a career as a social worker. Truc Tran recalled that she acclimated just as readily and came to appreciate the differences between American and Vietnamese cultures. A resident of Salt Lake City who received degrees in business management and computer science, she not only learned "how to speak English correctly, how to act in an institutional environment that is going to deal with students, the American way," but liked the "outward thinking for independence" that characterized Americans. "You hold on to it, you grab it, you take it," she continued, unlike the Vietnamese, who "are more reserved. And that is good, but not good in the professional environment."[123]

The director of the Amerasian Resettlement Program, Anita Menghetti, acknowledged the hardships Amerasians like Tung, Memon, Tran, and Miller confronted, but also stressed their gains in education and employment. In a statement announcing the program's end in 1993 as migrations subsided, she stressed their successes rather than problems.[124] The pages of *Amerasian Update* certainly featured the disappointments and difficulties of Amerasians, but just as often it shared tales of Amerasians happily adjusting to American society. Son, an Amerasian, and his mother arrived in Philadelphia in 1991. Although he had never attended school in Vietnam, and knew very little English, he eventually landed a job at an auto remanufacturing plant and rose quickly through its hierarchy. As another example representative of the experiences of a larger class of Amerasians, Phoung found employment at a grocery store after he learned sufficient English and then won promotion to manager. With his steady income, he supported his mother and purchased a red sports car that he proudly displayed.[125]

Seeking to build a sense of community and opportunity among Amerasians that corrected or at least complicated the now prevalent belief that they remained loners on the margins of American society, their lives barely improved from their days in Vietnam, the young adults shared their positive experiences and ideas through conferences, social groups, and newsletters. In a piece titled "What Will We Do," Tu Le referenced the many films and articles about Amerasians that had shaped American impressions of the multiracial immigrants, but thought these representations distorted rather than revealed the lives of Amerasians in the United States.[126] Having just returned from a two-day conference in San Diego attended by hundreds of Amerasians from all over the United States, he coached his compatriots "to unite together to make our community stronger, and . . . show everyone that we are not useless people as Vietnamese people in Vietnam thought we were."[127] In a 1990 issue of *Amerasian Update*, Ho Thi Kim Nguyet agreed that many people had "the wrong idea about Amerasians." He emphasized that environment rather than character explained their struggles and predicted that their youth and enthusiasm would assure their eventual success, offering his own life as evidence.[128]

The resettlement of Amerasians and their families in the United States reenergized and revised American discussions about the duration and nature of U.S. responsibilities to Southeast Asia and its people that had structured the process and interpretation of Vietnamese adoptions a decade earlier. In Amerasians, Americans envisioned a second chance to prove the nation's good will and capacity for inclusion. However, the relative maturity, familial attachments, and independent ambitions of Amerasians complicated this conception of their migrations. Their arrival raised questions about gendered power relations and how broadly Americans might conceptualize the family. Moreover, the movement of Amerasians expressed the continued, creative efforts of Vietnamese families to reconnect, reestablish, and realize new lives after years of violence, disruption, and loss.

4 Living Legacies

Reflecting on the adoption of her daughter, Dolores Sloviter noted that she and her husband had "concentrated on the hope of adopting a Vietnamese orphan because we were both vehement opponents of the United States role in that war and wanted to make some effort, however small, to redress the damage. Also we knew there was a supply of orphans whom many prospective parents would reject because of the racial difference." On April 29, 1975, the couple realized their hopes of adopting a child, critiquing the Vietnam War, and defying conventional racial attitudes. They received a call from the Delaware Regional Adoption Council reporting the sudden availability of a Vietnamese girl evacuated from the An Lac Orphanage; they could immediately collect her at a shopping mall in Plymouth Meeting, Pennsylvania, a suburb of Philadelphia. Despite the lack of advance warning, the Sloviters hurried to the site where nearly one hundred other families eagerly awaited their new, Vietnam-born sons and daughters. The Sloviters named the small, frail girl placed in their arms Vikki. Not for Victoria—a name that Dorothy explained connoted war and conflict—but one that phonetically rendered the girl's Vietnamese name, Vu Thuy Quyen. Due to the rarity of interracial families in the 1970s, Dorothy noted, Vikki was an "oddity," a condition the Sloviters tried to remedy by hiring a Vietnamese nanny who could speak Vietnamese, cook Vietnamese dishes, and teach Vikki about Vietnam, as well as sending her to one of Philadelphia's more diverse, progressive private schools.[1]

Vikki did not always embrace these plans to protect her from prejudices and doubts about her identity. By her own admission, she was not interested in learning about Vietnamese culture and "patently refused" her mother's repeated proposals to visit Vietnam. "I never felt Asian or Vietnamese," she insisted, rarely identifying herself as such even though she recognized her physical appearance distinguished her from her white parents.[2] During college in the early 1990s, she resented solicitations by Asian American students to join their ethnic associations. Reflecting back on those days, Vikki interpreted her resentment as evidence of the dilemma confronted and rarely resolved by most adoptees about whether to identify based on "how one looked physically or how one was raised."³ However, a 1998 contest in *Life Magazine*, which invited essays of one hundred words or fewer describing the person one would most like to meet, changed Vikki's perspective. She entered and won the contest with a submission celebrating the altruism of Betty Tisdale, a woman central to Operation Babylift, the mass airlift that had brought Vikki to the United States in 1975; she had learned about the dramatic event and Tisdale's role after watching the film *The Children of An Lac*, originally released in 1980. As her reward, Vikki was flown to Seattle, where she met Tisdale and a host of reporters who documented the pair's reunion. The women hugged, shared photos, and examined keepsakes from the orphanage where Tisdale had worked and cared for Vikki before her departure.⁴ "One of the most emotional events in her life" and one that "made everything feel real," Vikki explained that afterward she no longer "denied" her Vietnamese past "as much." However, she never considered herself an immigrant, despite her foreign birth. Immigrants are those "who bring something with them," she remarked. "Because I did not bring any food, family or belongings and I was too young to retain a memory or connection to Vietnam, I have always considered myself American."⁵

Vikki's entry, assimilation, and eventual engagement with Southeast Asia reveal the complex and varied experiences of Vietnamese children who grew up and acted as living legacies of the Vietnam War. Folded into and sometimes stretched between American and Vietnamese families, adopted Vietnamese and Amerasians observed ongoing conversations about how to remember the war, played out in literature, film, memorials, and U.S. policy toward Vietnam. At the same time, a heightened appreciation and politicization of cultural differences by distinct ethnoracial groups problematized interracial families and recommended new strategies of parenting. Ideas of cultural preservation and pluralism championed by ethnoracial minorities and many whites directed adoptive parents and their children to discover Vietnamese traditions and connect with Vietnamese refugees in the late 1980s and 1990s, but oftentimes differences in geography, language, foods, education, and conceptions of race, gender, and sexuality complicated such connections. So did the lure of exceptionalist and apologetic conceptions of American actions in Southeast Asia, beliefs that dismissed or deemphasized the role of U.S. ambition and violence in the region.

Although a sense of cultural, political, and economic distinctions often divided adopted Vietnamese and Amerasians who immigrated in the 1980s from other Vietnamese, by the end of the 1990s and with the normaliza-

Vikki and her parents, Henri and Dolores Sloviter, on Thanksgiving, 1975. Courtesy of Vikki Sloviter.

tion of U.S.-Vietnam relations, both these groups increasingly sought to reconnect to Vietnam. They researched, documented, and interpreted their own histories with an energy, emotion, and attention to complexity that distinguished their work from earlier renderings. They designed and communicated via websites dedicated to transnational adoption and interracial identity; organized social events, reunions, and conferences in the United States; took photographs; sang songs; wrote memoirs; produced documentaries; joined tours of Vietnam; volunteered at heritage camps for the most recent generation of adopted Vietnamese; lobbied Congress to facilitate the naturalization of Amerasians; and launched DNA projects to ease the search for Vietnamese or American kin. These journeys, communions, and cultural productions changed how the adoptees, Amerasians, Vietnamese immigrants, and Americans generally thought about their pasts and contributed to more elaborate understandings of refugees. Rather than confirm the "determined incomprehension" that defines the general public's stance on the Vietnam War—one that too often obscures Vietnamese suffering and violence and American culpability—they have tried to expose a history of racial difference, damage, and dislocation that highlights both the uniqueness and the commonality of their places within the larger diaspora of Vietnamese.[6] Many gained a sense of belonging, rediscovered and formed attachments with extended Vietnamese kin within Vietnam and the United States, expressed ideas of closure or new beginnings, or committed to improving conditions in Vietnam. Others admitted feelings of estrangement from Vietnamese people and culture, a greater appreciation for their adoptive families, and a surer belief in their American identities. At times, these affirmations of whiteness and Americanness reproduced rather than unraveled a Cold War discourse that had motivated American initiatives in Asia. Overall, the adoptees' conclusions suggest the fluidity and complexity of their assimilations. The demographics of their American communities and families, popular assumptions about the poverty and precariousness of Vietnamese refugees, memories of or discoveries about wars in Southeast Asia, the adoptee's gender,[7] and persistent anti-Asian sentiment conditioned the belonging of these uncommon immigrants.

Like the Sloviters, many American parents sought to reinforce or introduce Vietnamese culture to their adoptive offspring, embracing the insights of cultural nationalists and families who adopted from other regions of Asia, especially Korea. Many had highlighted their respect for cultural differences in their appeals to adoption agencies, as explored earlier in this book, and now wished to practice those ideals. In doing so, they contributed to a critical change in the practices and ideas of adoptive families in the mid-1960s and early 1970s, one that heralded a broader shift in national culture. Much like the white adoptive parents of domestic minority children, especially African Americans, who rejected still-prevalent community opinion, adoptive parents of Vietnamese chose to recognize, even emphasize racial and cultural differences without expecting their disappearance.[8] This recognition could also reinforce their search for forgiveness and sense of responsibility to Vietnamese within and outside the United States. In her 1977 memoir Gretchen Duling depicted her and her husband's efforts to teach the black Vietnamese boy whom they had adopted in 1973 about his biracial heritage, efforts she encouraged others to emulate. "We wanted to be able to assist in learning black-American culture but also Vietnamese culture," Joe[9] she said, even though the Dulings felt unsure "what difference this would make to him, but at least we could provide him with more knowledge to back up the decisions he would need to make later in this life." Gretchen argued that adoptive parents had an obligation to appreciate "not only the differences between the world's peoples, but the reasons for these differences," because such an awareness might help "bring about the lifting of racial barriers." Anticipating Joe's possible struggles with racial prejudice and questions of identity, she pledged to "handle these times as well as I can," and expressed gratitude for the proximity of other multiracial families and for her residence in a community of "relative open-mindedness and acceptance."[10] Indeed, during their time in Boston, the Dulings met monthly with a community of Vietnamese and adoptive families to discuss shared experiences and learn Vietnamese culture. Parents commiserated about the disapproval of relatives and emotional outbursts of their children. Gretchen also recalled the friendliness of Vietnamese participants who "were very accepting and helpful to us," teaching about Vietnamese cuisine and customs.[11] Jan De Hartog, the father of two Korean adoptees and a member of FMSVC, similarly instructed adoptive parents to moderate American cultural influences and maintain the child's history. He cautioned against expecting a quick transformation of the child and the ability "to dazzle him out of memories of his past," as these "children are not our own." Such doubts about the redemptive and assimilative powers of the American family shaped the expectations of adoptive parents and the experiences of Vietnamese.[12]

Despite or perhaps because of these doubts, some adoptive American families invested more heavily in Vietnamese culture and politics, offering sustained support to Vietnamese refugees. Years after adopting an eight-year-old boy from Vietnam, Virginia and Bill Littauer fostered two Vietnamese children, sponsored Vietnamese refugees, and taught English at a local community center. Ken Armstrong, the Vietnam veteran who adopted Ri, a young Cambodian boy who had lost his family and his leg during wars in Southeast Asia, opened his home and heart to a series of Vietnamese families bewildered by their new environment. "We had one couple that lived in our house, that had two daughters, and then later we had another couple," he related during a 2012 interview. His advocacy did not end there. After working with Catholic and Lutheran organizations to help resettle refugees, Armstrong discovered the unique problems of Vietnamese children and began fostering them. Some remained with him and his wife for as long as nine years, others only a few months, till they felt ready for independence. In one case, Armstrong assumed care for seventeen-year-old Kien, who became "such a close part of the family" that while celebrating his twenty-third birthday, Kien asked "to be part of the family" and "have your [Armstrong's] last name." Armstrong formally adopted the refugee, who later married, moved out of Armstrong's household, and secured a job with Continental Airlines.[13]

A group of children, including Stephen Lester Ngo Duling (*second from right*), sitting on a stoop in Vietnam, 1973. Courtesy of Gretchen Duling.

Duling family (Stephen, his sister Teddie Anne, Henry, and Gretchen) and new kitten, 1973. Courtesy of Gretchen Duling.

Ri and Ken Armstrong, 2015. Courtesy of Ken Armstrong.

Perhaps the strongest statement of his commitment to Southeast Asian peoples and desire to mitigate the damages of war, Armstrong founded a nonprofit organization, Child Rescue, in 2003 to help orphans in Cambodia. He explained that when he returned to Southeast Asia with a group of nurses and medics in 2000, the relative wealth and restoration of Vietnam impressed him, while the extreme poverty and absence of orphanages in Cambodia made him despair and prompted him to intervene. Rather than facilitate the adoption of young babies—a role Armstrong noted other organizations fulfilled—Child Rescue helped older and injured children secure better education, homes, food, and security within the region.[14]

For Bill Popp, like Armstrong and the Littauers, becoming a parent to one Vietnamese child was the first rather than the final expression of service to Vietnamese, one that spurred an ongoing tug of obligation. After he and his Vietnamese wife, Lon, won the court battle and secured custody of her three sons, the pair turned their attention to Vietnamese refugees and Amerasians. Popp related that in 1980, the pair housed as many as ten Vietnamese; they helped the new arrivals find jobs, learn English, and obtain driver's licenses. Five years later, the Popps sponsored two Amerasian young girls and their mother, whom Popp described as "part of our family now," saying that they "have done exceedingly well."[15] Closeness to Vietnamese refugees could not only assuage an adoptive family's feelings of guilt about the

Living Legacies   123

consequences of war but also establish connections between adopted Vietnamese and Vietnamese communities. Trista's adoptive mother, Nancy Kalan, corresponded with, sponsored, and eventually housed the Vietnamese family who had fostered Trista for the one year prior to her migration in 1973. A pastor in Vietnam, Trista's foster father and his wife, mother, and four children lived with the Kalans for years before establishing a separate residence. Trista remembered them as a hardworking group who introduced her to Vietnamese celebrations, language, and foods. The orientation they offered to Vietnamese culture continued when she began waitressing at their Vietnamese restaurant at age fifteen.[16]

A general sense of responsibility for the struggles of Vietnamese and a specific prescription to expose adoptive children to Vietnamese culture proved so strong that even in families where adoptees remembered the absence of Vietnamese customs, their American parents had publicly professed openness to these traditions. During a 2009 interview, Kimberly Thompson referenced a 1975 newspaper article featuring her adoption and her parents' promise to preserve her ethnic heritage. But Thompson dismissed the stated promise as an empty claim intended to preserve the appearance of "bringing home this refugee and giving her a wonderful home and aren't we wonderful people." After the reporters disappeared, her parents raised her no differently from her white siblings, she insisted. Thompson puzzled over and acknowledged her bitterness over this choice, noting that in contemporary America, "if you put a black child with a white family you better believe they know what Kwanza is and better know how to cut black hair and cook certain foods."[17] Her parents' choice underscored a persistently different racialization of Asian girls as deferential and easy to direct, despite attention drawn to and the celebration of diverse cultural origins in the 1980s and 1990s.

LeChristine Hai expressed similar disappointment about her adoptive parents' decision to resist the cultural recommendations of the era's activists and educators. At age eleven, following the imprisonment of her Vietnamese mother by the Vietcong, Hai's desperate and destitute grandmother placed her in an orphanage. According to Hai's memoir, she reached the United States and the Willis family in 1975. The family changed her and her brother's names from Hai and Sang to Christi and Jason, respectively. Told that she and Jason "should forget our past" and find comfort in the "big house with our perfect family with plenty of food and television," Hai could not sustain her Vietnamese culture or connections to Vietnamese family, a loss that she deeply regretted when she reached adulthood.[18]

The disappointment registered by Hai and Thompson notably surfaced later in life. Even in the many adoptive families who accepted and sought to follow advice about explaining Vietnamese ways and the Vietnam War, their children typically resisted such explanations until they matured during the 1990s and early twenty-first century; they sought refuge in conventional constructions of a white, middle-class America, reiterating reductive conceptions of Vietnam and Vietnamese identity. Bob Burns remembered identifying "T.V. programs and books and other things on Vietnam," only to have his daughter, Jane, express "no real interest." Neither did Virginia Littauer's son, John, despite the visits she had arranged of a local Vietnamese woman who shared her language and foods.[19]

Adopted within a context of political conflict and war, few Vietnamese children wished to grapple with such troubling events and tackle the gendered and racialized power dynamics between the United States and Vietnam. Julie Davis noted that she avoided the subject of Vietnam because "what little I knew of the war was bad and I felt people would dislike [what] reminded them of such a painful period of our history." Hai pondered over how to explain the war to her American friends, because although she had lived in Vietnam as a young child before her migration and adoption, she "never knew it the way many Americans remember it" and was "too young to understand the political agenda that caused the war." So over time, she substituted her own vague and painful memories of Vietnam with what she learned "like any other children reading about a war that became a part of American History." When Hoang Purdy discovered a book of newspaper clippings regarding the circumstances of his adoption collected by his mother, Pam, he wondered why she had kept accounts critiquing the U.S. role in Vietnam and the airlift of Vietnamese children. "I guess your adoption had more to do with politics than Ron's [her other adopted son] did," she responded, prompting Hoang to ask, "What's politics anyway?" Praising the question, Pam replied, "I would say . . . because this country was committed to winning a war in Vietnam for so long, there was, and still is, more interest in your adoption." The thought of such attention and the reminder that he could not remember his Vietnamese mother brought Hoang to tears and inspired more questions about the possibilities of love and reproduction across political and cultural divides: "Mom, if my real father was a black American soldier, and my real mother was Vietnamese, how could they get together, if they were fighting on different sides?" Pam searched for a simple and soothing explanation that would clarify the American role in Vietnam and Hoang's separation from his birth mother. "Do you know what a civil war is honey? It's a war when one part of a country fights another part. It was the South Vietnamese against the North Vietnamese. Your father was in Vietnam because the United decided to take sides with the South," she asserted, "and that's why your mother, along with other mothers of half-American children decided you would be safe in this country." Hoang may have felt safe in the United States, but learning of his past only reinforced his desire to get along and disguise his differences. He longed for straight blond hair and confessed, "Mom, I guess what I'm saying is that I hate being called Blackie and Cotton Picker at school. I wish I were white." Although the Purdys believed that he should retain the name Hoang and highlight his Vietnamese origins, he found the name "unsettling" and preferred to use the American-sounding "Stephen."[20]

Many adoptees shared Hoang's resolve to forget or avoid attachments to Vietnam, a strategy of assimilation and cultural detachment often embraced by other children of Asian descent growing up in majority white, American communities, and one that neglected the problem of American will and violence in Asia. "[I] shed everything that resembled Vietnam" and "determined to mold myself into any other form but Asian," Brad Davis recalled of his youthful efforts. "I always wanted to be white for a long time," Jay Sheridan similarly confessed; rather than rice, he savored "hot dogs and McDonalds."[21] Kim Delevett explained that she did not wish to talk about Vietnam, "a foreign place," but wished "to fit in and be like other friends who were blond and blue eyed." So dismayed was she by her "being Vietnamese American," she said, "[I] used to pull at my nose because I wanted it to be more pointy." In eighth grade, she was embarrassed when her classmates attended her naturalization ceremony because she "didn't want to talk about [her] past or associate with being Vietnamese, or just being different."[22] Neither did Julie Davis, who recalled how she "embraced American culture" and "felt completely disjointed from my Vietnamese heritage." Rather than troubled by this break from her origins or critical of dominant social patterns that discouraged their investigation or expression, she contended, "[I] was never bothered by my inability to explain who I was and where I came from."[23] Even Trista, who had regular contact and communication with her Vietnamese foster family, initially decided against engagement. Although in retrospect she appreciated how having "them [her foster family] around" offered her "a sense of it [Vietnamese culture] throughout my childhood that I wouldn't have had if I didn't have them," she acknowledged her disinterest in the language and her foster family's frustration that "I didn't want to embrace my heritage."[24]

A reluctance to connect with or claim the unsettled legacies of the Vietnam War certainly shaped the early integration of adopted Vietnamese, but so did a sense of separation from other Vietnamese refugees. Jared Rehberg remembered "trying my best to be the best kid I could in the town of Northborough, Massachusetts. I didn't live in L.A., I didn't live near Asian people. I think the closest Asian community was in the town . . . or city called Worcester, which was about 25 miles from my house." Rehberg avoided visiting the Vietnamese community because of its distant location and because "the reputation of the Vietnamese in Worcester was gangs and bad kids."[25] Whether an accurate description of the adjustment difficulties of young Vietnamese or not, Rehberg's impressions highlighted the socioeconomic and cultural distinctions that set him and other adopted Vietnamese apart from others. Sheridan also felt physically and culturally distant from Vietnamese refugees. When his father brought him to a Vietnamese mass in the mostly white city of Hartford, Connecticut, a woman "poked and prodded him" and marveled at how much bigger than a typical Vietnamese he appeared, an observation that reinforced his perception of difference.[26]

If young, adopted Vietnamese attempted a course of assimilation that steered them away from Vietnamese culture, Vietnamese refugees, and the Vietnam War, their attempts met resistance and encouraged revisions. So committed to a white identity was Thompson that she felt shock when the father of a friend labeled her Vietnamese and forbade his son to accompany her to a school dance. "What the hell is Vietnamese," Thompson remembered thinking, and from that moment forward she expressed confusion: "I really started to feel like the square peg in a round hole and not understanding where I fit in or who I was." Rehberg recalled similar surprise on learning that others viewed him as someone other than white. At the age of ten, when "I first started to experience some bullying and racism, it was confusing to me because I had seen myself differently," Rehberg confessed. Rather than "becoming a Vietnamese person," he understood himself as "looking like my parents, beginning to sound like my parents, sharing my parents' mannerisms," a development called into question by classmates who defined him as an outsider.[27]

Adopted Vietnamese confronted generalized anti-Asian sentiments as often as Vietnamese-specific ones, slurs that highlighted the continued conflation of Asian ethnicities in the 1990s, prompted new anxieties about their belonging and showcased the strength of racist and orientalist traditions even after the Cold War's end. Thompson related that her maternal grandfather called her "Fu Man Chu and never called me by name," while an uncle "always called me Chinaman." If expressed in jest, Thompson did not like the joke. In a 1993 diary entry, Jane Burns (Nguyen Thi Van) described her realization that "I am the only minority in the school," a realization made all the more painful by a classmate's accusation during gym that she was "a Jap" who should "go back to the rice paddies." When a black student spontaneously shouted, "Watch yourself, fucking chink, VC!" Hai regrettably reached for her own racial epitaph, calling the classmate "you damned nigger!" Stung by the incident, she now believed she would "always be categorized as the Asian, a foreigner with the face of the enemy."[28]

Adopted black Vietnamese navigated communities where their African American heritage precipitated as much comment, and often complaint, as did their Vietnamese ancestry. After an angry shopper shouted "Half-Pint Nigger" at and assaulted Hoang Purdy in a convenience store in 1981 near his home in Massachusetts, his father, David, wrote an editorial published by the local newspaper. Reminding readers of his son's and other Vietnamese children's paths to the United States, he explained that the U.S. government had airlifted the youth "for fear that the orphan children of American GIs would be poorly treated by the new Communist government. In the USA, it was believed, they would be free, they could live in peace, they would have a chance." David had tried to convince Hoang that he was "better off here" rather than in Vietnam, where he may "have been killed by the Communists, maybe he'd be carrying a gun now as a young military recruit[,] maybe he'd be doing forced labor." However, recent events had deeply shaken David's own confidence in the comparative benefits of the United States. "When an 11 year old is called vicious racist names, is he free, can he be at peace, does he have a chance?" he asked readers, urging them to feel outrage over his son's attack in order to challenge racism.[29]

As a teacher who had worked in urban schools and witnessed prejudice firsthand, Gretchen Duling anticipated and grew frustrated with her black Vietnamese son Stephen's treatment by administrators who misunderstood at best and made painful assumptions at worst. When entering an Ohio kindergarten in the late 1970s, a teacher believed Stephen to be a "boat child" and recommended applying for grants supportive of Vietnamese refugees. When Gretchen protested this designation, the teacher explained that "we [the Duling family] can get all this money," seemingly insensitive to the differences in political status, paths of migration, and family affiliation that Gretchen found so important. As Stephen reached high school, he confronted a different set of assumptions based on his black heritage and gender. "He did something . . . that a Caucasian child would do that would be overlooked," Gretchen recalled. Once during an overnight field trip, Stephen and friends grew rowdy and smeared mustard over a building's windows. Although Stephen had not acted independently, "he got blamed for the whole thing" and the principal called Gretchen to her office, where Gretchen defended Stephen's behavior, insisting that the official "was making an awful big issue about something. You take a hose and you rinse it off. I don't understand why you're picking on our son." When Stephen did not join the meeting as anticipated, Gretchen searched for him in the hallway, where she found him quietly waiting, and he explained that the secretary had refused his admittance. The secretary then glanced at Gretchen and gasped, "He's your son?," a remark Gretchen understood as "stupid" and all too common.[30]

Encounters with racial prejudice, entrance into adolescence, popular constructions of the Vietnam War, and the warming of U.S. diplomatic relations with Vietnam persuaded many adopted Vietnamese to investigate their origins. And new forms of social media and technology introduced in the early 1990s facilitated these searches and ultimately the creation of a community of adopted Vietnamese. By the early 1980s, Vietnam's invasion of Cambodia, the resulting loss of aid from China, the limits of its centralized planning, rife political corruption, and long-standing trade embargos created severe economic problems; industry contracted, agriculture stagnated, imports increasingly exceeded exports, and rice shortages caused widespread hunger. The formal end of the Cold War also generated new security and financial pressures. In response to the crisis, new party leadership beginning in 1987 relaxed central planning, permitted greater market influences, made the painful political choice to withdraw from Cambodia, began to repay loans the United States had made to the former Saigon regime, and accepted U.S. efforts to dig through government documents and Vietnamese soil in search of POWs and MIAs.[31] This last concession assuaged lingering American anxieties about the abandonment of imprisoned and missing servicemen. Although the 2,500 Americans who did not return from the Vietnam War were far fewer than those unrecovered or unidentified during the Civil War, World War II, or even the Korean War, American presidents ranging from Ronald Reagan and George Bush to Bill Clinton stated their commitment to the issue. They did so because after 1975, talking about American men lost in Vietnam, like discussions of Vietnamese adoptees and refugees, remained a means of exploring the costs and responsibilities of U.S. intervention in the region.[32]

Reforms dramatically improved Vietnam's economic health, attracting foreign investors and allowing Southern Vietnamese to leave despised cooperatives and pursue entrepreneurial activities. Winning membership in the Association of Southeast Asian Nations—a regional organization that promotes economic and political cooperation—reintroduced Vietnam to world markets and contributed to an enviable rate of economic growth unfazed by the Asian financial crisis in 1997 and the global recession at the end of the twentieth century. Indeed, the shift from a managed to a market economy brought the Southeast Asian nation out of poverty and into relative prosperity. Political and economic changes in Vietnam also facilitated a new relationship with the United States, which sought normalization as a means of strengthening its position in Asia. Between 1994 and 1995, under the guidance of Clinton, the United States ended a two-decade-old trade embargo, restored diplomatic relations, and increased its investments in Vietnam.[33] Relaxed travel restrictions and discussions of shared security interests and prospects for collaboration also resulted. In his remarks announcing the decision in July 1995, Clinton brought attention to Vietnam's past and promised support in locating American prisoners of war as well as the endorsement of Vietnamese veterans.

These changes eased and even encouraged the efforts of adopted Vietnamese to devise their own interpretations of and connections to Vietnamese families, refugee communities, Vietnam, and its wars. An adoption discourse previously strangled by the United States' long antipathy toward Vietnam—embedded in hostile rhetoric and restrictive policies since 1975—finally emerged. Tiffany Chi Goodson was adopted at the age of four months in 1974 by a white couple who raised her in what she described as "pretty white-bread, homogenous" neighborhoods in Illinois, Washington, and New Jersey. Realizing at the age of sixteen or seventeen that she "was never going to be one of the popular people" or "fit with the mainstream status quo," Goodson claimed that she "accepted it at that point and embraced it." During her first year in college, her confidence had further evolved, and she surrendered her childhood hopes of having "blond hair and blue eyes and look like my Barbie dolls basically," in favor of "seeing the advantage of being unique," she asserted. In shifting her aspirations away from white, middle-class norms, she discovered sources of identity and criticisms of U.S. empire that energized the experiences of Vietnamese refugees. Previously reluctant, Goodson now chose to take "an interest in circumstances surrounding my relinquishment and what was this country's part in it" and realized "that had a huge impact on so many people and so many families." She understood this impact not only through her own readings and reflections, but also through public memorials and the presumptions of others. While waiting in line at an Arby's restaurant one day, a man with a Hawaiian shirt, whom she suspected was a veteran, approached her and tried to communicate in Vietnamese, perhaps seeking some connection or solace, prompting Goodson to explain that she only spoke English. On other occasions, she would "see someone who looked like a veteran and it looked like you were giving him a flashback." Goodson acknowledged that she had first thought these encounters "invasive," but later accepted that those who experienced the Vietnam War "went through quite a lot psychologically and physically" and continued to recover in the United States and "even over in Vietnam as well," where "people don't talk about [it] and probably should to enable healing." Goodson's respect for the pains of remembrance eventually led her to the Vietnam War Memorial in Washington, D.C., where she had "mixed feelings about being there" and wondered, "Do you celebrate those lives, do you cry over those lives, a little of both?" Bert Ballard's direct encounters with Vietnam veterans and memories of the war raised questions as well. In the 1990s, while visiting a pawnshop with his parents, the proprietor asked if he was adopted and Vietnamese. After hearing Ballard's confirmation, the man explained that he had served as a translator in Da Nang during the war, insisted "it was a good thing [Ballard] got out of there," and spoke repeatedly in Vietnamese despite Ballard's insistence that he had arrived in the United States as a baby and did not comprehend the language. The exchange led Ballard to wonder, "How do I respond—point out the ignorance, or leave the store?"[34]

This sense of uncertainty about and unique responsibility for the violence and consequences of the war structured how other adopted Vietnamese thought about their pasts. Although Anh Đào's upbringing in an international, multicultural community in the Middle East, where her American parents had taken jobs, protected her from "an obsessive need to figure out who I was racially, ethnically, in regards to that," and deflected the pressures of whiteness that had enticed other adoptees, she still grew curious about her origins during high school and "carried around a quiet sadness because you hear all the stereotypical things of these young women being raped by soldiers, or falling in love and then being dumped."[35] Such alternating frames of sexual violence and romantic tragedy shaped how adopted Vietnamese imagined their parents' first meeting and then their separation. Some adoptees labored under the burden of these popular stories about Vietnam and the relations between American soldiers and Vietnamese women.

Bree Cutting Sibble regretted not only that so many Americans "expect me to be an authority on the war" and asked for "her insight on the cause of the conflict," but also that her physical appearance forced her to represent "so many things . . . the war, the sexual exploits of soldiers and the face of the enemy that killed U.S. troops."[36] However, Delevett credited *Miss Saigon*, a successful musical of the 1990s about the tragic love affair between an American GI and a Vietnamese barmaid, for sparking her search for her Vietnamese heritage. When her boyfriend bought tickets to the production, she attended without enthusiasm or expectations. However, during the show, she recalled "becoming extremely emotional" as what unfolded on stage so "eerily mirrored" her own thoughts about her past. As she left the theater, she told her boyfriend, "I'm ready to go back and find my roots," and she "felt it was time, I had denied my heritage and being Vietnamese."[37]

Others rejected familiar conceits about the Vietnam War and the tragic contexts of their migration, fashioning their own stories and artistic expressions. Merrie Li Camp and her siblings and cousins took offense and sought to correct the interpretation of a well-publicized, made-for-television movie, *The Last Flight Out*. Debuting in 1990, it presented itself as a fact-based dramatization of the Pan Am flight crew that transported 300 Vietnamese children out of Vietnam. Although she did not appear in the movie, Merrie Li and a group of other adopted Vietnamese attended the premier, after which they gathered at a nearby hotel and expressed their disapproval. "There was a lot of, I don't want to say resentment," she noted in a 2013 interview, "but a lot of issues that were going on there that weren't very positive." Among the criticisms leveled against the movie were its exaggeration of napalm burns suffered by select individuals, inattention to the resolve displayed by Vietnamese family members, and glorification of American caregivers. Moreover, the film brought unwanted attention to many adopted Vietnamese. The spotlight became so intense, Merrie Li related, that "I couldn't walk down the street without people calling me and tracking me down, and so forth." One particular man, who was likely motivated by tropes of alluring, accessible Vietnamese women, became so fascinated with the movie's depiction that he located Merrie Li's phone number and incessantly called her until she told him "you don't need to know about me," just as she had no right to meddle in or presume details about his life.[38]

Rehberg acknowledged the influence of "enough movies" and "enough stories," like the ones that troubled Merrie Li, which taught him "my mother could have been a prostitute, my mother could have been raped . . . all these horrible things could have happened to my parents." Rather than allow

Jared Rehberg with his first guitar. Courtesy of Jared Rehberg.

these narratives to direct his life, Rehberg chose to "have control over my message." A musician, after an emotional reunion with other adopted Vietnamese in 2000, he turned his attention to writing and performing songs that explored his adoption and integration in the United States. He released his first CD, *Waking Up American*, in 2003 and a second, *Somewhere in the Middle*, which explored similar themes of transition, uncertainty, loss, and rediscovery, in 2010.[39]

Anh Đào sought to revise visions of Vietnamese adoption, dominated by assumptions of rescue and salvation, through her photography. "I don't like the word grateful per se," she stated during an interview, believing the prescription to feel thankful simplified the experience of migration and imposed unjust obligations on the adoptee. "I am appreciative that I was adopted," she stated, "but at the same time please understand the sort of emotional, mental, and physical burden I've had to carry that comes along with that." In explaining her "motivations of being a photographer, being a mentor, going into the field of social work," she faulted "survivor's guilt." Among the most personal and descriptive of the adopted experience is her portrait series titled "Misplaced Baggage: Same, Same but Different," displayed at the Wing Luke Museum in Seattle in 2014. The forty-seven pictures feature individuals who attended a 2010 reunion and tour of Vietnam organized by Trista Goldberg. "Misplaced Baggage" emphasizes the individuality of its subjects. The adopted Vietnamese appear in different postures, express different emotions, and sport different fashions. While Tuyet Cam tosses her head away from the camera and wears a bright black-and-red top evocative of traditional Vietnamese clothes, Matt Ryan stares into the camera, a subtle grin on his face, and the tattoos covering his arms readily visible. We learn that they are a global group, growing up in the United Kingdom, Europe, Australia, and the United States. Yet these portraits also convey what Anh Đào calls "the ways in which we are more alike than unlike." The juxtaposition and common composition of the photos invite the viewer to see adoptees as sharing backgrounds and experiences despite their disparate locations and uniqueness. In text accompanying the photos, Anh Đào makes clear her desire to document the adoptees in order to raise their visibility.[40]

Through his scholarship, counseling of youth, and activism, Ballard has also animated and altered adoption discourse. A professor of communications, he has blended theory and personal experience in his writings about the process and practices of adoption over the course of almost fifteen years. In 2001, he penned a reflective essay in the popular magazine *Adoption Help* about the joy of meeting Tisdale, discovering more about his Vietnamese past, and connecting to other adoptees during a 2000 reunion. Rather than feeling "so alone or abandoned," he believed himself "blessed to be a part of one of the most unique communities to ever exist."[41] Such sentiment shaped his decision to serve as a counselor at Vietnamese Heritage Camp in Colorado, where he would learn more about Vietnamese culture and "how Vietnamese have adapted to the United States," and "be a role model for young adopted Vietnamese."[42] Ballard's engagement with and analysis of adoption, though, would disrupt this confident, almost celebratory story of self-discovery and a will to serve that so many adoptees told at the beginning of the twenty-first century. In 2011 he published an article about the idea of "sacred" or unseen and unspoken forms of communication. He traced his and his wife's exhausting efforts to adopt from Vietnam, "to have a son from my birth country." Ballard attributed the decision to "our origin stories and family composition" (his wife had four siblings adopted from Korea) and an emotional encounter with a Vietnamese baby whom they met at an adoption culture camp. However, his critical studies of adoption and the interruption of adoptions from Vietnam following a U.S. embassy report in 2008 alleging fraud, corruption, bribery, and human trafficking highlighted the political and ethical complexities of the modern process. He noted an important shift by 2009, "with many scholars and adult adoptees calling for an end to and stricter standards for international adoption," a call that posi-

Tuyet Cam, "Misplaced Baggage," photo taken by Anh Dào. Courtesy of Anh Dào Kolbe.

tioned him, an adoptee seeking to adopt, as a betrayer: "Promoting the event that has caused us pain, made us search and question for who we are, and adopting from Vietnam, I am perpetuating the structure of oppression and occupation."[43] Proclamations of loyalty and accusations of treachery have also marked the language of Vietnamese refugee and homeland communities as they struggle to find their place and direct history. Yet, in successfully adopting a young Vietnamese boy in 2011 after years of delays and complications, Ballard tested and reformulated this characterization of duplicity, exploring the ways in which inherited and imagined stories shape the identities fashioned by transnational families.[44]

These ideas about adopted Vietnamese possessing a unique place and assuming unsettling obligations resonated in Ballard's more recent investigation of the cultural and structural factors that constrain. He noted the burden he and other adoptees carry because they have inherited "a narrative, one of a certain kind of skin color, one of being evacuated from

Mike Ryan, "Misplaced Baggage," photo taken by
Anh Dào. Courtesy of Anh Dào Kolbe.

a war-ravaged country, one of being adopted into a white family, one of living in a small town, one where growing up [they] felt anything but normal." Because their stories proved uncommon, they regularly elicited confusing and uncomfortable questions about their origins, appearance, and attachments that challenged their sense of belonging. However, Ballard proposed the possibility of finding some space and commonality among the adoptees "not to account for difference, but to constitute our unique selves."[45] His formulation suggested that even as adopted Vietnamese have revised thoughts of immigration, war, and family since the 1990s, their attempts to author alternatives remain arduous.

Explorations of their pasts convinced some adoptees to reconsider and reach out to Vietnam veterans, often redirecting notions of gratitude that had dominated explorations of adoption, namely that they should appreciate how fortunate they were to be rescued. Although Hai regretted that friends in the late 1970s, "influenced by their parents[,] saw in our young faces an enemy from the unpopular Vietnam War," by the late 1990s, she came to appreciate that "so many veterans of war needed healing" and thought there was no one "better than I, a former orphan and veteran of many battles[,] to help them." Thus, in 2000, she created a nonprofit organization dedicated to humanitarian efforts between Vietnam and the United States, and she delivered a speech before veterans gathered at a Rotary Club meeting in 2009. Emphasizing her feelings of duty toward this population, Hai closed her memoir by professing that, "from the deepest place in my heart," she wished to "wipe one less tear from the faces of these soldiers who fought for my freedom." As he aged, Sheridan also came to comprehend the struggles of soldiers and appreciate their service in Vietnam. The father of one of his first girlfriends, a Vietnam veteran who suffered night terrors and flashbacks triggered by his wartime memories, discouraged his daughter from dating Sheridan. Other encounters with veterans proved similarly upsetting. Sheridan remembered that most often "the soldiers he met were more hostile and I didn't understand because in school" one did not learn "the nuances, they more or less teach what the government wants you to learn." At the age of twelve, while sitting next to a veteran on a bench during a funeral, the man "made some comment about how I shouldn't be here." Years later, Sheridan understood the utterance as part of the veteran's grieving and felt "a deep sense of gratitude for soldiers who gave their lives" and wished to thank them for their service.[46]

Given the propensity of Americans since 1965 to discursively use veterans and Vietnamese children to negotiate the meanings of wars in Southeast Asia and U.S. foreign policies, the appreciation for veterans articulated by adopted Vietnamese in the late twentieth and early twenty-first centuries seemed both disruptive and conclusive. Choosing to accept, even celebrate, the service of veterans, adopted Vietnamese spoke rather than were spoken for, and their voices contained an authority drawn from their histories as refugees of the wars in which American soldiers fought. To a large degree, their perspective matched that at which the broader public had arrived by the early twenty-first century. Rather than fault veterans, Americans now viewed these men and women as casualties of unfortunate events. The shift reflected not only improved official relations between the United States and Vietnam but also the activism of veterans and their families, including those of prisoners of war, whose persistent public appeals to search for loved ones made the fate of veterans what historian Michael Allen has called "the dominant means through which millions of Americans addressed their nation's defeat in Vietnam."[47]

As they tried to make sense of their beginnings and place, adopted Vietnamese reached out to Vietnamese refugees, with whom they shared a location of birth and experiences of war, migration, and resettlement. Yet, these seeming commonalities often proved too shallow to support substantive connections. During his freshman year in college, Ballard attended a gathering of Asian American students who questioned his Vietnamese credentials. "Well, you don't look very Asian, and you certainly don't sound Asian," one girl insisted, and then she said something in Vietnamese he did not comprehend. When Ballard did not respond, she pronounced, "You're not Vietnamese" and walked away, leaving him to wonder whether "he should leave the room feeling like I've lost a part of myself."[48] Tuan-Rishard Schneider noted that during high school other Vietnamese students "didn't really have anything to say to me, as I didn't to them." He credited the division to the different "worlds" he and they inhabited. While his white, middle-class parents had exposed him to the diversity of innercity Minneapolis, he longed for acceptance or recognition among Vietnamese. Thompson also sought recognition. In college she approached the local Vietnamese association, but soon withdrew because she feared "not fitting in" and "never felt comfortable," a sense of unease that made her feel "sad because I want to be able to connect with the culture of Vietnam and show to [Vietnamese] kids [that I could fit in]." Discomfort and regret have continued to define Thompson's encounters with Vietnamese. During a 2009 interview, she recalled entering Vietnamese-run nail salons in Orange County, where she chafed under their seeming disapproval and intrusive questions. "They are disgusted and appalled that I don't know the language, the food, the customs," she explained. "I don't mean to stereotype," she added, "but all Vietnamese pry into my life, and I try to skirt it." If she trusted their sincerity, she sometimes disclosed part of her story, but admitted being "burned too many times" by Vietnamese promising to return to Vietnam and look for her mother.[49]

As much as her own experiences with Vietnamese refugees, the cautionary tale of a dispiriting reunion between an adopted Vietnamese and her Vietnamese mother portrayed in the Academy Award–winning documentary *Daughter from Danang* swayed Thompson's interpretation of the Vietnamese community and reinforced her feelings of estrangement. The film follows the return of Heidi to Vietnam in 1997, where she reunites with her Vietnamese mother, Mai, and explores the complicated feelings and cultural misunderstandings that surface. In its closing scenes, the documentary stresses the seemingly irreconcilable differences that divide the two women and the depth of their mutual disappointment. *Daughter from Danang* has received its fair share of criticism. Gregory Paul Choy and Catherine Ceniza Choy fault the piece for privileging a narrative of culture clash while obscuring the political, economic, and cultural contexts of adoption. Jodi Kim has similarly argued that *Daughter from Danang* elides larger processes of imperial violence and inequality that structure Heidi's and Mai's fraught exchanges.[50] Reductive and problematic though the documentary may be, Thompson and other adopted Vietnamese found it compelling, perhaps because of the paucity of popular sources that chronicled their experiences, the film's depiction of loss and disorientation, and the positive attention it received from mainstream media. Indeed, Linh Nguyen has recently proposed a rereading of the film, one that shifts attention toward Heidi's motivations for reunion and treats her as a subject whose feelings of separation and longing echo those of other refugees.[51] Thompson described Heidi's expectations as "exactly like mine. I just wanted to know. I just wanted the answers to know what I never knew. I wanted to fit in finally," but feared a resolution in which Vietnamese family would see her primarily as "an American benefactor" who would send them money. Rather than confront that possibility of fraud, Thompson accepted that "it's better off making stories in my head about how it happened," including one in which her mother was a nurse and her father an American soldier. Anh Đào also expressed concerns about her reception among and critiques by Vietnamese refugees. While Americans articulated the adoption experience in the language of gratitude, she insisted that the Vietnamese community spoke of betrayal: "You left us, you don't speak Vietnamese, you aren't one us, how are you one of us?"[52] Although accusations of treachery had followed diasporic Vietnamese, the allegations seemed especially troubling to adoptees who remembered so little about Vietnam and whose disruption and migration were chosen by others.

Although Goodson did not have the same misgivings about the motives and expectations of Vietnamese, she, too, found her efforts to enrich her identity through contacts with Vietnamese both unsatisfying and a reminder of her orientation to what she perceived as more egalitarian, American gender roles. At a Vietnamese dance she attended near her American university, she "felt uncomfortable" because she found the women so shy and the men so presumptuous. Goodson recalled trying to tell a story to one man, when her Vietnamese date unceremoniously interrupted and attempted to finish on her behalf. She concluded that "there was a different level of place and position in their culture," and despite sharing the "same genealogy," they had few other commonalities.[53] A white, American man may have similarly overstepped and underlistened, but Goodson's perception of Vietnamese social norms—that women are passive and men dominant—guided her reactions and ultimately limited her engagement with the community.

If attempts to find common ground with Vietnamese immigrants did not always create a sense of kinship or place, some adopted Vietnamese sought reassurances by recovering or inventing ties to other adopted Vietnamese, Vietnamese relatives, and Vietnam. Enabled by new forms of technology that debuted in the 1990s and matured through the beginning of the twenty-first century, adoptees searched for information about their pasts and connected to one another. Commemorations of Operation Babylift organized by adoption agencies provided the initial framework and occasion for adoptees to gather, but the community and its conversations would grow beyond those airlifted in 1975, beyond the space of local reunions, and beyond the intentions of its sponsors. Like others in her cohort, Goldberg recalled trolling the Internet in the late 1990s for every possible video, news article, photograph, and website that addressed adoption from Vietnam. In the process, she located the Vietnamese Adoptee Network (VAN) and Adopted Vietnamese International (AVI). Founded in 2000 by a small group of Vietnamese adoptees following reunions in Baltimore, Maryland, and Estes Park, Colorado, coordinated by Holt International, Tressler Adoption Services, and the Evan B. Donaldson Institute, VAN used its website to link Vietnamese adoptees to one another and relevant resources. Claiming both a responsibility for and right to make sense of events about which others had imposed meaning, VAN's members asserted their belief that "the time has come for the torch to be passed to the adoptee community, and that the stewardship of our history, and the direction of our adoptee community would take, was now in our hands."[54] AVI, an Australia-based network also launched on the twenty-fifth anniversary of the close of the Vietnam War, made similar assertions. More global in its membership and spirit, AVI expressed its ambitions to help adoptees connect and explore their histories. Equally important, the group wished to "promote our unique insights on adoption" and create relationships with not only "adoptive parents and birth parents, other trans-racial adoption communities, younger generations of adopted Vietnamese," but also "general members of the Vietnamese Diaspora and other cultural communities."[55]

A sense of relief and kinship with other adopted Vietnamese developed from these collective, adoptee-directed efforts to construct an expansive community of individuals who were most affected by the Vietnam War. After meeting other adoptees, Goodson remembered "feeling that I am not alone . . . wow I have this clan who knows what it was like . . . challenging to be different, challenging to find a sense of belonging . . . a lot still on the path and [we] can walk it together." Ballard described such contacts as akin to finding lost brothers and sisters "who could understand the uniqueness that came with being multiracial and multi-ethnic," while Goldberg gushed that finding "soul mates in almost each and every one of them" helped "enhance my own self-respect and knowledge of my inner self and strength that I didn't even know I had."[56] Such realizations developed through discussions about their migrations and incorporation into largely white families; adoptees asked and answered questions about the planes that had transported them, meetings with their birth families, and the characteristics of their adoptive parents. Some had envied the web of connections spun by adopted Koreans—connections Eleana Kim has defined as a "self-conscious community, consolidated out of disparate spaces of social activity and discourses"[57]—and thus appreciated the emerging visibility and authority of the Vietnamese. Schneider noted that he had "lived in the shadow of adopted Koreans," in whose community "there were always support groups, weekly summer camps, and other Korea adoptees for others to talk with."[58]

Reunions, discussions, and exchanges among adopted Vietnamese and Vietnamese immigrants often encouraged tours of Vietnam. In his study of "birthright tourism" in Israel by Jewish immigrants and their progeny—part of a larger scholarship about forms of tourism among immigrants and their descendants in the more globalized world of the late twentieth and early twenty-first centuries—Shaul Kelner argued that the category of home is especially unstable among populations shaped by migration and dispersion who visit homelands to "untangle the complexities that bind self, community, culture and place—if not to resolve the tensions, then at least to find some modus vivendi."[59] Sponsoring or cooperating nations have recognized the political and economic advantages of homeland trips that tie immigrants and their descendants to the state. In its reception of adoptees, the South Korean government positions the immigrants as both reminders of the nation's past economic and political troubles and harbingers of a future in which Korea will enjoy full integration and prosperity in a more globalized society.[60] However, the tourists seek more personal and transformative meanings. Many covet a sense of rootedness and comfort, an opportunity to ease anxieties about their incompleteness.[61] The photos taken, souvenirs purchased, journals kept, and stories told become ways of consuming a place and reintegrating one's identity.

Such experiences are mediated by a birthright organization's set itineraries, guides, and one's fellow tourists, with whom one presumably shares an ethnic or historical connection and a common desire to know more about one's past. Through dialogue and reflections with these fellows, a diasporic tourist may better navigate terrain that seems both familiar and strange. Anh Đào confessed that she had "felt very invested and connected to the forty-seven adoptees" whom she met in 2010, but came to the "insight that just because you're Vietnamese and adopted doesn't mean that you are going to be BFFs for the rest of your lives." Not only did adoptees have unique experiences and react differently to their encounters in Vietnam, but they also diverged in their educations, economic resources, sexual preferences, religious and political beliefs, employment, and regions. As the only "out" person on her tour, Anh Đào felt "her isolation because I can't talk to these people as I would as if I had my LGBT community," concluding that "my Vietnamese adopted community understand me to a certain extent in what it feels to be a Vietnamese adoptee, but then they fail to see what it means to be a lesbian as well." Rehberg noted the importance of political and regional distinctions among the adopted Vietnamese. "We sound so different in person . . . our values are different," and "I don't de-friend them because they are my brothers and sisters, but I am *so* lucky that I went north, y'know."[62] Overall, although intended to reassure, deepen an individual's sense of connection, and reenergize ethnic communities outside the homeland, the birthright visits also created feelings of alienation and uncertainty.

Recognizing that individuals adopted internationally and their families occupy a unique place within diaspora populations, entrepreneurs and states have created specialized tours. In addition to the typical sites and experiences packaged in conventional homeland tours, these incorporate visits to orphanages, hospitals, court houses, and welfare centers intended to help one reimagine one's origins and the process of adoption. They offer extensive cultural orientations prior to departure; propose, but do not promise, the possibility of reunions with birth families; and invite humanitarian work. Overall, they try to help adoptees comprehend an uneasiness rooted in perceptions of abandonment and distinction from traditional families.[63] Despite their separation from Vietnam and integration into primarily white, American families, the adoptees hope to find or build roots within their country of origin.⁶⁴ Sample itineraries from homeland tours to Vietnam, which have increased in number and sophistication since the early 1990s, include cruises along the Mekong Delta River, encounters with local fishermen, tours of coconut tree manufacturers, and meals at Vietnamese restaurants. While operators such as Vietnam Journeys, Motherland Heritage, and Holt International highlight how enjoyable and convenient their packages are, they also recognize the social and cultural significance of returns to Vietnam. Thus, they provide supportive social workers and chances to help local communities. Through acts of organized kindness—the donation of a sampan; a visit to the Children Village, where one may go "toe-to-toe with its children in a game of soccer"; or participation in playtime with infants and toddlers at Bo Da Pagoda (a refuge for homeless children and elderly)—adopted Vietnamese may better appreciate local poverty and feel connected, even obligated, to Vietnam.⁶⁵ Such service also perpetuates themes of American responsibility to the children of Vietnam that had shaped the process and reception of adoptees decades earlier.

Tours that marketed returns to Vietnam as a form of commemoration of Operation Babylift offered an even more directed experience, one that narrowed the space for an adoptee's own engagements. One of the earliest occurred in 1985 on the tenth anniversary of the mass airlifts and helped establish a template for future excursions in 1995, 2000, 2005, and 2010. Among the organizations responsible were FFAC, who supported a twenty-fifth-anniversary venture, and World Airways, which flew twenty-one Vietnamese adults as well as former pilots, flight attendants, World Airways personnel, and veterans back to Vietnam to mark the thirtieth anniversary of the airlifts. Media coverage of these tours replayed familiar ideas of rescue, American abundance, and shadowed memories of the Vietnam War. In his celebratory account of World Airways' trip, reporter Bob Shane described the first airlift of fifty-seven children initiated by the company's "maverick president" as a "heroic act" and complimented the crew who "had risked their lives to save orphan children and refugees." As the carefully choreographed and deliberately sentimental conclusion to the tour, participants gathered at the Presidential Palace with Vietnamese hosts and cheered the presentation of a signed quilt stitched from remnants of clothing worn by adopted Vietnamese during the airlift. Although Shane acknowledged the emotional intensity of the tour, he suggested that adopted Vietnamese universally felt love and thanks for those Americans who had orchestrated the airlift and offered them American homes. Indeed, World Airways' return and Shane's coverage did not so much provide an open pathway for adopted

Vietnamese to investigate their pasts and revise their identities as encourage them to perform scripted roles as grateful, contented adults.[66]

In 2013, a Vietnamese immigrant and critic of Communism sponsored a local variant of this commemoration in Southern California, a gathering designed to celebrate the humanitarianism of American veterans and the common struggles of a generation of Vietnamese born during war. As the daughter of an ARVN soldier held captive for seven years while his wife and children struggled to survive in Vietnam's New Economic Zones, Julia Nguyen had little but contempt for the nation's Communist government and cheered her family's eventual immigration to the United States in 1993. Her residence in the United States and accidental friendship with American veterans, to whom she felt connected as common survivors of war, convinced her to establish a nonprofit that would educate and celebrate those who had served in Vietnam. Her advocacy and imagination also supported her sense of kinship with other children of the Vietnam War: adopted Vietnamese and Vietnamese refugees of the late 1970s. In Torch 1975's mission's statement, Nguyen wrote that "as the North Vietnamese Army took control of the South, the lives of thousands of children were affected in many different ways. Some—like myself—were victims of the New Economic Zone. Others, escaping by boat, became victims of pirates or were lost at sea," while "Operation Babylift children experienced their early years in new countries throughout the world." Because Nguyen recognized similarities and shared histories among a cohort of Vietnamese that too often went unobserved, she facilitated a gathering of adoptees on the anniversary of Operation Babylift. Yet, as in the case of earlier commemorations, Torch 1975's event repeated a specific message about the heroism of Americans and the good fortune of the adopted Vietnamese, one that left little room for the adoptee's own interventions and exonerated rather than disputed American neocolonialism in South Vietnam. More veterans than adoptees prepared to attend, and the planned itinerary reflected this imbalance. Participants could play golf, attend a historical forum, or watch a heartwarming reenactment of the airlift. Among the featured speakers selected by Nguyen was Nikki Logan, the first Vietnamese baby carried off the plane by President Gerald Ford, an identity and gesture central to defenders of the airlift and the United States' honorable withdrawal from Vietnam. Indeed, Nguyen and the veterans with whom she collaborated stressed the importance of praising the efforts of Ford and other Americans who, as Nguyen told an Orange County reporter covering the story, "sacrificed to get the children out of Vietnam."[67]

Adopted Vietnamese acted within and against these versions of their reunions and tours, designing their own interpretations of place and redesigning their identities. Disappointed by the motives and message of reunion tours funded by Holt, FCVN, and World Airways, adopted Vietnamese chose to initiate and finance their own visit in 2010, a feat coordinated by Operation Reunite, a nonprofit founded by Goldberg in 2003 to offer "search support to help reunite Vietnamese families separated by war." In its mission statement, the organization acknowledged the difficulty of discovering one's past, but pledged to facilitate adoptees' preparation for this task by teaching about the Vietnam War, Vietnamese culture, language, and family customs. In addition, it encouraged adopted Vietnamese and Vietnamese to take a DNA test in the interest of expanding a genetic database that would aid their searches.[68] Goldberg noted that use of the DNA kits and the discovery of familial ties increased after 2003 due to greater publicity and the heightened interest of Vietnamese birth families. As a result of this biological mapping, adoptees have realized filial relationships with other adopted Vietnamese and found parents, uncles, aunts, and cousins.[69]

Curiosity and accounts of successful discoveries also persuaded forty Vietnamese adoptees, many of whom had never explored Vietnam, to join the 2010 trip. Alongside pool parties, a nighttime tour of Saigon on motor bikes, a water puppet show, an adoptee photo shoot by Anh Đào, an appearance on a Vietnamese television show, and a memorial at the site where the first plane evacuating Vietnamese children and caregivers had crashed in 1975, the adoptees had ample volunteering opportunities. At the Go Vap Orphanage in Saigon, they painted rooms in disrepair, fed babies, taught English, and took its school-age children bowling. Despite surface similarities in the tour's agenda and spirit, one of the attendees, Dominic Golding, emphasized its departure from previous efforts. "Other reunions have been organized on our behalf," he asserted, "but they also serve the aims and objectives of the principle organizers of benevolence." In contrast, "the Operation Reunited Vietnamese Tour is what I call soft activism; where adoptees take charge of our history and narratives and journey back to Vietnam." Golding explained his desire to document the events not as "an objective observer/mainstream reporter" but as an "insider" who would show "we cannot be defined as child victims of war. We are adults who share a unique social/familial 'experiment': intercountry adoption and Operation Babylift."[70]

Indeed, adopted Vietnamese attempted to define the meanings of their migration and return. Some experienced Vietnam as a foreign space that reinforced alternate attachments and their choice of white, middle-class conventions. With the encouragement of his Illinois-based, adoptive family, Khanh Duy Nguyen first attended a reunion of adopted Vietnamese in 1985, an event that would inspire regular visits to Vietnam. He recalled the fascination of locals who discovered he knew almost nothing about his Vietnamese family. He typically countered their expressions of sympathy by explaining his contentment and good fortune: "My family in America is everything anyone could ever ask for.... They must have done something right enough so that I came back, right?" For Rehberg, who first visited Vietnam as part of a Motherland Tour sponsored by Holt and purchased by his adoptive parents, the country similarly appeared an unfamiliar and inhospitable place that made him more aware of his American sensibilities. Although he enjoyed the amenities and structured activities, he disliked the food, the congestion (he was hit by a motor bike), and the petty crime (his wallet was stolen). Other adopted Vietnamese and homeland tourists have confessed similar feelings of disorientation, even alienation, as encounters with other places brought into sharp relief cultural differences that defined them as American. Although Rehberg concluded that he had no admiration for Vietnam, he believed the trip helped him realize "that there will always be missing pieces, and this is my life to create, and I am moving forward." Oktober, the adopted son of Nhu and Tom Miller, arrived at a similar conclusion. The release of *Daughter from Danang* prompted his Vietnamese mother, with whom Nhu had kept in close contact for over two decades, to confess that Oktober had a brother, adopted by three Chinese sisters in Vietnam. The revelation persuaded Oktober to visit Vietnam, where he and his older brother had the opportunity to compare experiences. When his brother expressed regret that he had not had his younger sibling's luck to be raised in the United States, Oktober newly appreciated his position and embraced the material ease and political stability Americans conceive as their natural national condition. According to Nhu, Oktober had "felt sorry for himself because he was not the biological son" and had made "invidious comparisons about what could have been rather than seeing the advantages of what is," but after the visit and exchange, decided "the past is past, there is nothing we can do about it," came back much happier, applied to law school, and eventually married.[71]

Other adopted Vietnamese spoke of their trips as rewarding returns that resolved uncertainties, renewed commitments to Vietnam, and reintegrated them into Vietnamese families and communities. This proved especially true for those who possessed some specific information (photographs, birth documents, stories) that linked them to peoples, institutions, and places in Vietnam. Joshua Woerthwein returned as part of a special tour in 1997, during which he visited historic sites and his orphanage. "I don't know if I'll ever be able to articulate what was going through my head when I saw my birthplace . . . when I cried and cried," he confessed. "It felt good inside for the first time in a long, long time." Yet these sentiments of relief and release were tempered by "a cloud of guilt and self-hate that surfaced to hang over my head," as he saw himself as an outsider who did not speak the language and whose physical size distinguished him. In summing up the consequences of the tour, he believed it diminished his sense of "inadequacy" and resolved some "internal conflicts."[72] Nol also appreciated the ways in which going to Vietnam opened up new stories and sources of belonging. While attending the University of San Francisco, he received a brochure advertising a study abroad program in Vietnam. Determined to "know something about the Vietnamese side of me," Nol spent part of 1993 there, exploring the Santa Maria orphanage in Saigon and determining that "I understand who I am and what I have become is because of my past." Indeed, the notion that being in Vietnam was a form of fixing oneself in history and fabricating a Vietnamese identity shaped the impressions of other adoptees. Struck by the beauty of the Delta, the friendliness of Vietnamese, the seeming simplicity of rural life, and an emotional meeting with the Catholic nun who facilitated her evacuation, Julie Davis believed "she was more confident than ever to be Vietnamese: and thirty years after being adopted into America, she insisted she now had adopted Vietnam." Her inversion of the usual architecture and agency of adoption highlighted the success of adopted Vietnamese in becoming authors of their own migrations.[73]

Many of the adopted Vietnamese wished not only to visit the landscapes, official historic sites, and orphanages of Vietnam, but to locate and reunite with Vietnamese family, searches that could as often lead them to other regions of the United States and other nations where Vietnamese relations had resettled. In the late 1990s, during a two-week trip to Vietnam, Thu-Hien found her entire Vietnamese family, including her mother, Lam. Journalists reporting the dramatic encounter noted that the girl was never forgotten; her mother had prayed for her daughter's return and kept the toys with which Thu had played nearly two decades prior neatly stacked in the china cabinet.[74]

Delevett enjoyed a similarly euphoric conclusion to her search for her past, one that would challenge the portrait of failed reunion featured in

Daughter from Danang and reveal the prominence of adopted Vietnamese within a larger diaspora. In 1994, she and her boyfriend flew to Hanoi and spent a month traveling the country before reaching Soc Trang, the small fishing town in the Mekong Delta where Delevett's family originated. Armed with an old address and a letter in Vietnamese explaining Delevett's identity, the pair found and knocked on the door of the house where Delevett's cousins had once resided. The man who answered the door read the letter and led them down the street to another house, where an old man lay asleep; with shock, Delevett recognized him as her uncle Sam. After their tears of joy and excitement had subsided, Sam shared photos and stories of Delevett's mother, Nuoi. Delevett learned the date of her own birth, the details of how they had been separated, and her mother's failed attempt to reach the United States. While bidding her brother Sam good-bye and fighting through the chaotic streets of Saigon to reach the airport, Nuoi missed her scheduled flight and lost contact with Delevett and her brother, Lam. Despondent, Delevett mother's tried for many years to escape Vietnam. Finally, in 1979, following the footsteps of Uncle Sam's son, Hiep, she fled by boat. However, while waiting almost two years at a Malaysian refugee camp for clearance, she died suddenly of a heart attack. Despite this tragic end, Delevett took comfort in unearthing a specific story of her past—especially one that highlighted her mother's affections and desire for reconciliation—and the discovery of Vietnamese kin in Vietnam and the United States. She enjoyed meeting and swapping tales with Vietnamese cousins who had immigrated in the late 1970s to Texas, Nevada, and Germany. One of the proverbial boat people, Hiep had bid his father good-bye, boarded a leaky motorboat, evaded pirates, and eventually arrived in the United States, where he would open a successful nail shop and acquire the American-sounding name Tony. Overall, Delevett depicted the experience "as the homecoming that I thought I would never have. . . . I found my place in the world."[75]

Others also found their place in the world by tracking down and building relationships with Vietnamese relatives, thus reweaving the threads of Vietnamese migrations split by war and resettlement programs. Their searches replicated and resuscitated investigations instigated in the 1970s and 1980s by Vietnamese kin, especially mothers, who had attempted reunion with lost children. Against their expectations, their pursuit of Vietnamese family sometimes led them to other regions of the United States. In 1975, at the age of four, Ginger's Vietnamese aunt, who was caring for her in the unexplained absence of her mother, convinced the girl's father to put

Kim Delevett (on horse), her cousin Lan Phan (*left*), brother, Lam (*middle*), and mother, Nuoi, on the balcony of their Saigon home in April 1975 just before the children left for the United States. Courtesy of Kim Delevett.

her up for adoption. The Seevers, an American family who resided in Kansas, eagerly accepted and raised Ginger. Although she had invested in conventionally American activities as a young girl—acting in plays, reading fashion magazines, and studying—and expressed no interest in Vietnam, she grew curious at the age of twenty. She expressed shock on discovering that she had a brother, Jeff, and a sister, Brigitte, from whom she was separated during Operation Babylift. While Brigitte had grown up in Germany, Jeff was raised in the United States. The trio organized a reunion in September 1995 at Ginger's apartment in Overland Park, positively chronicled in *People* magazine. Despite Jeff's anxiety (he confessed to downing two beers to relax on the plane en route), the siblings enjoyed their two weeks together, dancing, cooking, and looking in the mirror to identify similarities. "There was a bond there that none of us could really explain,"

Kim Delevett and her brother, Lam, with their adoptive American siblings. Courtesy of Kim Delevett.

Jeff noted, because "maybe deep, deep down, we could remember each other." Ginger agreed, suggesting that "it's like finding the pieces of a missing puzzle, Now we're all one again." Trista and Jeffrey's search for their Vietnamese mother and sibling, detailed in this book's introduction (the adopted siblings reunited with and built ties with their kin who had immigrated and been resettled under the Amerasian Homecoming Act in 1991), similarly revealed the twisting paths of Vietnamese migrations and the complexities of family reformation.[76] Like the first generation of adopted Vietnamese, Amerasians who arrived in the 1980s have articulated a history of war and displacement that complicates the imperfect renderings embraced by many Americans. Angelina Memon, who came to the United States with her mother in 1989, wrote a memoir in 2007 to strengthen community among Amerasians, affirm their self-esteem, and correct misperceptions about them. "From the bottom of my heart, I dedicate this story to the more than fifty thousand Amerasian children who faced a very similar fate—prejudice and rejection, abandon, unwanted and isolated," she asserted, but she urged her "friends" to "stop playing the victims because nobody cares unless we do." By accepting "who we are" and letting "people recognize the Amerasian existence," Memon wrote, Amerasians would find some peace and facilitate connections between Vietnam and the United States because "we hold the blood of both within."[77]

Memon belongs to a group, Amerasians without Borders, led by Jimmy Miller that has championed Amerasians within both the United States and Vietnam, bringing attention to and calling for political solutions to problems of poverty and exclusion. During a 2013 interview, Miller expressed his and other Amerasians' disappointment that the "U.S. don't see us as Americans because they see us like other refugee people," a perception that denied their paternity, history, and the U.S. government's responsibility. "So our father sacrificed for their country to die to protect freedom and now their children come here and now our government ignore it, and they don't treat us as the children of the G.I. [even] while they make the name of the act really beautiful, 'Amerasian Homecoming Act.'" Among the difficulties Amerasians confronted, Miller emphasized, were limited education, facility with English, and employment prospects, conditions that discouraged their becoming more than legal residents and enjoying the full benefits of the United States. Miller and others have also spoken on behalf of Amerasians who suffer discrimination in Vietnam, their exits blocked by their poverty and restrictive U.S. laws. Such advocacy expressed many Amerasians' sense of duty to reinterpret their pasts and moderate the consequences of war and displacement. Tung Nguyen, who learned of Miller's efforts through social media, became involved because he "felt bad. I felt remorse for not knowing them sooner," since his military service kept him "detached from America." Now, having discovered that "there's still a lot of them stuck behind in Vietnam today," he wished "to help them get to the U.S. after all these years . . . do whatever contribution I could do to help."[78]

These concerns prompted national gatherings of Amerasians and the formation of the Amerasian Fellowship Association and the Amerasian Independent Voice in 2007. The nonprofits successfully lobbied Congress and convinced Zoe Lofgren, representative for California's Sixteenth District, to sponsor HR 4007, the Amerasian Paternity Recognition Act, which would confer automatic citizenship on all Amerasians residing in the United

States born between 1962 and 1976.[79] To enable the immigration of Amerasians in Vietnam, of whom U.S. officials demand more onerous proof of ancestry than in the past, Miller has written letters to Congress and funded use of Family Tree DNA, a company that helps to determine one's genealogy. He has also solicited and secured the support of Goldberg's Operation Reunite. "Since we already have the project set up for the Vietnamese adoptees," Goldberg stated, "we welcomed them into our group," a welcome that translated into DNA samplings of more than eighty Amerasians in Vietnam during a recent visit. Operation Reunite shared the results with the U.S. consulate and hoped it would help resolve pending cases.[80]

Through his career in the U.S. military and involvement in the POW/MIA program, Tung Nguyen, an Amerasian resettled in Rochester, New York, in the mid-1980s, has offered perhaps the most poetic revision of narratives about the Vietnam War, one that crosses and concludes two stories previously kept parallel: those of American prisoners of war and Amerasians. Americans used both groups to examine and reexamine the meanings of the war and U.S. responsibilities in the region. On the eve of retirement in 2009 after twenty years of service, Nguyen accepted an invitation to lead searches for POWs and MIAs in Vietnam. "That's something that I have always wanted to do the whole time I was in the military," he related, because "I always felt my dad was a military member, a U.S. military member. . . . So I wanted to be a part of it. I wanted to be able to contribute to sacrifices, to try to bring them home. These are the men that never made it back to the U.S., and so it's always been my dream to be able to repatriate them to the U.S." Nguyen explained that on his first of four missions, he and his team found more remains than had been discovered since the early 1980s. His desire to locate and return the remains of American soldiers suggested the continued longing of Amerasians for what was lost during the Vietnam War and the possibilities of selective resolution, even as formal campaigns and public recognition of such recovery efforts become less salient. And his relationship to and understanding of Vietnam's politics and economy changed as he noticed the country's transformation. "Everything is different. . . . So just grew and grew so fast, and the culture is completely different. Kids are a lot happier now. Most of them have money, and it's not like what I grew up with." Moreover, it seemed easier to travel without restrictions and enjoy everyday life without a sense of fear.[81]

At the close of the twentieth century and the beginning of the twenty-first, as Amerasians, adopted Vietnamese, and Vietnamese refugees have matured, resettled, and returned, they have also recovered or reinvented familial ties and reinterpreted the legacies of the Vietnam War. In doing so, they have altered their positions in discussions about U.S. interventions in Asia and relations with Vietnam, immigration policies, the definition of family, and constructions of identity, becoming authors and activists rather than simply subjects. What they have argued for and created, ranging from congressional legislation and DNA databases to humanitarian organizations and photos, suggests the diversity of Vietnamese experiences of assimilation and definition, the unexpected ties that bind once-separated migrants, and an understanding of war and displacement that breaks down familiar binaries of rescued versus stolen, gratitude versus guilt, and loss versus gain. Instead, almost five decades after Americans began to think about and engage with Vietnam and its children, we have new ideas about how military actions and migrations have shaped the formation of families and community, the responsibilities that should attach to U.S. citizenship, and ways to remember.

Conclusion

2015: Tung Nguyen and Merrie Li—siblings born in Vietnam who reconnected in the United States in the 1980s—mourned the passing of their Vietnamese mother and puzzled over the discovery that the American man whom Tung believed was his father was not. A large group of Amerasians organized by Jimmy Miller gathered in Seattle for an annual celebration, reflection, and call to political action. During the festive evening of dancing and dining, they honored their successes, paid tribute to Vietnam veterans, and recommitted to helping those who remained in Vietnam. Adoptee Tiffany Chi Goodson, who spent one year in Hanoi, where she taught English and yoga, hosted monthly music events, and served street youth under the auspices of the nonprofit Blue Children's Foundation, relocated to South Africa with and soon married Chris, a fellow volunteer and traveler whom she met in Southeast Asia. "Operation Babylift: Perspectives and Legacies," an exhibit documenting and inviting exchanges on the subjects of adoption and the airlifts, opened in San Francisco's Presidio. The bilingual, interactive space featured artifacts from Operation Babylift, text panels interpreting key events, a set of dialogues that paired adoptees with Presidio volunteers, and notecards—each asking a question such as "What conversation do you want to begin?" "What memories or stories do you want to share?" and "What question do you have about Operation Babylift?"—for visitors to complete and display on a peg-filled wall. National and regional media outlets used the occasion of the fortieth anniversary of the U.S. withdrawal from Vietnam to explore the recollections of aging veterans and the status of Vietnamese communities stretching from Philadelphia and Houston to San Jose and Garden Grove, California. The coverage not only replayed familiar themes of exile, anti-Communism, despair, and courageous adaptation but also noted the waning poignancy of the war and shifting priorities among American-born Vietnamese.

These nearly simultaneous events suggest the many ways in which the unexpected migrations, memories, and communities generated by wars in Southeast Asia continue to resonate in disparate locations. This book has spotlighted specific populations within the larger diaspora of Vietnamese to understand the division, revision, and restoration of families in contexts of violence, trauma, and uncertainty since 1965. Indeed, many of the accounts that animate the narrative convey the pain, agony, and sadness of Vietnamese and Americans entangled in complicated and often intimate ways by war and its long-reaching repercussions. However, they also suggest the endurance and hope that have guided new lives, strategies of survival, and reflections on responsibility.

Children of Reunion underscores the rhetorical and practical power of foreign children in debating and explicating U.S. foreign policies and immigration laws, especially as the gender and racial rules that defined American families changed in the wake of tumultuous social movements at midcentury. After World War II, falling fertility rates increased the demand of children available for adoption domestically while a softening stigma against single mothers reduced the supply. At the same time, Americans articulated new confidence that they could and should help foreign children by removing them from places of unrest and poverty rather than investing and stabilizing distant families and systems of social welfare. Whether brought from Europe, Latin America, or especially Asia, the children not only received the affection and protection associated with individual American families but also represented the hopes and ideals of the national family. Thus, as the United States' position and strategies in the world changed between 1945 and 1965, so did its conceptions of and policies toward children. First entwined with efforts to rebuild Japan and nations of Europe devastated by World War II, thus shoring up capitalism and asserting U.S. influence in those regions, adoption became part of an evolving Cold War doctrine of containing Communism and evangelizing Christian democracy, most notably in Korea. As the clearest evidence of the importance and heightened visibility of foreign children in the postwar period, the United States for the first time established permanent provisions for adoption, ones that arguably favored the adoptees more than any other category of migrant. Yet, as the United States escalated its global commitments, and diverse movements for social justice challenged the authority of established institutions and principles, the meanings attached to helping foreign children shifted. Beginning in the 1960s, Americans seeking to care for Southeast Asian children were interrogating mixed feelings about intervention in the region, the broader logic and virtues of U.S. foreign policy, and ways to assimilate while respecting racial and cultural diversity within the bounds of family. Reflecting and reinforcing divisions of the era that pitted champions of tradition, law, and order against opponents of conventional hierarchies, the discussion of adoption became more heated than ever before. Like those adopted prior, whose immaturity and helplessness Americans presumed, Vietnamese youths appeared ideal sites for the projection of roiling sentiments and beliefs.

Yet no one remains a child forever, and even during their childhoods, many Vietnamese adoptees voiced misgivings about their position as objects in a divisive and dramatic discourse. As the adoptees grew older, their voices grew louder, often accompanied by those of Vietnamese kin and Amerasians who migrated in the 1980s and 1990s. Their varied and distinctive assertions about remembrance, obligation, and identity have expanded discussions of war and migrations that were caught in all-too-familiar, narrow, and oppositional grooves. These migrants disrupt explanations that emphasize rescue and redemption as readily as ones that stress misery and misuse. Instead, their cultural expressions—photographs, songs, memoirs, and documentaries—organizations, travels, and everyday interactions convey how their longing and loss are tempered by discovery, connection, and creation. As a group united by common characteristics of dislocation, migration, and incorporation into new families, they are also divided by geography, education, class, sexuality, religion, and gender, divisions that make their contributions to interpretations of the past and projections for the future dissonant as often as harmonious. This lack of melody may frustrate, as it has previously, American attempts to find a singular, ultimately uplifting tune about the Vietnam War and Vietnamese immigration, but it may also prompt new approaches and practices as the twenty-first century advances.

The histories of adopted Vietnamese may help us think about where and how the United States should conduct itself internationally and whether it should privilege children, or, in the parlance of today, "unaccompanied minors," in its immigration policies. Americans have shown a great willingness to adopt healthy children under the age of five severed from birth families but also a reluctance to admit those who are older or who have suspended, but not erased or eased, family connections. Echoing the painful but often calculated choices of Vietnamese who placed their children with Americans and hoped to secure better opportunities for and eventually reclaim their kin, recently residents of El Salvador, Guatemala, and Nicaragua—confronting violence, poverty, and political chaos—dispatched tens of thousands of young children to cross the U.S.-Mexico border alone, wishing and waiting for reunion. In doing so, they have reversed the usual sequence of immigration, in which young adult men come first, and their female relatives and children follow. Uncertain how to react to children as the forerunners in a larger effort of family migration, but perhaps recounting criticisms leveled against Vietnamese, Americans have delayed them, detained them, and debated how best to care for them, educate them, and reconnect them with family members in the United States or Central America. Lax U.S. policies and weak border enforcement may have encouraged the migration of minors, highlighting themes of ambivalence and altruism within our approach to immigration. Outraged and empathetic, Americans have called for immigration reforms and actions in Central America that would discourage the practice of child migration but still revere familial ties and the idea of the United States as a refuge. Whether explicit or not, these responses reprise past uncertainty about and criticisms of Vietnamese families who used adoption as a diasporic strategy.

Given heightened environmental, political, and economic instability in the twenty-first century, the United States has and will likely continue to face more pressure to admit refugees, a class of migrant that reflects U.S. foreign policy objectives and demands declarations of gratitude. As the second-largest refugee group of the twentieth century (second only to Soviet Jews), and one whose departure from Vietnam triggered the creation of a comprehensive U.S. refugee policy in 1980 (ad hoc measures prevailed through the 1970s), the case of Vietnamese and Amerasians is illustrative and may prove instructive. The United States admitted large numbers of Southeast Asians because it believed them both enemies and victims of Communism. Measured relief and resettlement services reinforced the idea that refugees deserved support that other immigrants did not. However, such attention did not come without costs. Americans asked for more contributions and appreciation from Vietnamese refugees than from other newcomers. And while Vietnamese have often fulfilled these demands and successfully deployed the language of anti-Communism and hyperpatriotism to their advantage, such constructions of the grateful and readily assimilated refugee obscure real economic and social difficulties as well as other political vocabularies. The children of Vietnamese, Amerasians, and adoptees will likely fracture these ideas about refugees, opening up new spaces to manifest grief, implicate U.S. actions abroad, and design different versions of Vietnamese American identity. Their efforts and an understanding of the history of Vietnamese migrations may prompt Americans to reevaluate the classification of and expectations placed on the latest generation of refugees.

This book also makes clear the tenacious and intricate ties that Vietnamese conjured and often sustained or reimagined across time and space.

Adoptees and Amerasians were part of a larger migratory process directed by extended Vietnamese families. Amid the political confusion and destruction of Vietnam, Vietnamese designed plans for survival and even success that included separation, departure, and hopeful reunions. They huddled together and debated who should go, who could stay, and how to distribute responsibilities and resources across members. Putting relatives up for adoption was among their most difficult decisions. Recognizing the odds against recovery and reconciliation, many expected never to see their young kin again and wished them better lives in Europe, Australia, or especially the United States, where the majority resettled. Yet, others beat the odds, reached American shores, and began searches for related children because they had promised themselves or their siblings or cousins or parents that they would. These investigations required patience, serendipity, and a willingness to confront American adoptive parents, institutions, and ideals that scripted all Vietnamese children as orphans best suited for more prosperous, stable, American homes. Discovering the presence and parental claims of Vietnamese caused panic and pain among unsuspecting Americans, but also raised doubts about what the United States owed Vietnam and the ways in which those debts could be paid.

Vietnamese refugees seeking children, Vietnamese adoptees seeking birth families, and Amerasians seeking fathers sometimes found whom they sought. Their attempts at and actual reunions revealed the sprawl and intrigue of Vietnamese migrations and the possibility of reshaping families often divided over long periods of time and distance: an American veteran located his son and rekindled relations with his Vietnamese paramour; adopted siblings raised as cousins hugged their Vietnamese mother and Amerasian siblings, who had resettled in the United States; a Vietnamese man shared tears and photos with his niece, whom he had not seen since she left Vietnam and was adopted by an American couple. Most encounters proved emotional and awkward as parties struggled to find commonality and manage the weight of their expectations, shaped in part by the assertions of veterans organizations, adoptee social networks, the media, Vietnamese and American governmental organizations, and adoption agencies. In some cases, first meetings were the last, either because they sufficiently satisfied a simple need to know or because they increased more than they relieved feelings of loss and dislocation. However, in other cases, the rendezvous with relatives initiated a habit of revelation and connection that felt like restitution. Adopted Vietnamese, Amerasians, Vietnamese, and Americans knitted themselves into patterns that did not so much deny or erase the threads of U.S. imperialism and wars in Southeast Asia that had initially brought them together as identify common strands of inquiry and reflection.

Adoptive parents have participated in these patterns, sometimes resisting but often respecting and even facilitating their adoptive children's desire to discover their Vietnamese beginnings. In encouraging these searches for place and people, they have sustained a perspective on raising children that they embraced years earlier. More than their predecessors who adopted internationally, the Vietnam generation began to popularize race- and culture-conscious parenting practices intended to prepare children for the identity dilemmas of their adolescence; many demonstrated a willingness to integrate the era's liberal wisdom about teaching Vietnamese traditions and explaining global inequalities to their offspring. Adoptees preferring to fit in rather than stand out may have deflected these prescriptions at first, but they often revisited them as they aged. Such ideas would shape how couples and singles adopting in the late twentieth and early twenty-first centuries approached family formation and spawned an industry of heritage camps and birthplace tours intended to guide their efforts. Through structured travel, mediated activities, and orientation sessions, these programs attempted to educate, reassure, and root the most recent wave of adoptees.

Overall, this book notes the importance of Vietnamese adoptions to the larger process through which Americans and Vietnamese have tried to assign responsibility and find belonging in the aftermath of wars in Southeast Asia that ruptured their respective senses of identity, community, and place. It also proposes that Americans will continue to explore and explain their obligations to families in poorer regions touched by U.S. power, many of whom may seek refuge or opportunity in the United States, by making promises to their children. If and as they do so, Americans might respect the muddled experiences of violence and migration that complicate kinship and national will.

Notes

Introduction

1. Author's interview with Trista Goldberg, September 18, 2013.

2. Although some individuals adopted from Vietnam stated a preference for the designation "adopted Vietnamese," a term that they argued suggested greater action and affirmation, others expressed greater comfort with the more common "adoptee." I use the former appellation more regularly than the latter.

3. Author's interview with Trista Goldberg; author's interview with Jeffrey Corliss, November 10, 2013.

4. Author's interview with Jeffrey Corliss.

5. U.S. Department of Defense statistics reproduced by CNN and cited in Yên Lê Espiritu, *Body Counts: The Vietnam War and Militarized Refuge(es)* (Berkeley: University of California Press, 2014), 17; Vu Hong Lien and Peter D. Sharrock, *Descending Dragon, Rising Tiger: A History of Vietnam* (Chicago: University of Chicago Press, 2014), 240.

6. Espiritu, *Body Counts*, 16–18.

7. Carl Bon Tempo argues that the prominence of anti-Communism as the rationale for refugee policy during the early Cold War had receded by the 1970s; human rights became the principle most cited by politicians and the public. Carl J. Bon Tempo, *Americans at the Gate: The United States and Refugees during the Cold War* (Princeton, N.J.: Princeton University Press, 2008). Other scholars have challenged this interpretation, highlighting the persistence of political motives in defining refugee policy. Heather Marie Stur, "'Hiding behind the Humanitarian Label': Refugees, Repatriates, and the Rebuilding of America's Benevolent Image after the Vietnam War," *Diplomatic History* 39, no. 2 (April 2015): 223–24. Espiritu and others have noted an absence of scholarly attention to refugee experience and have begun to fill the gap. Espiritu, *Body Counts*; Aihwa Ong, *Buddha Is Hiding: Refugees, Citizenship, the New America* (Berkeley: University of California Press, 2003), 78; Mimi Thi Nguyen, *The Gift of Freedom: War, Debt, and Other Refugee Passages* (Durham, N.C.: Duke University Press, 2012).

8. Mae Ngai, *Impossible Subjects: Illegal Aliens and the Making of Modern America* (Princeton, N.J.: Princeton University Press, 2004); Erika Lee, *At America's Gates: Chinese Immigration during the Exclusion Era, 1882–1943* (Chapel Hill: University of North Carolina Press, 2003); Aristide Zolberg, *A Nation by Design: Immigration Policy in the Fashioning of America* (Cambridge, Mass.: Harvard University Press,

2008); Hiroshi Motomura, *Americans in Waiting: The Lost Story of Immigration and Citizenship in the United States* (New York: Oxford University Press, 2007).

9. Bon Tempo, *Americans at the Gate*; Maria Cristiana Garcia, *Seeking Refuge: Central American Immigrants to Mexico, the United States, and Canada* (Berkeley: University of California Press, 2006).

10. Among the most noteworthy works that explore the evolution and broader meanings of adoption are Ellen Herman, *Kinship by Design: A History of Adoption in the Modern United States* (Chicago: University of Chicago Press, 2008); Catherine Cezina Choy, *Global Families: A History of Asian International Adoption* (New York: New York University Press, 2014); Julie Berebitsky, *Like Our Very Own: Adoption and the Changing Culture of Motherhood, 1851-1950* (Lawrence: University of Kansas Press, 2000); Laura Briggs, *Somebody Else's Children: The Politics of Transracial and Transnational Adoption* (Durham, N.C.: Duke University Press, 2012); Arissa Oh, *To Save the Children of Korea: The Cold War Origins of International Adoption* (Palo Alto, Calif.: Stanford University Press, 2015); Rachel Winslow, "Immigration Law and Improvised Policy Making, 1948-1961," *Journal of Policy History* 24, no. 2 (April 2012): 319-49.

11. Christina Klein, *Cold War Orientalism: Asia in the Middlebrow Imagination, 1945-1961* (Berkeley: University of California Press, 2003); Margaret Peacock, *Innocent Weapons: The Soviet and American Politics of Childhood* (Chapel Hill: University of North Carolina Press, 2014); Donna Alvah, *Unofficial Ambassadors: American Military Families Overseas and the Cold War* (New York: New York University Press, 2007); Mary Dudiak, *Cold War Civil Rights: Race and the Image of American Democracy* (Princeton, N.J.: Princeton University Press, 2001); Shana Bernstein, *Bridges of Reform: Interracial Civil Rights Activism in Twentieth-Century Los Angeles* (New York: Oxford University Press, 2011).

12. David Kieran, *Forever Vietnam: How a Divisive War Changed American Public Memory* (Amherst: University of Massachusetts Press, 2014); Michael Allen, *Until the Last Man Comes Home: POWs, MIAs, and the Unending War in Vietnam* (Chapel Hill: University of North Carolina Press, 2012); Scott Laderman, *Tours of Vietnam* (Durham, N.C.: Duke University Press, 2009); Patrick Hagiopan, *The Vietnam War in American Memory: Memorials and the Politics of Healing* (Amherst: University of Massachusetts Press, 2011); Robert Schulzinger, *A Time for Peace: The Legacy of the Vietnam War* (New York: Oxford University Press, 2008); G. Kurt Piehler, *Remembering War: The American Way* (Washington, D.C: Smithsonian Institution Press, 1995).

13. This book joins an emerging collection of scholarly works exploring ideas of loss and violence associated with refugees. See the writings of Yên Lê Espiritu, Victor Bascara, Lan Duong, Ma Vang, Viet Thanh Nguyen, Khatharya Um, and Mimi Thi Nguyen. Diplomatic historians have tried to temper these themes of anguish and vulnerability, emphasizing the political and military events that created refugees and the ways in which refugees shaped those events. Peter Nyers, *Rethinking Refugees: Beyond States of Emergency* (New York: Routledge, 2006); Lisa H. Malkki,

"Speechless Emissaries: Refugees, Humanitarianism, and Dehistoricization," *Cultural Anthropology* 11, no. 3 (August 1996): 377–404.

Chapter One

1. Letter to Friends Meeting for the Suffering of Vietnamese Children from Sandstroms, September 15, 1967, Box 5, Friends Meeting for Suffering of Vietnamese Children Records, DG111, Swarthmore Peace Collection (hereafter cited as FMSVCR-SPC).

2. Sophie Quinn-Judge, "Through a Glass Darkly: Reading the History of the Vietnamese Communist Party, 1945–1975," in *Making Sense of the Vietnam Wars: Local, National, and Transnational Perspectives*, ed. Mark Philip Bradley and Marilyn B. Young (New York: Oxford University Press, 2008), 111–34.

3. Mark Atwood Lawrence, "Explaining the Early Decisions: The United States and the French War," in Bradley and Young, *Making Sense of the Vietnam Wars*, 23–44. Recent studies of the Vietnam War have complicated conventional wisdom about what drew the United States and Soviet Union into the region. Edward Miller and Tuong Vu, "The Vietnam War as a Vietnamese War: Agency and Society in the Study of the Second Indochina War," *Journal of Vietnamese Studies* 4, no. 3 (Fall 2009): 1–16. More generally and using Vietnamese sources, a set of scholars has shifted attention toward the experiences and intentions of Vietnamese, asking new questions and providing different answers to old ones. Tuong Vu and Wasana Wongsurawat, eds., *Dynamics of the Cold War in Asia: Ideology, Identity and Culture* (New York: Palgrave, 2009); Christopher Goscha and Christian Ostermann, eds., *Connecting Histories: The Cold War and Decolonization in Asia, 1945–1962* (Palo Alto, Calif.: Stanford University Press, 2009).

4. Lien-Hang T. Nguyen, "Cold War Contradictions: Toward an International History of the Second Indochina War, 1969–1973," in Bradley and Young, *Making Sense of the Vietnam Wars*, 221.

5. Mitchell Hall, "The Vietnam Era Anti-war Movement," *OAH Magazine*, October 2004; Tom Wells, *The War Within: America's Battle over Vietnam* (Berkeley: University of California Press, 1994); Charles DeBenedetti and Charles Chatfield, *An American Ordeal: The Antiwar Movement of the Vietnam Era* (Syracuse, N.Y.: Syracuse University Press, 1990); Terry Anderson, *Rethinking the Anti-war Movement* (New York: Routledge, 2011); Penny Lewis, *Hardhats, Hippies, and Hawks* (Ithaca, N.Y.: Cornell University Press, 2013). Judy Tzo-Chun Wu, *Radicals on the Road: Internationalism, Orientalism, and Feminism during the Vietnam Era* (Ithaca: Cornell University Press, 2013).

6. For more about the social, political, and cultural turmoil aggravated by the Vietnam War, see Robert Schulzinger, *A Time for Peace: The Legacy of the Vietnam War* (New York: Oxford University Press, 2008); Daniel Lucks, *Selma to Saigon: The Civil Rights Movement and the Vietnam War* (Lexington: University Press of Kentucky, 2013); Meredith Lair, *Armed with Abundance* (Chapel Hill: University

of North Carolina Press, 2013); Bradley and Young, *Making Sense of the Vietnam Wars*.

7. Among the scholars who have asserted and explored the broader significance of families are Christina Klein, *Cold War Orientalism: Asia in the Middlebrow Imagination, 1945–1961* (Berkeley: University of California Press, 2003); Barbara Melosh, *Strangers and Kin: The American Way of Adoption* (Cambridge, Mass.: Harvard University Press, 2006); Elaine Tyler May, *Homeward Bound* (New York: Basic Books, 1999); Sara Dorow, *Transnational Adoption: A Cultural Economy of Race, Gender, and Kinship* (New York: New York University Press, 2006).

8. Historians such as Margaret Peacock, Donna Alvah, Heide Fehrenbach, and Karen Balcom have documented the use of children to express and enact the United States' policy objectives during the Cold War. Margaret Peacock, *Innocent Weapons: The Soviet and American Politics of Childhood in the Cold War* (Chapel Hill: University of North Carolina Press, 2014); Donna Alvah, *Unofficial Ambassadors: American Military Families Overseas and the Cold War, 1946–1965* (New York: New York University Press, 2007); Heide Fehrenbach, *Race after Hitler: Black Occupation Children in Postwar Germany and America* (Princeton, N.J.: Princeton University Press, 2007); Karen Balcom, *The Traffic in Babies: Cross-Border Adoption and Baby-Selling between the United States and Canada, 1930–1972* (Toronto: University of Toronto Press, 2011).

9. Antiwar veterans would employ the "baby killer" image to discredit the U.S. presence in Vietnam, blaming the U.S. military for programming and tolerating random, civilian-directed violence. Andrew J. Huebner, *The Warrior Image: Soldiers in American Culture from the Second World War to the Vietnam Era* (Chapel Hill: University of North Carolina Press, 2008), 225.

10. Heather Marie Stur, Susan Jeffords, and Andrew Huebner examine the diverse cultural and political meanings of American soldiers. Heather Marie Stur, *Beyond Combat: Women and Gender in the Vietnam War Era* (Cambridge: Cambridge University Press, 2011); Susan Jeffords, *The Remasculinization of America: Gender and the Vietnam War* (Bloomington: Indiana University Press, 1989); Huebner, *The Warrior Image*. Huebner notes the multiplication of "routes to honor" in understandings of military service during Vietnam. Manliness was not realized simply or strictly through acts of classic heroism such as jumping on a grenade, but through expressions of compassion, loneliness, even depression in the face of war's challenges. Huebner sees these varied versions of manliness not as inventions of the Vietnam War era but as revisions and intensifications of more sentimental images dating to World War II.

11. Jeffords, *Remasculinization*.

12. Sara Fieldston, "Little Cold Warriors: Child Sponsorship and International Affairs," *Diplomatic History* 38, no. 2 (2014): 240–50.

13. Rachel Winslow, "Immigration Law and Improvised Policy Making, 1948–1961," *Journal of Policy History* 24, no. 2 (April 2012): 324.

14. Ellen Herman, *Kinship by Design: A History of Adoption in the Modern United States* (Chicago: University of Chicago Press, 2008), 13.

15. Fehrenbach, *Race after Hitler*; Arissa Oh, "From War Waif to Ideal Immigrant: The Cold War Transformation of the Korean Immigrant," *Journal of American Ethnic History* 31, no. 2 (2013): 34–55.

16. Michael Hunt and Steven Levine, *Arc of Empire: America's Wars in Asia from the Philippines to Vietnam* (Chapel Hill: University of North Carolina Press, 2012).

17. Case 60-495, Box 125, International Social Service, American Branch Papers, Social Welfare History Archives (hereafter cited as ISS-USA, SWHA).

18. Catherine Cezina Choy, *Global Families: A History of Asian International Adoption* (New York: New York University Press, 2014), 49.

19. Created in 1924, ISS offered services through national branches in Europe and the United States. After World War II, intercountry adoptions became the single largest category of assistance provided by ISS. Rather than a formal adoption agency, it mediated between interested parties.

20. Choy, *Global Families*, 68–70.

21. Ibid., 71. Scholars have also argued that positive representations of Asian war brides in popular culture helped assuage American anxieties about racial integration and imperialist ventures. The interracial marriages suggested that American society could safely absorb newcomers and that Asians felt fondly toward Americans despite or even because of U.S. actions in the region. See Caroline Chung Simpson, *An Absent Presence: Japanese Americans in Postwar Culture, 1945–1960* (Durham, N.C.: Duke University Press, 2002); Shirley Jennifer Lim, *A Feeling of Belonging: Asian American Women's Public Culture, 1930–1960* (New York: New York University Press, 2006); Traise Yamamoto, *Masking Selves, Making Subjects: Japanese American Women, Identity, and the Body* (Berkeley: University of California Press, 1999).

22. Lily Anne Yumi Welty, "Advantage through Crisis: Multiracial American Japanese in Post–World War II Japan, Okinawa, and America, 1945–1972" (Ph.D. diss., University of Santa Barbara, 2012); Robert Fish, "The Heiress and the Love Children: Sawada Miki and the Elisabeth Saunders Home for Mixed-Blood Orphans in Post-war Japan" (Ph.D. diss., University of Hawaii, 2002); Richard Weil, "International Adoptions: The Quiet Migration," *International Migration Review* 18 (Summer 1984): 276–93. In her analysis of an article penned by Norman Cousins for a 1949 issue of *Saturday Review*, Laura Briggs noted the expressions of regret made by some Americans to Japanese children. While one woman offered a "small tax payment for my share in the guilt of belonging to a race which dropped the first atomic bomb," a former World War II pilot wrote that helping Japanese children financially might "soothe an elusive feeling of collective guilt." Laura Briggs, *Somebody's Children: The Politics of Transracial and Transnational Adoption* (Durham, N.C.: Duke University Press, 2012), 187–88.

23. Susie Woo, "'A New American Comes Home': Race, Nation, and the Immigration of Korean War Adoptees, 'GI Babies,' and War Brides" (Ph.D. diss., Yale University, 2010), 206.

24. Oh, "War Waif to Ideal Immigrant," 34–55; Choy, *Global Families*; Elise Prebin, *Meeting Once More: The Korean Side of International Adoption* (New York: New York University Press, 2013).

25. By the early 1960s, the government and social workers came to the conclusion that international adoption was an imperfect solution to the problem of child abandonment and began to implement programs to promote family preservation, facilitate the integration of mixed-race children, and encourage domestic adoptions. Eleana J. Kim, *Adopted Territory: Transnational Korean Adoptees and the Politics of Belonging* (Durham, N.C.: Duke University Press, 2010), 73.

26. Ibid., 72.

27. Woo, "'A New American Comes Home,'" 17.

28. Oh, "War Waif to Ideal Immigrant." SooJin Pate considers the role Korean children played in easing neocolonial relations between Korea and the United States. SooJin Pate, *From Orphan to Adoptee: U.S. Empire and Genealogies of Korean Adoption* (Minneapolis: University of Minnesota Press, 2015).

29. Although Latin American countries more rarely drew the attention of prospective adoptive parents until the 1980s and 1990s, the U.S. government did arrange special visas for 14,000 Cuban children between 1960 and 1962, a program the press nicknamed Operation Pedro Plan. Responding to and encouraging rumors that Fidel Castro would take children away from their families—sending them to Russian camps or government hostels—the State Department granted a Catholic priest in Miami authority to give a visa waiver to Cuban children between the ages of six and sixteen who wished to come to the United States. Paired with the Bay of Pigs Invasion, the effort revealed and reinforced American claims about the cruelty of Communism and the Cuban people's opposition to Castro. It also demonstrated the continued, post–World War II desire to support children by taking them out of their native contexts and raising them as Americans. Most of the youth grew up in foster homes, orphanages, refugee camps, or Catholic monasteries. Briggs, *Somebody's Children*.

30. Beginning in the late 1940s, American officials identified refugee children from newly Communist China as among the most in need of American homes. Agencies in the United States and Hong Kong (where the children had resettled) gave priority to Chinese and Chinese American families seeking to adopt. An ISS report noted that 75 percent of the couples who adopted Chinese children from Hong Kong between 1968 and 1969 were of Chinese descent. For more about the optimism and commitment to colorblindness expressed by American adopters in the 1950s, see Klein, *Cold War Orientalism*, and Tobias Hübinette, *Comforting an Orphaned Nation: Representations of International Adoption and Adopted Koreans in Korean Popular Culture* (Seoul: Jimoondang, 2006).

31. Letter to Margaret Watts from Morgan Sibbett, March 28, 1968, Box 2, FMSVCR-SPC; Ann Bryan, "The Unwanteds: Thousands of GI War Babies Face a Grim Future in Vietnam," June 26, 1971; Loren Jenkins, "Vietnam's War-Torn Children," *Newsweek*, May 28, 1973, 52–61; D. E. Ronk, "The Forgotten Victims of the

War in Vietnam," *Parents' Magazine and Better Family Living*, August 1969, 43–44, 90–91; Klein quoted in Jean Yavis Jones, "Vietnamese Adoption and Child Care," July 18, 1973, part of a report compiled by Education and Public Welfare Division, Congressional Research Service; "New Methods Sought to Take Care of Children Fathered by GIs in Vietnam," *Philadelphia Evening Bulletin*, December 27, 1966.

32. Buck quoted in Sidney Fields, "Aid for Unwanted Babies," *Daily News*, December 13, 1971.

33. Letter to Friends Meeting for the Suffering of Vietnamese Children from Connie and Harvey Bartz, December 12, 1967, Box 3, FMSVCR-SPC.

34. From newspaper clippings and letters to FMSVC, Box 3, FMSVCR-SPC; David Barnett Jr., "Matthew's Saga: Saigon to Southampton: Welcome House Had Been Saving Children for 30 Years," April 29, 1979, Welcome House Parents' Association, Scrapbook, 1979–1980, RG1, S1, Papers of the Pearl S. Buck Foundation, Archives of the Pearl S. Buck House, Pearl S. Buck International (hereafter cited as APSBH); Marlene Simons, "Help for 'Amerasian' Children," *Los Angeles Times*, August 9, 1971, E3; Bryan, "The Unwanteds."

35. Jones, "Vietnamese Adoption and Child Care."

36. Mary Graves, Welcome House Adoptive Parents Group, Scrapbook, 1973–1975, APSBH.

37. Ministry of Social Welfare and Land Development and Hamlet Building, "Child Welfare in the Republic of Vietnam," in *Vietnam Children's Basic Problems* (Saigon, 1974), a series of pamphlets prepared for the International Conference on Children and National Development. Between 1955 and 1974, the number of orphanages had increased from 14 to 134 (ibid., 6).

38. The Committee of Child Welfare was organized in preparation for the International Conference on Children and National Development in Saigon in December 1974. It consisted of senior members of the Ministry of Social Welfare and Land Development, Health, Culture Education and Youth as well as representatives of USAID, UNICEF, UNESCO, WHO, and Vietnamese and international voluntary agencies.

39. Ministry of Social Welfare and Land Development and Hamlet Building, "Child Welfare in the Republic of Vietnam," 10–12.

40. Rosemary Taylor, *Orphans of War: Work with the Abandoned Children of Vietnam, 1967–1975* (London: Collins, 1988), 133.

41. Morgan Sibbet, "Reports and Notes," Box 3, FMSVCR-SPC.

42. Letter to Charge de Mission, Office of Prime Minister, South Vietnam, from Jan De Hartog, May 9, 1967, ISS-Box 21, Folder FMSVC, ISS-USA, SWHA.

43. Wells Klein, "The Special Needs of Vietnamese Children—a Critique," February 1972, quoted in Jones, "Vietnamese Adoption and Child Care," 12.

44. Ibid.

45. Walter R. Sherman, "Report to the Board of Directors of ISS, American Branch, regarding Visit to Vietnam, Jan 14–21 1966," Box 7, FMSVCR-SPC; Letter to Friends Meeting for the Suffering of Vietnamese Children from Sandstroms, 1967, Box 3, FMSVCR-SPC. For a more detailed discussion of the competition and conflict

between ISS and the social welfare community of the 1950s, see Winslow, "Immigration Law," and Choy, *Global Families*.

46. It was not until 1976, with the passage of an amendment permitting single persons to adopt foreign children, and 1978, when new bills allowed petitioners to adopt more than two foreign children and expedited the naturalization of children adopted from abroad, that Congress made any significant revisions to the process outlined in 1961; "Alien Adopted Children," *Hearing before the Subcommittee on Immigration, Citizenship and International Law Committee of the Judiciary, House 95th Congress, June 15, 1977* (Washington, D.C.: Government Printing Office, 1978); Gerald Adcock, *Intercountry Adoptions: Where Do They Go from Here* (Dearborn, Mich.: Bouldin-Haigh-Irwin, 1979).

47. Jones, "Vietnamese Adoption and Child Care."

48. Stuart Harverson, *God's Orphans in Vietnam* (London: Page Bros., 1971), 26.

49. LeAnn Thieman and Carol Dey, *This Must Be My Brother* (Wheaton, Ill.: Victor Books, 1995), 58.

50. Ibid., 34.

51. Mary Graves, Welcome House Adoptive Parents Group, Scrapbook, 1973–1975, APSBH.

52. Robbie Lieberman, *The Strangest Dream: Communism, Anticommunism, and the U.S. Peace Movement, 1945–1963* (New York: Syracuse University Press, 2000); Avital H. Bloch and Lauri Umansky, eds., *Impossible to Hold: Women and Culture in the 1960s* (New York: New York University Press, 2005). Feminists often took issue with women peace activists whose politics drew narrowly on their identities as mothers, caretakers, and kin workers. Sara Ruddick, *Maternal Thinking: Toward a Politics of Peace* (Boston: Boston University Press, 1989).

53. Howard Rusk quoted in Committee of Responsibility document, undated, File COR, Box 7, FMSVCR-SPC.

54. Author's interview with Tom Miller, May 29, 2012. Pierre Gaisseau's documentary *Gooks* details the work of Barsky in Vietnam. *Gooks*, directed by Pierre Gaisseau (Canadian Broadcasting Corporation, 1972), 56 minutes; David Dunlap, "Dr. Arthur Barsky Dies at 83," *New York Times*, February 11, 1982.

55. Author's interview with Tom Miller.

56. Letters to Committee of Responsibility, Box 30, Committee of Responsibility Records, Swarthmore Peace Collection (hereafter cited as CORR-SPC).

57. Form letter to prospective parents from Holt International, undated, Folder "Holt Adoption Program, Inc.," Box 2, FMSVCR-SPC; Letter to Rev. John E. Adams [executive director of Holt International] from Rachel Lee, March 9, 1968, Box 2, FMSVCR-SPC.

58. Letter to Margaret Watts from Morgan Sibbett, March 28, 1968, Box 2, FMSVCR-SPC.

59. Cherie Clark, *After Sorrow Comes Joy: One Woman's Struggle to Bring Hope to Thousands of Children in Vietnam and India* (Westminster, Colo.: Lawrence and Thomas, 2000).

60. Letter to COR from Susan Tracy, January 4, 1967, Box 30, FMSVCR-SPC.

61. Letter to Jan De Hartog from Mrs. Donald Smith, March 31, 1967, Box 2, FMSVCR-SPC; Letter to Mrs. Smith from Tullis Inglese, March 6, 1968, Box 30, CORR-SPC; Letter to Morgan Sibbett from Wanda Knight, February 28, 1968, Box 2, FMSVCR-SPC.

62. Letter to FMSVC from Beverly Ann Rayor, December 16, 1967, Box 2, FMSVCR-SPC.

63. Clark, *After Sorrow Comes Joy*, 22; Era Bell Thompson, "The Plight of Black Babies in South Vietnam," *Ebony*, December 1972, 105.

64. Pamela Chatterton Purdy, *Beyond the Babylift: A Story of an Adoption* (Nashville: Abingdon, 1987), 15.

65. Letter to Jan and Marjorie De Hartog from Mrs. Bryan P. Michener, October 19, 1966, Box 1, and Letter to Jan and Marjorie De Hartog from Wendy Grant, December 6, 1966, Box 2, FMSVCR-SPC.

66. Letter to Mrs. Richard Burton from Frank Ortoloff, January 6, 1967, Box 3, FMSVCR-SPC.

67. "A Poor Argument," *Boston Herald*, January 9, 1967; "Suffering Little Children," *Boston Globe*, January 9, 1967.

68. Patricia Nye, "First Asia-Oceania Conference Report of International Social Service," March 18–23, 1973, Box 44, and *Frontiers in Adoption*, May 1972, Box 19, ISS-USA, SWHA.

69. Letter to FMSVC from California resident (unnamed), September 26, 1966, Box 3; Response to FMSVC questionnaire about ability to adopt, foster, or provide forms of care for Vietnamese children by Mary Ellen Tjossem, 1966, Box 2; and Letter to FMSVC from Wilma Brown, October 25, 1966, Box 1, FMSVCR-SPC.

70. "National Association of Black Social Workers Position on Transracial Adoption," September 1972, accessed July 5, 2016, http://c.ymcdn.com/sites/nabsw.org/resource/collection/E1582D77-E4CD-4104-996A-D42D08F9CA7D/NABSW_Trans-Racial_Adoption_1972_Position_(b).pdf.

71. Response to FMSVC questionnaire, 1967, Box 4; Response to FMSVC questionnaire by James and Carol Urquhart, 1967, Box 4; and Letter of inquiry from Rev. Irving C. Beveridge, December 5, 1966, Box 1, FMSVCR-SPC; Frank Chinook, *Kim, a Gift from Vietnam* (New York: World Publishing, 1969), 10.

72. Karen Dubinsky, "'We Adopted a Negro': Interracial Adoptions and the Hybrid Baby in 1960s Canada," in *Creating Postwar Canada: Community, Diversity, and Dissent, 1945–1975*, ed. Magna Fahrni and Robert Futherdales (Vancouver, B.C.: University of British Columbia Press, 2008); Margaret Jacobs, "Remembering the Forgotten Child: The American Indian Child Welfare Crisis of the 1960s and 1970s," *American Indian Quarterly* 37, nos. 1–2 (Spring/Winter 2013): 136–59. Jacobs estimates that in states with large American Indian populations, as many as 25–30 percent of their children were removed during the duration of the program. For an exhaustive treatment of U.S. policies toward American Indian children and the challenges

mobilized by American Indian families to these policies, see Margaret Jacobs, *White Mother to a Dark Race: Settler Colonialism, Maternalism, and the Removal of Indigenous Children in the American West and Australia, 1880–1940* (Lincoln: University of Nebraska Press, 2009), and Margaret Jacobs, *A Generation Removed: The Fostering and Adoption of Indigenous Children in the Postwar World* (Lincoln: University of Nebraska Press, 2014).

73. Letter to FMSVC from Dorothy and Harvey Smith, March 12, 1967, Box 3; Letter to FMSVC from Dorothy and Harvey Smith, January 16, 1967, Box 3; and Letter to FMSVC from Paul and Amy Kaplan, 1967, Box 1, FMSVC-SPC; Case 72-183, Box 318, ISS-USA, SWHA.

74. Marjorie Margolies, *They Came to Stay* (New York: Coward, Mccann and Geoghegan, 1976), 38.

75. Ibid., 205.

76. Ibid., 209.

77. Ibid., 210.

78. Ibid.

79. Ibid., 220.

80. Chinook, *Kim*, 42.

81. Ibid., 8.

82. Ibid., 197.

83. Ibid., 51.

84. Author's interview with Ken Armstrong, May 5, 2012.

85. George Allen, *Ri* (New York: Prentice Hall, 1978), 96.

86. For more about the exchanges and relationship between American soldiers and local boys, see Kori Graves, "Domesticating Foreign Affairs: The African American Family, Korean Orphans, and Cold War Civil Rights" (Ph.D. diss., University of Wisconsin–Madison, 2011); Stur, *Beyond Combat*.

87. Allen, *Ri*, 91.

88. Ibid., 112.

89. Ibid., 240.

90. Ibid., 283.

91. Elsie Hower quoted in Rose Perlberg, "When a GI Adopts a Vietnamese Waif—Happiness or Heartbreak," *Family Weekly*, January 29, 1967.

92. Perlberg, "When a GI Adopts."

93. Case 72-146, Box 318, ISS-USA, SWHA.

94. U.S. hearings referenced in Rachel Winslow, "Good Samaritans or Baby Brokers? Conflicting Responses to the Holt Adoption Program, 1956–1964" (M.A. thesis, California State University, Sacramento, 2007).

95. "House Bill #2037," *Insight/Asia Newsletter* 2, no. 5 (1971).

96. "Suffer the Little Children," *New York Times*, February 15, 1973; 119 Cong. Rec. (1973) (address of Sen. Kennedy of Massachusetts).

97. 119 Cong. Rec. (1973) (statement of Sen. Steiger of New York).

98. Buck quoted in Tom Tiede, "U.S. Passes Buck on GI Babies," *Union*, January 1971.

99. James Reston, "Vietnamese Children of GIs Require Help," *Providence Journal*, February 28, 1973; Lawrence O'Rourke, "Vietnam War Left Over 700,000 Orphans," *Philadelphia Evening Bulletin*, opinion and review, October 5, 1973.

Chapter Two

1. The Paris Peace Accords, signed by the United States, the DRV, RVN, and PRG, which represented the region's revolutionary minorities, provided for a ceasefire between North and South Vietnam, the withdrawal of U.S. troops within sixty days, negotiations between the RVN and the PRG to establish a popular government, and steps toward the reunion of North and South Vietnam.

2. Christine D. Leivermann quoted in Rosemary Taylor, *Orphans of War: Work with the Abandoned Children of Vietnam, 1967–1975* (London: Collins, 1988), 171.

3. "Ford Vows to Continue Operation Babylift," *Los Angeles Times*, April 4, 1972, 4.

4. Tsongas and Marrs quoted in "The Orphans Saved or Lost?," *Time*, April 21, 1975, 13.

5. Figures from the Socialist Republic of Vietnam cited in Vu Hong Lien and Peter D. Sharrock, *Descending Dragon, Rising Tiger: A History of Vietnam* (Chicago: University of Chicago Press, 2014), 240.

6. "The Orphans Saved or Lost?," *Time*, April 21, 1975, 10–13.

7. Shana Alexander, "A Sentimental Binge," *Newsweek*, April 28, 1975, 88.

8. Grace Paley, "Other People's Children: The Young Shoots of Vietnam," *Ms.*, September 1975, 68.

9. "Rescuing Vietnam Orphans: Mixed Motives," *Christian Century*, April 16, 1975, 374.

10. Desmond Smith, "Second Hand Babies," *Nation*, April 19, 1975, 454; Judith Coburn, "The War of the Babies," *Village Voice*, April 14, 1975, 15.

11. Smith, "Second Hand Babies," 454; Gloria Emerson, "Operation Babylift," *New Republic*, April 26, 1975, 9; Susan Abrams, "The Vietnam Babylift," *Commonweal*, September 24, 1976, 617–21.

12. Herbert quoted in Nancy Hicks, "Black Agencies Charge Injustice in Placing of Vietnam Children," *New York Times*, April 19, 1975, 11; "And Now a Domestic Babylift," *Ebony*, June 1975, 134.

13. As quoted in Colburn, "War of the Babies," 17.

14. Ibid., 15; Emerson, "Operation Babylift," 9.

15. Reporter's Partial Transcript, May 19 and 20, 1975, Box 11, RG 276, United States District Court of California, San Francisco, National Archives at San Francisco (hereafter cited as NARA-SF). I accessed court records stored at the National Archives in two visits separated by two years. During this interval, the court records

were reorganized and the box numbers changed. Box numbers in the 500 range reflect the most recent iteration.

16. Dana Sachs, *The Life We Were Given: Operation Babylift, International Adoption, and the Children of War in Vietnam* (Boston: Beacon, 2010); Reporter's Partial Transcript, June 25, 1975, Box 11, RG 276, NARA-SF.

17. Plaintiff's Memo in Support of Entry of Preliminary Injunction Incorporating Provision of Consent Order and Petition for Rehearing and Suggestion for Rehearing En Banc, 1975, Box 520, RG 276, NARA-SF.

18. Ibid.; Complaint for Declaratory Relief, Box 4, RG 276, NARA-SF; Affidavit of Joyce Ladner, January 20, 1976, Box 520, RG 276, NARA-SF.

19. Affidavit of Tran Tuong Nhu [Nhu Miller], April 28, 1975, Box 520, RG 276, NARA-SF.

20. Heather Marie Stur labeled the competing types of Vietnamese women conceived by Americans as "damsels in distress" (those in need of rescue from Communist aggression) and "dragon ladies" (those whose duplicitous behavior compromised U.S. ambitions and invited censure). *Beyond Combat: Women and Gender in the Vietnam War Era* (Cambridge: Cambridge University Press, 2011), 176.

21. Author's interview with Nhu Miller, May 29, 2012. Oktober is the boy's "Berkeley, California," name; "A." is a pseudonym for Oktober's birth mother.

22. Ibid.

23. Author's interview with Le Thi Hang, October 13, 2011.

24. Helle Rydstrom, "Gendered Corporeality and Bare Lives: Local Sacrifices and Sufferings during the Vietnam War," *Signs* 37, no. 2 (January 2012): 275–99; Lan Duong, *Treacherous Subjects: Gender, Culture, and Trans-Vietnamese Feminism* (Philadelphia: Temple University Press, 2012); Nathalie Huynh Chau Nguyen, *Memory Is Another Country: Women of the Vietnamese Diaspora* (Santa Barbara, Calif.: Praeger, 2009).

25. Reporter's Transcript, n.d., Box 12, RG 276, NARA-SF. Although excluded from the specific class represented by Tom Miller in the lawsuit because the children had arrived in the United States earlier than 1975, their stories resonated, and Nguyen Thi Phuc had stepped forward because of the lawsuit.

26. Affidavit of Thomas Miller, July 1975, Box 6, Folder 2, RG 276, NARA-SF.

27. Certificate of Attorney, March 24, 1976, Box 33, RG 276, NARA-SF.

28. Letter to John F. Cooney Jr., Assistant U.S. Attorney, from Thomas Miller, November 1, 1975, and Certificate of Thomas R. Miller, n.d., Box 520, RG 276, NARA-SF; "The Tragic End to Operation Babylift," *San Francisco Bay Guardian*, February 20, 1976.

29. Letter to Mr. Davidson, Acting District Director, U.S. INS, March 19, 1976, RG 276, NARA-SF.

30. Letter to Hoang Van Thanh c/o Buddy Randall from Helen Miller, Supervisor of Social Services, Holt Adoption Agency, August 4, 1975, RG 276, NARA-SF.

31. Letter to Ms. Tran Tuong Nhu [Nhu Miller], August 6, 1975, from Hoang Van Thanh, September 6, 1975, Translation Box 5, Folder 2, RG 276, NARA-SF.

32. *Tin Sang*, advertisement with translation in folder, Certificate of Thomas R. Miller, January 30, 1976, Box 33, RG 276, NARA-SF.

33. Cherie Clark, *After Sorrow Comes Joy: One Woman's Struggle to Bring Hope to Thousands of Children in Vietnam and India* (Westminster, Colo.: Lawrence and Thomas, 2000).

34. Affidavit of Rosemary Taylor, July 30, 1975, Box 33, RG 276, NARA-SF. In 1967 Australian Rosemary Taylor arrived in Vietnam attached to Catholic Refugee Services. Awakened to the struggles of Vietnamese children, she soon separated from this organization and opened her own nursery. Eventually she operated three nurseries and between 1968 and 1972 orchestrated the adoption of more than 1,000 children by overseas families. In 1973, when new registration requirements were enacted, she began an affiliation with FCVN, one of the organizations recently licensed as an adoption agency by the Vietnamese government. Susan McDonald interviewed in Larry Engelmann, *Tears before the Rain: An Oral History of the Fall of South Vietnam* (New York: Oxford University Press, 1990), 22–25.

35. Pamela Chatterton Purdy, *Beyond the Babylift: A Story of an Adoption* (Nashville: Abingdon, 1987), 92.

36. Clark, *After Sorrow Comes Joy*.

37. Affidavit of Cherie Clark, Overseas Director of Adoption for Friends of Children of Vietnam, March 9, 1976, File 7, Box 520, RG-276, NARA-SF.

38. Affidavit of Terre Super, March 11, 1976, Box 520, RG 276, NARA-SF.

39. Affidavit of Cherie Clark.

40. Ibid.; Affidavit of Le Thi Nga, February 7, 1976, and Affidavit of Nguyen Khang, February 7, 1976, File 8, Box 33, RG 276, NARA-SF. Affidavits of Nguyen Phuoc Loc (second cousin), Lam Hoag Lan (aunt), and Lam Hung Tam (uncle) corroborate these depictions.

41. Affidavit of Cherie Clark.

42. Affidavit of Wende S. Grant, March 10, 1976, Folder "Record of Appeal vol 7 and 8," Box 8, RG 276, NARA-SF.

43. Letter to Parents from Wende Grant, FFAC, November 24, 1975, Box 520, RG 276, NARA-SF.

44. Suzanne Dash, letter published in response to Paley's "Other People's Children" (September 1975) in *Ms.*, February 10, 1976, 10.

45. "Viet Tots, Adopted, Then Returned to Parents," *Independent Gazette*, January 8, 1976; "U.S. Family Loses Viet Orphans," *Los Angeles Times*, January 8, 1976, B9.

46. "Tragic End to Operation Babylift"; Deposition, Elisabeth S. Brodyaga, December 1975, Box 520, RG 276, NARA-SF.

47. Affidavit of Elisabeth (Lisa) Brodyaga, November 14, 1975, RG 276, NARA-SF.

48. Letter to Concerned Members of Congress from Lisa Brodyaga, December 1, 1975, RG 276, NARA-SF.

49. Letter to Parents from Friends of Children of Vietnam, January 27, 1976, RG 276, NARA-SF.

50. Thompson quoted in Abrams, "The Vietnam Babylift," 620.
51. Affidavit of Kathleen J. Strand, re: Interview of Children, June 21, 1976, File 8, Box 33, RG 276, NARA-SF.
52. INS Report of Investigation, October 24, 1975, Adoptive Home Study, Department of Health and Social Service, August 1, 1975, Box 10, RG 276, NARA-SF.
53. Affidavit of Kathleen J. Strand.
54. Affidavit of Dale E. Strand, April 13, 1976, File 8, Box 33, RG 276, NARA-SF.
55. Author's interview with Merrie Li Camp, December 8, 2013.
56. The plaintiffs' attorneys asserted that the first progress reports submitted by INS concluded that *all* children were eligible for adoption, a conclusion they found dubious and suggested the agency's errors or indifference. "Brief for Plaintiffs-Appellants," June 1, 1976, Box 10, RG 276, NARA-SF; "U.S. Expert Finds Few Viet Orphans Adoptable," *East-West: The Chinese-American Journal* 10, no. 34 (August 25, 1976): 3. In correspondence with the author on July 11, 2015, Tom Miller noted that the plaintiffs' attorneys found numerous instances where the INS investigator's initial finding was that the child was "not eligible for adoption," but was told by higher authorities to "review" the finding, and then reversed the decision.
57. Certificate of Attorney, March 19, 1976, Box 33, RG 276, NARA-SF.
58. Nguyen Da Yen v. Kissinger, 528 F.2d 1194 (U.S. Court of Appeals, 9th Cir., Nov. 5, 1975). The judge's concerns about the emotional costs of searches likely shaped his decision to seal the case files rather than appoint special masters to review the files. This effectively frustrated the efforts of the plaintiffs' attorneys, in cooperation with the International Red Cross and Vietnamese government, to help families in Vietnam locate children in the United States. Author's correspondence with Tom Miller, July 11, 2015.
59. Letter to Judge Spencer from Muoi McConnell, September 17, 1976, Folder 2, Box 2, RG 276, NARA-SF.
60. Ibid.
61. *Nguyen Da Yen et al. v. Henry Kissinger et al.*, U.S. District Court for the Northern District of California 70 R.D. 656 (1976).
62. Letter of Nguyen Dang Tuc as Appendix to Petition for Writ of Mandamus Filed by Attorneys for Petitioners, February 28, 1975, Addressed to Nguyen Thi Phuong, Attorney Case Files, Box 2, RG 276, NARA-SF.
63. Huynh Thi Anh v. Levi, 586 F.2d 625 (1978).
64. For most of the airlifted children, INS exercised a form of administrative relief known as parole in place; aliens were admitted for urgent humanitarian reasons and could remain lawfully in the United States.
65. Affidavit of Cherie Clark collected in *Nguyen Da Yen et al. v. Kissinger et al.*
66. Duong Bich Van v. John T. Dempsey, individually and as director of Social Services and the Michigan Department of Social Services, and David and Barbara Pederson, jointly and severally, Civil Action No. 76-140 499 (June 23, 1976).
67. "Parents Farewell to Adopted Son," *San Francisco Chronicle*, October 19, 1976.

68. Dexter Waugh, "The Orphan with Three Parents," *San Francisco Chronicle*, May 3, 1977, 1.

69. Peter Brennan, "Tug of Love: A Boy's Tough Choice between Two Mothers," *US Magazine*, June 28, 1977, 71–73; Le Thi Sang v. Knight, California Superior Court, San Joaquin County, docket no. 125898 (April 26 and September 22, 1977).

70. He was also identified as Vo Huy Tung.

71. William Popp distributed a twenty-six-page "report" to friends and family composed of e-mails and letters sent to Reed Dilbeck, a fellow crew member at the Flying Tigers, and his adopted Vietnamese daughter, Tanya, as she prepared to return to Vietnam as part of a heritage tour. He shared the report, completed on June 11, 2005, with me in correspondence in August 2011.

72. Hao Thi Popp v. Richard Lucas et al., 182 Conn. 545 (1980).

73. Davis quoted in Barry Siegel, "Child Custody Battle Rooted in Vietnam," *Los Angeles Times*, December 26, 1976, F1.

74. Tracy Johnson, "An Agonizing Mother's Day Dilemma," *Los Angeles Times*, May 9, 1976, E1.

75. People of the State of Colorado in the interest of Le Thanh Tung, aka Vo Huy Tung, aka Le Hoang Tung, aka Brice Zenk, County of Adams, State of Colorado, Dependency Action No. J6-5679-N, May 31–June 10, 1977.

76. Popp's report; Siegel, "Child Custody Battle," F1.

77. Michael Knight, "Vietnamese Mother, Now in U.S., Denied Custody of Children," *New York Times*, April 23, 1977.

Chapter Three

1. Drawn by the French during the 1930s, these borders resembled those established during the seventeenth and eighteen centuries when Vietnam acquired Cambodian territories. Although Vietnam accepted the status quo, Cambodian nationalists objected.

2. Michael Hunt, *A Vietnam War Reader: A Documentary History from American and Vietnamese Perspectives* (Chapel Hill: University of North Carolina Press, 2010).

3. Carol Bon Tempo has argued that the 1975 law represented a shift in U.S. refugee policy away from traditional Cold War rationales and toward the notion that the nation had an obligation to defend and protect human rights. Carl J. Bon Tempo, *Americans at the Gate: The United States and Refugees during the Cold War* (Princeton, N.J.: Princeton University Press, 2008).

4. As cultural phenomena whose popularity outlasted the 1960s, *The Sound of Music* and *Mary Poppins* have attracted much scholarly attention. Although some have interpreted the films as conservative texts that reinforce and romanticize traditional family values, others have noted their subversive and feminist meanings. Martin Gorsky, "'Raindrops on Roses': *The Sound of Music* and the Political Psyche of the Sixties," *The Sixties: A Journal of History, Politics and Culture* 6, no. 2 (2013): 199–224; Bruce Babington, "Song, Narrative, and the Mother's Voice: A Deepish

Reading of Julie Andrews," in *British Stars and Stardom: From Alma Taylor to Sean Connery*, ed. Bruce Babington (Manchester: Manchester University Press, 2001); Desiree Garcia, *The Migration of Musical Film: From Ethnic Margins to American Mainstream* (New Brunswick, N.J.: Rutgers University Press, 2014).

5. Richard Stirling, *Julie Andrews: An Intimate Biography* (New York: St. Martin's, 2007).

6. Andrews quoted in Kathleen Hendrix, "Andrews Can't Ignore the Orphans of Southeast Asia," *Los Angeles Times*, September 22, 1982, F1.

7. Heather Marie Stur, *Beyond Combat: Women and Gender in the Vietnam War Era* (Cambridge: Cambridge University Press, 2011).

8. Amerasian Immigration Proposals, *Hearings before the Subcommittee on Immigration and Refugee Policy of the Committee on the Judiciary United States Senate, Second Session, S. 1698, June 21, 1982* (Washington, D.C.: Government Printing Office, 1982), 78–79.

9. Angelina Wentz Memon, *The Misplaced* (Baltimore: Publish America, 2007), 23; author's interview with Jimmy Miller, August 15, 2013.

10. Susanna McBee with Walter A. Taylor, "The Amerasians: Tragic Legacy of Our Far East Wars," *U.S. News and World Report*, May 7, 1994.

11. *Nightline*, ABC News, October 7, 1982.

12. John Shade, *America's Forgotten Children: The Amerasians* (Perkasie, Pa.: Pearl S. Buck Foundation, 1980); Amerasian Immigration Proposals, *Hearings before the Subcommittee*, 13.

13. Memon, *The Misplaced*, 25.

14. Author's interview with Truc Tran, September 9, 2013.

15. Author's interview with Jimmy Miller, August 15, 2013.

16. Amerasian Immigration Proposals, *Hearings before the Subcommittee*, 63–64.

17. Immigration and Nationality Act, amendment, Pub. L. No. 97-359, 96 Stat. 1716 (1982), accessed February 10, 2016, http://library.uwb.edu/guides/usimmigration/96%20stat%201716.pdf.

18. Peter W. Rodino, chairman, quoted in *Public Law 97-359 Amerasian Processing Manual: M-254* (Washington, D.C.: Government Printing Office, 1985).

19. Ibid.

20. Bon Tempo, *Americans at the Gate*, 187.

21. Ronald Reagan, "Remarks on Signing a Bill Providing for the Immigration of Certain Amerasian Children," October 22, 1982, accessed June 15, 2015, http://www.reagan.utexas.edu/archives/speeches/1982/102282c.htm.

22. Bob Sector, "11 Vietnam Children Fly to a New World—the U.S.," *Los Angeles Times*, October 1, 1982, 1.

23. "11 Amerasian Kids Leave Vietnam and Happy Families Embrace Them," *People Weekly*, October 18, 1982, 34–37; "Coming Home—at Last," *Newsweek*, October 11, 1982, 78.

24. Andrew MacLeod, "Amerasian Girl Finally Finds a Home," *Los Angeles Times*, April 22, 1983, D7.

25. "To Bring His Daughter Home," *20/20*, ABC News, November 20, 1987.

26. Nikki Finke, "For Vietnam Vet Barry Huntoon, a Never Ending Story," *Los Angeles Times*, February 18, 1988, 1.

27. Ibid.

28. According to a U.S. State Department pamphlet, Vietnamese authorities unilaterally suspended interviewing applicants in Vietnam for the ODP, resuming the process only after negotiations with U.S. officials under the auspices of the United Nations High Commissioner for Refugees generated a bilateral program that permitted more participation from the Vietnamese government and the eventual definition of Amerasians as immigrants, not refugees.

29. Ilana Debare, "Rescue Registry Group Seeks to Reunite American Father with Vietnamese Children," *Los Angeles Times*, March 31, 1987, 3. A state of California special report recommended the International Red Cross, Pearl S. Buck Foundation, and Amerasian Registry as the three best sources for tracing the fathers of Amerasians. Department of Social Services, "Amerasians' Special Needs Report," August 1989.

30. *Nightline*, ABC News, October 7, 1982; Ellen Goodman, "Amerasians Caught in Our Lopsided Ethics," *Los Angeles Times*, October 11, 1982, C9.

31. Luncheon Address by Joseph Cerquone at "Amerasian Settlement: Enhancing the Homecoming" Conference Proceedings, Washington, D.C., n.d., Interaction Amerasian Resettlement Program Office of Refugee Resettlement Family Support Administration, U.S. Department of Health and Human Services.

32. "We'll Accept Them All," *American Legion*, February 1989, 46–47.

33. Letter to Marta Brenden from Howard Killingbeck, February 23, 1989, Folder "Volunteer Inquiries," Box 2, InterAction Records, 1987–1994 (hereafter cited as IAR).

34. Letter to Marta Brenden from Sang and Lina Le, February 20, 1989, Folder "Volunteer Inquiries," Box 2, IAR.

35. Letter to Gloria and Charles Wilson from Marta Brenden, March 1, 1989, Folder "Volunteer Inquiries," Box 2, IAR.

36. Kieu-Linh Caroline Valverde, "From Dust to Gold: The Vietnamese Amerasian Experience," in *Racially Mixed People in America*, ed. Maria Root (New York: Sage, 1992), 151.

37. Sophie Quinn-Judge, "Children of the War Start Leaving for America," *Indochina Issues* 35 (March 1983), 24–50.

38. 133 Cong. Rec. (May 4, 1987).

39. Pub. L. No. 100-202, December 22, 1987, *United States Statutes at Large* (Washington, D.C.: Government Printing Office, 1987); "Amerasian Processing," U.S. ODP Embassy of the United States of America Pamphlet, 1989, Folder 10, Box 1, IAR.

40. "Amerasian Processing," U.S. ODP Embassy of the United States of America Pamphlet, 1989, Folder 10, Box 1, IAR.

41. Stephen Debonis, *Children of the Enemy: Oral Histories of Vietnamese Amerasians and Their Mothers* (London: McFarland, 1995), 12.

42. Tuan Den, interview with Debonis, in ibid., 48; Vu, interview with Debonis, in ibid., 115; Memon, *The Misplaced*, 38.

43. Thanh Thi Nguyen and her family's story introduces the central ideas of this book.

44. Author's interview with Trista Goldberg, September 18, 2013.

45. Loan and Be, interviews with Debonis, in *Children of the Enemy*, 136.

46. William Branigin, "Vietnamese Try to Buy the American Dream," *Washington Post*, February 19, 1993.

47. Letter to Charles A. Bowsher from Robert J. Mrazek, October 11, 1991, Folder 50, Box 1, IAR.

48. Branigin, "Vietnamese Try to Buy the American Dream."

49. Letter to Charles A. Bowsher from Robert J. Mrazek, October 11, 1991, Folder 50, Box 1, IAR.

50. Katie Kelly, *A Year in Saigon: How I Gave Up My Glitzy Job in Television to Have the Time of My Life Teaching Amerasian Kids in Vietnam* (New York: Simon and Schuster, 1992), 244.

51. GAO Report, November 16, 1992, Folder 50, Box 1, IAR; Letter to Robert J. Mrazek from Eleanor Chelimsky, November 16, 1992, Folder 50, Box 1, IAR.

52. Loan and Be, interviews with Debonis, in *Children of the Enemy*, 136.

53. Letter to Consular Office of ODP from Hoan Thi Thanh, April 26, 1993, Folder 12, Box 1, IAR.

54. Kelly, *Year in Saigon*, 242.

55. GAO Report, November 16, 1992, Folder 50, Box 1, IAR.

56. Phuong, interview with Debonis, in *Children of the Enemy*, 12.

57. Be, interview with Debonis, in ibid., 136; report referenced in "Amerasian Update, 1990–1991," n.d., Folder 11, Box 2, IAR.

58. Loc, interview with Debonis, in *Children of the Enemy*, 12.

59. Branigin, "Vietnamese Try to Buy the American Dream."

60. Ahn Do, "Alleged Killer Says Love Brought Him, Victim to the United States," *O.C. Register*, October 31, 1991.

61. Letter to Charles A. Bowsher from Robert J. Mrazek, October 11, 1991, Folder 50, Box 1, IAR.

62. Author's interview with Truc Tran.

63. Author's interview with Merrie Li Camp, December 8, 2013.

64. Author's interview with Tung Joe Nguyen, November 16, 2013.

65. Ibid.

66. Ibid.

67. Ibid.

68. Author's interview with Merrie Li Camp.

69. Author's interviews with Tung Joe Nguyen and Merri Li Camp.

70. Ibid.

71. As quoted in Dianne Klein, "Vietnam's Castoffs Come Home," *Los Angeles Times*, June 30, 1991, A1, A28.

72. Kelly, *Year in Saigon*, 251.

73. Yên Lê Espiritu, *Body Counts: The Vietnam War and Militarized Refuge(es)* (Berkeley: University of California Press, 2014), 54.

74. Vietnam Veterans of America Foundation, *Report on the Amerasian Issue* (Washington, D.C.: August 1989). At the camps, education was limited to classes that introduced "survival English"—competence in the most common expressions—and familiarity in basic American customs. A study published by the Bilingual Education Office of California's Department of Education also noted problems with the food supply and security at the PRPC. Chung Hoang Chuong and Le Van, "The Amerasians from Vietnam: A California Study," 1994, Bilingual Education Office, California Department of Education, Box 1, Van Le Files on Southeast Asian Refugees (hereafter cited as VLF); Debonis, *Children of the Enemy*, 4.

75. For more about the practices and ideas that guided the evacuation of Vietnamese after 1975 as well as the responses triggered, see Jana K. Lipman, "A Refugee Camp in America: Fort Chaffee and Vietnamese and Cuban Refugees, 1975–1982," *Journal of American Ethnic History* 33, no. 2 (Winter 2014): 57–87; Jana K. Lipman, "A Precedent Worth Setting: Military Humanitarianism: The U.S. Military and the 1975 Vietnamese Evacuation," *Journal of Military History* 79, no. 1 (2015): 151–79; Espiritu, *Body Counts*, 49–80; Heather Marie Stur, "'Hiding behind the Humanitarian Label': Refugees, Repatriates, and the Rebuilding of America's Benevolent Image after the Vietnam War," *Diplomatic History* 39, no. 2 (April 2015): 223–44.

76. Other prominent volags were the U.S. Catholic Bishops and Lutheran Immigration and Refugee Services. GAO, *Vietnamese Amerasian Resettlement: Education, Employment, and Family Outcomes in the United States*, report to congressional requesters submitted to Subcommittee on International Law, Immigration and Refugees, Committee on the Judiciary, House of Representatives, March 31, 1994.

77. Author's interview with Tung Joe Nguyen.

78. Espiritu, *Body Counts*; Ayako Sahara, "Theater of Rescue: Cultural Representations of U.S. Evacuation from Vietnam," *Journal of American and Canadian Studies*, no. 30 (March 2012): 55–84; Thuy Vo Dang, "The Cultural Work of Anticommunism in the San Diego Vietnamese American Community," *Amerasian Journal* 31, no. 2 (2005): 65–86; Yên Lê Espiritu, "The 'We-Win-Even-When-We-Lose' Syndrome: U.S. Press Coverage of the Twenty-Fifth Anniversary of the 'Fall of Saigon,'" *American Quarterly* 58, no. 2 (2006): 329–52. Donald Ranard and Douglas Gilzow, "Update," *In America: Perspectives on Refugee Resettlement*, no. 4 (June 1989), includes a helpful map illustrating the geography of Vietnamese resettlement. *In America* was published under cooperative agreement with the U.S. Bureau of Refugee Programs. For more about the secondary migrations and community formation among Vietnamese in the United States, see Hien Duc Do, "The Formation of a New Refugee Community in Orange County" (M.A. thesis, University of California, Santa Barbara, 1988).

79. Robert S. McKelvey, *The Dust of Life: America's Children in Vietnam* (Seattle: University of Washington Press, 1999); GAO, *Vietnamese Amerasian Resettlement*.

80. Chung Hoang Chuong and Le Van, "The Amerasians from Vietnam: A California Study," 1994, Bilingual Education Office, California Department of Education, Box 1, VLF.

81. "World Vision's Amerasian Mentor Program," 1990, Folder 4, Box 1, St. Anselm's Cross-Cultural Community Center Records (hereafter cited as SAR); J. Kirk Fesman and March C. Johnson, "Amerasians at Risk in Public Schools?," *In America: Perspectives on Refugee Resettlement*, no. 4, June 1989; Letter to Robert J. Mrazek from Eleanor Chelimsky, November 16, 1992, Folder 50, Box 1, IAR.

82. Anderson quoted in Carmen Ramos Chandler, "Amerasian Youths Struggle to Fit In," *Daily News*, June 24, 1991.

83. "World Vision's Amerasian Refugee Assistance Program," undated pamphlet, Folder 33, Box 1, IAR.

84. *African-American Veterans and Community: Post-Traumatic Stress Disorder and Related Issues, Hearing before the Subcommittee on Oversight and Investigations of the Committee on Veterans' Affairs, 103rd Congress, First Session, H.R., September 15, 1993* (Washington, D.C.: Government Printing Office, 1994).

85. "Reflections on the Amerasian Experience," speech delivered by Ruben Conner as part of Amerasian Resettlement Conference Proceedings, March 15–17, 1991, Los Angeles, Box 1, St. Anselm's Amerasian Records, SAR.

86. Linda Ralph Kern interviewed in *Amerasian Update*, October 1991.

87. "Reflections on the Amerasian Experience," speech delivered by Ruben Conner as part of Amerasian Resettlement Conference Proceedings, March 15–17, 1991, Los Angeles, Box 1, St. Anselm's Amerasian Records, SAR.

88. David Gonzalez, "For Afro-Americans, Tangled Emotions," *New York Times*, November 16, 1992, B1.

89. Chandler, "Amerasian Youths Struggle."

90. Trina Trent, "Black American History," *Amerasian Update*, January 1993.

91. Melinda Beck with Frank Gibney, "Where Is My Father?," *Newsweek*, April 15, 1985, 57.

92. Douglas Gilzow and Donald Ranard, "Update," *In America: Perspectives on Refugee Resettlement*, no. 9 (October 1990). Not until 1990 would the State Department agree to maintain a formal file of American fathers searching for their Amerasian offspring.

93. Chandler, "Amerasian Youths Struggle."

94. Nguyen Huynh Tuyet Trinh, "The Dream of Meeting with the Blood Father," *Amerasian Update*, 1991.

95. Author's interview with Tung Joe Nguyen.

96. Author's interview with Jimmy Miller. Memon, *The Misplaced*, 69.

97. Excerpt from presentation by Thuc Nguyen, YMCA International Services, *Amerasian Update*, June 1991.

98. Gilzow and Ranard, "Update" (1990).

99. Memon, *The Misplaced*, 54.

100. Author's interview with Jimmy Miller.

101. Letter to Marla Brenden, Lutheran Immigration and Refugee Service, from David Brigham, Veterans Assistance Service Program Volunteer, June 14, 1989, Folder 10, Box 1, IAR.

102. "Alleged Fathers of Amerasian Unaccompanied Minors Guidelines," 1989, United States Catholic Conference, Interaction Folder 10, Box 1, St. Anselm's Amerasian Records, SAR.

103. Henry Yu and Bill Ong Hing cited in Karin Aguilar-San Juan, *Little Saigons: Staying Vietnamese in America* (Minneapolis: University of Minnesota Press, 2009). Thomas Bass reported the successful suit filed by War Babes against the U.S. Department of Defense requesting that the National Personnel Records Center in Saint Louis open its files to the children of soldiers. Prior to the court decision, such requests for information had been denied in the interests of respecting the father's privacy. Bass made clear that he thought a child's right to know outweighed the father's right to conceal. Thomas Bass, *Vietnamerica: The War Comes Home* (New York: Soho, 1996), 189.

104. Memo to Lutheran Immigration and Refugee Services from Julie MacDonald, July 20, 1989, Folder 10, Box 1, IAR.

105. Ibid.

106. "Clinical Considerations for Counselors Working with Amerasians in Search of Their U.S. Fathers, a Developmental Perspective," n.d., Folder 10, Box 1, IAR.

107. Memo from MacDonald, IAR.

108. *Amerasian Update*, November 1991.

109. Tim Padgett and Judy Howard, "Like Meeting My Dad," *Newsweek*, April 9, 1990, 65–66.

110. Note from Gary Vancena, Vietnam Veterans of America, in Workshop Summaries of Amerasian Resettlement Conference Proceedings, June 25–27, 1992, Arlington, Virginia, Box 1, SAR.

111. Kelly, *Year in Saigon*, 237.

112. Ibid., 238.

113. Like St. Anselm's, Mohawk Valley Resource Center was created to aid Amerasians; it was established in 1979 and incorporated in 1981.

114. Bass, *Vietnamerica*, 257.

115. Le Ha quoted in ibid., 181.

116. GAO, *Vietnamese Amerasian Resettlement*.

117. Ibid.

118. Gilzow and Ranard, "Update" (1990).

119. Hoa Bui quoted in Steve Walker, "A Welcome Home," *Kansas City Live*, February 1991, 10–11.

120. GAO, *Vietnamese Amerasian Resettlement*.

121. Evelyn Hsu, "3 Men Learning Auto Mechanic Skills as Bridge to New Life," *New York Times*, December 30, 1990, reprinted in *Amerasian Update*, July–August 1991.

122. Author's interview with Angelina Memon, September 9, 2013.

123. Author's interview with Truc Tran.

124. *Amerasian Update*, no. 53 (December 1993).

125. "Cluster Citings," *Amerasian Update*, December 1991.

126. Among the feature films, made-for-television movies, and fictional works about Amerasians produced and released in the early 1990s were *Out of the Dust, Twice Under, Life and Times, Đêm Hoang Tu'o'ng, Missing in Action*, Tony Hillerman's *Finding Moon*, and Anthony Hyde's *Formosa Straits*.

127. Tu Le, "What Will We Do," *Amerasian Newsletter* (U.S. Catholic Charities, 1993), Box 2, IAR.

128. Ho Thi Kim Nguyet, *Amerasian Update*, September 1990.

Chapter Four

1. Dolores K. Sloviter, "The Vietnam Babylift: A Personal Story," *Philadelphia Lawyer* (Fall 2005): 34–36.

2. Vikki Sloviter, telephone interview with author, June 25, 2009.

3. Ibid.

4. Vanessa Bush, "*Life* Readers Who Won the 'I Want to Meet' Contest," *Life Magazine* 22 (January 1999): 83; author's interview with Vikki Sloviter.

5. Author's interview with Vikki Sloviter.

6. Yên Lê Espiritu, "Thirty Years after War: The Endings That Are Not Over," *Amerasian Journal* 31, no. 2 (2005): xiii–xxii; Yên Lê Espiritu, "The 'We-Win-Even-When-We-Lose' Syndrome: U.S. Press Coverage of the Twenty-Fifth Anniversary of the 'Fall of Saigon,'" *American Quarterly* 58, no. 2 (2006): 329–52; Yên Lê Espiritu, *Body Counts: The Vietnam War and Militarized Refuge(es)* (Berkeley: University of California Press, 2014).

7. Although adoptive families expressed a preference for girls, whom they envisioned as more docile and dependent—Orientalist images manufactured and communicated by the media, social workers, and popular culture—my sources suggest that as many boys as girls were adopted. In parenting their Vietnamese children, American couples acknowledged no gendered differences in forms of discipline and support, but variations may have existed. This chapter may reference adopted women's searches for their mothers more than those of men, but this does not prove that they were more likely to search and reunite with their biological mothers than their male counterparts.

8. Ellen Herman, *Kinship by Design: A History of Adoption in the Modern United States* (Chicago: University of Chicago Press, 2008), 252.

9. "Joe" is a pseudonym for Stephen Ngo Duling. Gretchen had changed her son's name in the memoir to disguise his identity and protect his privacy.

10. Gretchen Duling, *"Adopting Joe": A Black Vietnamese Child* (Rutland, Vt.: Charles E. Tuttle, 1977), 70.

11. Author's interview with Gretchen Duling, September 20, 2013.

12. Jan De Hartog, *The Children: A Personal Record for the Use of Adoptive Parents* (New York: Atheneum, 1969), 217.

13. Author's interview with Ken Armstrong, May 5, 2012.

14. Child Rescue website, accessed June 3, 2014, http://www.childrescueinc.org/.

15. William Popp distributed a twenty-six-page "report" to friends and family composed of e-mails and letters sent to Reed Dilbeck, a fellow crew member at the Flying Tigers, and his adopted Vietnamese daughter, Tanya, as she prepared to return to Vietnam as part of a heritage tour. He shared the report, completed on June 11, 2005, with me in correspondence in August 2011.

16. Author's interview with Trista Goldberg, September 18, 2013.

17. Author's interview with Kimberly Nguyen Thompson, May 28, 2009.

18. LeChristine Hai, *In the Arms of Grace: One Saved Child's Journey* (Atlanta: UniVoice International, 2003), 92–93.

19. Bob Burns quoted in Brent M. Eastwood, "Skygirl," Adopt Vietnam website, 2000, accessed July 7, 2015, http://www.adoptvietnam.org/adoption/babylift-brent.html; author's interview with Virginia Littauer, March 30, 2012.

20. Brad Davis and Julie Davis, "Homeward Bound," Adopt Vietnam website, accessed April 12, 2013, http://www.adoptvietnam.org/adoption/babylift-julie.html; Hai, *In the Arms*, 9; Pamela Chatterton Purdy, *Beyond the Babylift: A Story of an Adoption* (Nashville: Abingdon, 1987), 65, 122.

21. Author's interview with Jay Sheridan, December 8, 2008.

22. Kim Delevett, interview with Jason Stewart, April 30, 2010, Virtual Vietnam Center and Archive, Texas Tech University, accessed June 22, 2013, http://www.virtualarchive.vietnam.ttu.edu.

23. Davis and Davis, "Homeward Bound."

24. Author's interview with Trista Goldberg.

25. Author's interview with Jared Rehberg, August 16, 2013.

26. Author's interview with Jay Sheridan.

27. Author's interviews with Kimberly Nguyen Thompson and Jared Rehberg.

28. Author's interview with Kimberly Nguyen Thompson; Jane Burns [Nguyen Thi Van], quoted in Eastwood, "Sky Girl"; Hai, *In the Arms*, 105.

29. Purdy, *Beyond the Babylift*, 152.

30. Author's interview with Gretchen Duling.

31. Edwin Martini, *Invisible Enemies: The American War on Vietnam, 1975–2000* (Amherst: University of Massachusetts Press, 2007); Bill Hayton, *Vietnam: Rising Dragon* (New Haven, Conn.: Yale University Press, 2010).

32. Michael Allen, *Until the Last Man Comes Home: POWs, MIAs, and the Unending War in Vietnam* (Chapel Hill: University of North Carolina Press, 2012).

33. Vu Hong Lien and Peter D. Sharrock, *Descending Dragon, Rising Tiger: A History of Vietnam* (Chicago: University of Chicago Press, 2014), 245.

34. Author's interview with Tiffany Chi Goodson, January 12, 2010; Bert Ballard, "Narrative Burden: A Qualitative Investigation of Transnational, Transracial

Adoptive Identity," *Qualitative Communication Research* 2, no. 3 (Fall 2013): 229–54, 231.

35. Author's interview with Anh Đào, August 16, 2013.

36. Bree Cutting Sibble, "What Happened to Those Babies," in *Chicken Soup for the Adopted Soul: Stories Celebrating Forever Families*, ed. Jack Canfield, Mark Hansen, and LeAnn Thieman (Deerfield Beach, Fla.: Health Communications, 2008), 331.

37. Delevett, interview with Stewart.

38. Author's interview with Merrie Li Camp, December 8, 2013.

39. Author's interview with Jared Rehberg; Chasing Dragonflies: The Music of Jared Rehberg website, accessed March 2010, http://jaredrehberg.virb.com.

40. Anh Đào, *Portraits of Vietnamese* (blog), accessed March 10, 2014, http://vadportraits.wordpress.com.

41. Bert Ballard, "Legacy Fulfilled," *Adoption Today*, April–May 2001, 1–2.

42. Ibid., 2.

43. Bert Ballard, "I Heard the Call, but He Wasn't Actually There: Sacred Communication with My New Son," *International Review of Qualitative Research* 4, no. 3 (Fall 2011): 175–91.

44. Bert Ballard and Sara J. Ballard, "From Narrative Inheritance to Narrative Momentum: Past, Present and Future Stories in an International Adoptive Family," *Journal of Family Communications* 11, no. 2 (April 2011): 69–84.

45. Ballard, "Narrative Burden," 251.

46. Hai, *In the Arms*, 280; author's interview with Jay Sheridan.

47. Allen, *Until the Last Man Comes Home*, 3.

48. Ballard, "Narrative Burden," 231.

49. Author's interview with Bert Ballard, June 23, 2014; Tuan-Rishard F. Schneider, "Adoptee Connection," Adopt Vietnam website, accessed May 5, 2015, http://www.adoptvietnam.org/adoption/babylift-tuanschneider.html; author's interview with Kimberly Nguyen Thompson.

50. Gregory Paul Choy and Catherine Ceniza Choy, "Reframing *Daughter from Danang*," in *Outsiders Within: Writings on Transracial Adoption*, ed. Jane Jeong Trenka, Julia Chinyere Oparah, and Sun Yung Shin (Cambridge, Mass.: South End Press, 2006); Jodi Kim, "An 'Orphan' with Two Mothers: Transnational and Transracial Adoption, the Cold War, and Contemporary Asian American Cultural Politics," *American Quarterly* 61, no. 4 (2009): 855–80.

51. Linh Nguyen, "Recalling the Refugee: Culture Clash and Melancholic Racial Formation in *Daughter from Danang*," *Amerasian Journal* 39, no. 2 (2013): 103–41.

52. Author's interviews with Kimberly Nguyen Thompson and Anh Đào.

53. Author's interview with Tiffany Chi Goodson.

54. "Vietnamese Adoptee Network," Vietnamese Adoptee Network website, accessed April 28, 2014, http://www.van-online.org.

55. "Home," Adopted Vietnamese International website, accessed April 28, 2014, http://www.adoptedvietnamese.org/avi-community/avi-social-networks-groups.

56. Author's interview with Tiffany Chi Goodson; Ballard, "Legacy Fulfilled," 2; author's interview with Trista Goldberg.

57. Eleana J. Kim, *Adopted Territory: Transnational Korean Adoptees and the Politics of Belonging* (Durham, N.C.: Duke University Press, 2010), 5. Her book explores the recent emergence of a collective identity among Korean adoptees and their returns to Korea.

58. Schneider, "Adoptee Connection."

59. Shaul Kelner, *Tours That Bind: Diaspora, Pilgrimage, and Birthright Tourism* (New York: New York University Press, 2010), 2.

60. Kim, *Adopted Territory*, 173. Kim tracks the return and sometimes residence of Korean adoptees in Korea since the 1990s. Increasing numbers have chosen not simply to visit but to live and work in South Korea, a choice made possible after they successfully lobbied the government to offer them F-4 visas. Maggie Jones, "Why a Generation of Adoptees Is Returning to South Korea," *New York Times Magazine*, January 14, 2015.

61. Jillian Powers, "Going Away to Find Home: A Comparative Study of Heritage/Homeland Tourism" (Ph.D. diss., Duke University, 2011).

62. Author's interviews with Anh Đào and Jared Rehberg. In his study of Jewish Americans who toured Israel, Kelner noted the importance of the small-group context "as a socializing agent that mediates the encounter with place," but also described the possibility of "arenas of differentiations and status competition." Kelner, *Tours That Bind*, 179.

63. Jillian Powers, "Going Away to Find Home: A Comparative Study of Heritage/Homeland Tourism" (Ph.D. diss., Duke University, 2011), 135.

64. Barbara Yngvesson studied the return to Chile of twelve Swedish families who had adopted from the Latin American country during the middle years of the Augusto Pinochet dictatorship. She noted the importance of parents and social workers, who witnessed and guided the investigations of adoptees. Barbara Yngvesson, "Going 'Home': Adoption, Loss of Bearings, and Mythology of Roots," in *Cultures of Transnational Adoption*, ed. Toby Alice Volkman (Durham, N.C.: Duke University Press, 2005).

65. Vietnam Journeys, "The Ties Program," Adoptive Family Travel website, http://www.adoptivefamilytravel.com/asia/vietnam; "Culture Tours," Catalyst Foundation website, http://catalystfoundation.org/cultural-tour-travel-program; "Viet Nam Motherland Tour," Motherland Heritage Company website, http://Motherland-heritage.com/tours; "Heritage Tours," Holt International website, http://www.holtinternational.org/tours, all accessed August 3, 2014.

66. Bob Shane, "Courage Revisited: World Airways Returns to Vietnam," Vietnam Babylift website, accessed January 5, 2014, http://www.vietnambabylift.org/World_Airways.html.

67. "Julia Nguyen's Narrative," Torch 1975 website, accessed June 9, 2014, http://torch1975.org/index.php/about-home/founder-narrative-company-history; Lindsey Ruta, "Reunion Set for 1975 Operation Babylift," *Orange County Register*, June 24,

2013, http://www.ocregister.com/articles/veterans-234842-ocprint-nguyen-reunion.html.

68. "About," Operation Reunite website, accessed May 10, 2014, http://operationreunite.org/.

69. Author's interview with Trista Goldberg.

70. Dominic Golding quoted in Tricia Houston, "The Right Time for Reunion: *Operation Reunite* Vietnamese Adoptee Tour, April Reunion in Vietnam," *Adoption Today*, May–June 2010.

71. Author's interview with Nhu Miller, May 29, 2012.

72. Joshua Woerthwein, "A Vietnamese-American Adoptee Visits Vietnam," Adopt Vietnam website, accessed July 9, 2015, http://www.adoptvietnam.org/adoption/babylift-joshua.htmladopthelp.org.

73. Nol quoted in Susan Reed and Vickie Bane, "To a New Home," *People* 43, no. 17 (May 1, 1995): 40; Davis and Davis, "Homeward Bound."

74. "Adopted by Family in U.S., Vietnamese Beauty Now Searches for Her Father, a Black Vietnam War GI," *JET* 96, no. 11 (October 11, 1999): 36–38.

75. Delevett, interview with Stewart; Peter Delevett, "Return to Vietnam," *Honolulu Advertiser*, June 19, 2005, B1, B4; author's interview with Kimberley Delevett, May 27, 2012.

76. Jeff and Ginger quoted in Reed and Bane, "To a New Home," 40; see the opening paragraphs of this book's introduction.

77. Angelina Wentz Memon, *The Misplaced* (Baltimore: Publish America, 2007), 31.

78. Author's interview with Tung Joe Nguyen, November 16, 2013.

79. Author's interview with Jimmy Miller, August 15, 2013; Amerasian Paternity Recognition Act, H.R. 4007, 110th Cong. (2007), accessed May 22, 2014, https://www.govtrack.us/congress/bills/110/hr4007. The bill has not yet been enacted.

80. Author's interview with Trista Goldberg.

81. Author's interview with Tung Joe Nguyen.

Bibliography

Primary Sources

Archival Collections

Archives of the Pearl S. Buck House, Pearl S. Buck International, Perkasie, Pa.
Committee of Responsibility Records, Swarthmore College Peace Collection, Swarthmore, Pa.
Friends Meeting for Sufferings of Vietnamese Children Records, Swarthmore College Peace Collection, Swarthmore, Pa.
InterAction Records, 1987–1994, Ethnic Studies Library, University of California, Berkeley
International Social Service, American Branch, Records, Social Welfare History Archives, University of Minnesota Libraries, University of Minnesota, Minneapolis
Robert Walsh Files on Southeast Asian Refugee Resettlement and Education, MS-SEA021, Special Collections and Archives, University of California Irvine Libraries, Irvine
St. Anselm's Cross-Cultural Community Center Records, MS-SEA027, Special Collections and Archives, University of California Irvine Libraries, Irvine
United States District Court, Northern District of California, Civil Case, 75-839, National Archives, San Francisco
Van Le Files on Southeast Asian Refugees, MS-SEA12, Special Collections and Archives, University of California Irvine Libraries, Irvine
Vietnam Center and Archive, Texas Tech University, Lubbock

Court Cases

County of Adams, State of Colorado, Dependency Action No. J6-5679-N (May 31, 1977)
Duong Bich Van v. John T. Dempsey, individually and as director of Social Services and the Michigan Department of Social Services, and David and Barbara Pederson, jointly and severally, Civil Action No. 76-140 499 (June 23, 1976)
Hao Thi Popp v. Richard Lucas et al., 182 Conn. 545 (1980)
Huynh Thi Anh v. Levi, 586 F.2d 625 (1978)
Le Thi Sang v. Knight, California Superior Court, San Joaquin County, docket no. 125898 (April 26 and September 22, 1977)
Nguyen Da Yen v. Kissinger, 528 F.2d 1194 (U.S. Court of Appeals, 9th Cir., November 5, 1975)

Interviews and Oral Histories

Ken Armstrong, interview by author, May 5, 2012
Ri Armstrong, interview by author, June 9, 1012
Bert Ballard, interview by author, June 23, 2014
Merrie Li Camp, interview by author, December 8, 2013
Jeffrey Corliss, interview by author, November 10, 2013
Anh Đào, interview by author, August 16, 2013
Kimberly Delevett, interview by author, May 27, 2012
Gretchen Duling, interview by author, September 20, 2013
Stephen Duling, interview by author, November 10, 2013
Trista Goldberg, interview by author, September 18, 2013
Tiffany Chi Goodson, interview by author, January 12, 2010
Le Thi Hang, interview by author, October 13, 2011
Virginia Littauer, interview by author, March 30, 2012
Angelina Memon, interview by author, September 9, 2013
Jimmy Miller, interview by author, August 15, 2013
Nhu Miller, interview by author, May 29, 2012
Tom Miller, interview by author, May 29, 2012
Tung Joe Nguyen, interview by author, November 16, 2013
Jared Rehberg, interview by author, August 16, 2013
Jay Sheridan, interview by author, December 8, 2008
Vikki Sloviter, interview by author, June 25, 2009
Kimberly Nguyen Thompson, interview by author, May 28, 2009
Truc Tran, interview by author, September 9, 2013

Memoirs and Published Oral Histories

Allen, George. *Ri*. New York: Prentice Hall, 1978.
Canfield, Jack, Mark Hansen, and LeAnn Thieman, eds. *Chicken Soup for the Adopted Soul: Stories Celebrating Forever Families*. Deerfield Beach, Fla.: Health Communications, 2008.
Chinook, Frank. *Kim, a Gift from Vietnam*. New York: World Publishing, 1969.
Clark, Cherie. *After Sorrow Comes Joy: One Woman's Struggle to Bring Hope to Thousands of Children in Vietnam and India*. Westminster, Colo.: Lawrence and Thomas, 2000.
Debonis, Stephen. *Children of the Enemy: Oral Histories of Vietnamese Amerasians and Their Mothers*. London: McFarland, 1995.
Duling, Gretchen. *"Adopting Joe": A Black Vietnamese Child*. Rutland, Vt.: Charles E. Tuttle, 1977.
Engelmann, Larry. *Tears before the Rain: An Oral History of the Fall of South Vietnam*. New York: Oxford University Press, 1990.
Hai, LeChristine. *In the Arms of Grace: One Saved Child's Journey*. Atlanta: UniVoice International, 2003.

Hartog, Jan De. *The Children: A Personal Record for the Use of Adoptive Parents.* New York: Atheneum, 1969.

Harverson, Stuart. *God's Orphans in Vietnam.* London: Page Bros., 1971.

Kelly, Katie. *A Year in Saigon: How I Gave Up My Glitzy Job in Television to Have the Time of My Life Teaching Amerasian Kids in Vietnam.* New York: Simon and Schuster, 1992.

Margolies, Marjorie. *They Came to Stay.* New York: Coward, McCann and Geoghegan, 1976.

Memon, Angelina Wentz. *The Misplaced.* Baltimore: Publish America, 2007.

Purdy, Pamela Chatterton. *Beyond the Babylift: A Story of an Adoption.* Nashville: Abingdon, 1987.

Shade, John. *America's Forgotten Children: The Amerasians.* Perkasie, Pa.: Pearl S. Buck Foundation, 1980.

Taylor, Rosemary. *Orphans of War: Work with the Abandoned Children of Vietnam, 1967–1975.* London: Collins, 1988.

Thieman, LeAnn, and Carol Dey. *This Must Be My Brother.* Wheaton, Ill.: Victor Books, 1995.

"Vietnam Adoption Stories." Adopt Vietnam website. http://www.adoptvietnam.org/adoption/babylift-index.htm#adoptees. Accessed July 7, 2015.

Newspapers and Popular Magazines

Adoption Today
Amerasian Update
American Legion
Boston Herald
Boston Globe
Christian Century
Commonweal
Ebony
Honolulu Advertiser
Independent Gazette
JET
Life Magazine
Los Angeles Times
Ms.
The Nation
New Republic
Newsweek
New York Times
O.C. Register
People Weekly
Philadelphia Evening Bulletin
Philadelphia Lawyer
Providence Journal
San Francisco Bay Guardian
San Francisco Chronicle
Time
US Magazine
Village Voice
Washington Post

Selected Secondary Sources

Aguilar-San Juan, Karin. *Little Saigons: Staying Vietnamese in America.* Minneapolis: University of Minnesota Press, 2009.

Allen, Michael. *Until the Last Man Comes Home: POWs, MIAs, and the Unending War in Vietnam.* Chapel Hill: University of North Carolina Press, 2012.

Alvah, Donna. *Unofficial Ambassadors: American Military Families Overseas and the Cold War, 1946–1965.* New York: New York University Press, 2007.

Anderson, Terry. *Rethinking the Anti-war Movement.* New York: Routledge, 2011.

Balcom, Karen. *The Traffic in Babies: Cross-Border Adoption and Baby-Selling between the United States and Canada, 1930–1972.* Toronto: University of Toronto Press, 2011.

Ballard, Bert. "I Heard the Call, but He Wasn't Actually There: Sacred Communication with My New Son." *International Review of Qualitative Research* 4, no. 3 (Fall 2011): 175–91.

———. "Narrative Burden: A Qualitative Investigation of Transnational, Transracial Adoptive Identity." *Qualitative Communication Research* 2, no. 3 (Fall 2013): 229–54.

Ballard, Bert, and Sara J. Ballard. "From Narrative Inheritance to Narrative Momentum: Past, Present and Future Stories in an International Adoptive Family." *Journal of Family Communications* 11, no. 2 (April 2011): 69–84.

Bass, Thomas. *Vietnamerica: The War Comes Home.* New York: Soho, 1996.

Berebitsky, Julie. *Like Our Very Own: Adoption and the Changing Culture of Motherhood, 1851–1950.* Lawrence: University of Kansas Press, 2000.

Bernstein, Shana. *Bridges of Reform: Interracial Civil Rights Activism in Twentieth-Century Los Angeles.* New York: Oxford University Press, 2011.

Bloch, Avital H., and Lauri Umansky, eds. *Impossible to Hold: Women and Culture in the 1960s.* New York: New York University Press, 2005.

Bon Tempo, Carl J. *Americans at the Gate: The United States and Refugees during the Cold War.* Princeton, N.J.: Princeton University Press, 2008.

Bradley, Mark Philip, and Marilyn B. Young, eds. *Making Sense of the Vietnam Wars: Local, National, and Transnational Perspectives.* New York: Oxford University Press, 2008.

Briggs, Laura. *Somebody's Children: The Politics of Transracial and Transnational Adoption.* Durham, N.C.: Duke University Press, 2012.

Choy, Catherine Cezina. *Global Families: A History of Asian International Adoption.* New York: New York University Press, 2014.

Choy, Gregory Paul, and Catherine Ceniza Choy. "Reframing *Daughter from Danang.*" In *Outsiders Within: Writings on Transracial Adoption,* edited by Jane Jeong Trenka, Julia Chinyere Oparah, and Sun Yung Shin. Cambridge, Mass.: South End Press, 2006.

Dang, Thuy Vo. "The Cultural Work of Anticommunism in the San Diego Vietnamese American Community." *Amerasian Journal* 31, no. 2 (2005): 65–86.

Dorow, Sara. *Transnational Adoption: A Cultural Economy of Race, Gender, and Kinship.* New York: New York University Press, 2006.

Dubinsky, Karen. "'We Adopted a Negro': Interracial Adoptions and the Hybrid Baby in 1960s Canada." In *Creating Postwar Canada: Community, Diversity, and Dissent, 1945–1975,* edited by Magna Fahrni and Robert Futherdales, 268–88. Vancouver, B.C.: University of British Columbia Press, 2008.

Dudiak, Mary. *Cold War Civil Rights: Race and the Image of American Democracy.* Princeton, N.J.: Princeton University Press, 2001.

Duong, Lan. *Treacherous Subjects: Gender, Culture, and Trans-Vietnamese Feminism.* Philadelphia: Temple University Press, 2012.

Espiritu, Yên Lê. *Body Counts: The Vietnam War and Militarized Refuge(es).* Berkeley: University of California Press, 2014.

———. "Thirty Years after War: The Endings That Are Not Over." *Amerasian Journal* 31, no. 2 (2005): xiii–xxii.

———. "The 'We-Win-Even-When-We-Lose' Syndrome: U.S. Press Coverage of the Twenty-Fifth Anniversary of the 'Fall of Saigon.'" *American Quarterly* 58, no. 2 (2006): 329–52.

Fehrenbach, Heide. *Race after Hitler: Black Occupation in Postwar Germany and America.* Princeton, N.J.: Princeton University Press, 2007.

Fieldston, Sara. "Little Cold Warriors: Child Sponsorship and International Affairs." *Diplomatic History* 38, no. 2 (2014): 240–50.

Garcia, Desiree. *The Migration of Musical Film: From Ethnic Margins to American Mainstream.* New Brunswick, N.J.: Rutgers University Press, 2014.

Garcia, Maria Cristiana. *Seeking Refuge: Central American Immigrants to Mexico, the United States, and Canada.* Berkeley: University of California Press, 2006.

Goscha, Christopher, and Christian Ostermann, eds. *Connecting Histories: The Cold War and Decolonization in Asia, 1945–1962.* Palo Alto, Calif.: Stanford University Press, 2009.

Hagiopan, Patrick. *The Vietnam War in American Memory: Memorials and the Politics of Healing.* Amherst: University of Massachusetts Press, 2011.

Hayton, Bill. *Vietnam: Rising Dragon.* New Haven, Conn.: Yale University Press, 2010.

Herman, Ellen. *Kinship by Design: A History of Adoption in the Modern United States.* Chicago: University of Chicago Press, 2008.

Hübinette, Tobias. *Comforting an Orphaned Nation: Representations of International Adoption and Adopted Koreans in Korean Popular Culture.* Seoul: Jimoondang, 2006.

Huebner, Andrew J. *The Warrior Image: Soldiers in American Culture from the Second World War to the Vietnam Era.* Chapel Hill: University of North Carolina Press, 2008.

Hunt, Michael. *A Vietnam War Reader: A Documentary History from American and Vietnamese Perspectives.* Chapel Hill: University of North Carolina Press, 2010.

Hunt, Michael, and Steven Levine. *Arc of Empire: America's Wars in Asia from the Philippines to Vietnam.* Chapel Hill: University of North Carolina Press, 2012.

Jacobs, Margaret. "Remembering the Forgotten Child: The American Indian Child Welfare Crisis of the 1960s and 1970s." *American Indian Quarterly* 37, nos. 1–2 (Spring/Winter 2013): 136–59.

Jeffords, Susan. *The Remasculinization of America: Gender and the Vietnam War.* Bloomington: Indiana University Press, 1989.

Kelner, Shaul. *Tours That Bind: Diaspora, Pilgrimage, and Birthright Tourism.* New York: New York University Press, 2010.

Kieran, David. *Forever Vietnam: How a Divisive War Changed American Public Memory.* Amherst: University of Massachusetts Press, 2014.

Kim, Eleana J. *Adopted Territory: Transnational Korean Adoptees and the Politics of Belonging.* Durham, N.C.: Duke University Press, 2010.

Kim, Jodi. "An 'Orphan' with Two Mothers: Transnational and Transracial Adoption, the Cold War, and Contemporary Asian American Cultural Politics." *American Quarterly* 61, no. 4 (2009): 855–80.

Klein, Christina. *Cold War Orientalism: Asia in the Middlebrow Imagination, 1945–1961.* Berkeley: University of California Press, 2003.

Laderman, Scott. *Tours of Vietnam.* Durham, N.C.: Duke University Press, 2009.

Lee, Erika. *At America's Gates: Chinese Immigration during the Exclusion Era, 1882–1943.* Chapel Hill: University of North Carolina Press, 2003.

Lieberman, Robbie. *The Strangest Dream: Communism, Anticommunism, and the U.S. Peace Movement, 1945–1963.* New York: Syracuse University Press, 2000.

Lien, Vu Hong, and Peter D. Sharrock. *Descending Dragon, Rising Tiger: A History of Vietnam.* Chicago: University of Chicago Press, 2014.

Lim, Shirley Jennifer. *A Feeling of Belonging: Asian American Women's Public Culture, 1930–1960.* New York: New York University Press, 2006.

Lipman, Jana K. "A Precedent Worth Setting: Military Humanitarianism: The U.S. Military and the 1975 Vietnamese Evacuation." *Journal of Military History* 79, no. 1 (2015): 151–79.

———. "A Refugee Camp in America: Fort Chaffee and Vietnamese and Cuban Refugees, 1975–1982." *Journal of American Ethnic History* 33, no. 2 (Winter 2014): 57–87.

Lucks, Daniel. *Selma to Saigon: The Civil Rights Movement and the Vietnam War.* Lexington: University Press of Kentucky, 2013.

Martini, Edwin. *Invisible Enemies: The American War on Vietnam, 1975–2000.* Amherst: University of Massachusetts Press, 2007.

McKelvey, Robert S. *The Dust of Life: America's Children in Vietnam.* Seattle: University of Washington Press, 1999.

Melosh, Barbara. *Strangers and Kin: The American Way of Adoption.* Cambridge, Mass.: Harvard University Press, 2006.

Miller, Edward, and Tuong Vu. "The Vietnam War as a Vietnamese War: Agency and Society in the Study of the Second Indochina War." *Journal of Vietnamese Studies* 4, no. 3 (Fall 2009): 1–16.

Motomura, Hiroshi. *Americans in Waiting: The Lost Story of Immigration and Citizenship in the United States.* New York: Oxford University Press, 2007.

Ngai, Mae. *Impossible Subjects: Illegal Aliens and the Making of Modern America.* Princeton, N.J.: Princeton University Press, 2004.

Nguyen, Linh. "Recalling the Refugee: Culture Clash and Melancholic Racial Formation in *Daughter from Danang.*" *Amerasian Journal* 39, no. 2 (2013): 103–41.

Nguyen, Mimi Thi. *The Gift of Freedom: War, Debt, and Other Refugee Passages.* Durham, N.C.: Duke University Press, 2012.

Nguyen, Nathalie Huynh Chau. *Memory Is Another Country: Women of the Vietnamese Diaspora.* Santa Barbara, Calif.: Praeger, 2009.

Nyers, Peter. *Rethinking Refugees: Beyond States of Emergency.* New York: Routledge, 2006.

Oh, Arissa. *To Save the Children of Korea: The Cold War Origins of International Adoption.* Palo Alto, Calif.: Stanford University Press, 2015.

Ong, Aihwa. *Buddha Is Hiding: Refugees, Citizenship, the New America.* Berkeley: University of California Press, 2003.

Pate, SooJin. *From Orphan to Adoptee: U.S. Empire and Genealogies of Korean Adoption.* Minneapolis: University of Minnesota Press, 2015.

Peacock, Margaret. *Innocent Weapons: The Soviet and American Politics of Childhood in the Cold War.* Chapel Hill: University of North Carolina Press, 2014.

Piehler, G. Kurt. *Remembering War: The American Way.* Washington, D.C.: Smithsonian Institution Press, 1995.

Root, Maria. *Racially Mixed People in America.* New York: Sage, 1992.

Rydstrom, Helle. "Gendered Corporeality and Bare Lives: Local Sacrifices and Sufferings during the Vietnam War." *Signs* 37, no. 2 (January 2012): 275–99.

Sachs, Dana. *The Life We Were Given: Operation Babylift, International Adoption, and the Children of War in Vietnam.* Boston: Beacon, 2010.

Sahara, Ayako. "Theater of Rescue: Cultural Representations of U.S. Evacuation from Vietnam." *Journal of American and Canadian Studies*, no. 30 (March 2012): 55–84.

Schulzinger, Robert. *A Time for Peace: The Legacy of the Vietnam War.* New York: Oxford University Press, 2008.

Simpson, Caroline Chung. *An Absent Presence: Japanese Americans in Postwar Culture, 1945–1960.* Durham, N.C.: Duke University Press, 2002.

Stur, Heather Marie. *Beyond Combat: Women and Gender in the Vietnam War Era.* Cambridge: Cambridge University Press, 2011.

———. "'Hiding behind the Humanitarian Label': Refugees, Repatriates, and the Rebuilding of America's Benevolent Image after the Vietnam War." *Diplomatic History* 39, no. 2 (April 2015): 223–44.

Vu, Tuong, and Wasana Wongsurawat, eds. *Dynamics of the Cold War in Asia: Ideology, Identity and Culture.* New York: Palgrave, 2009.

Weil, Richard. "International Adoptions: The Quiet Migration." *International Migration Review* 18, no. 2 (Summer 1984): 276–93.

Wells, Tom. *The War Within: America's Battle over Vietnam.* Berkeley: University of California Press, 1994.

Welty, Lily Anne Yumi. "Advantage through Crisis: Multiracial American Japanese in Post–World War II Japan, Okinawa, and America, 1945–1972." Ph.D. diss., University of Santa Barbara, 2012.

Winslow, Rachel. "Immigration Law and Improvised Policy Making, 1948–1961." *Journal of Policy History* 24, no. 2 (April 2012): 319–49.

Woo, Susie. "'A New American Comes Home': Race, Nation, and the Immigration of Korean War Adoptees, 'GI Babies,' and War Brides." Ph.D. diss., Yale University, 2010.

Wu, Judy Tzu-Chun. *Radicals on the Road: Internationalism, Orientalism, and Feminism during the Vietnam Era.* Ithaca: Cornell University Press, 2013.

Yamamoto, Traise. *Masking Selves, Making Subjects: Japanese American Women, Identity, and the Body.* Berkeley: University of California Press, 1999.

Yngvesson, Barbara. "Going 'Home': Adoption, Loss of Bearings, and Mythology of Roots." In *Cultures of Transnational Adoption*, edited by Toby Alice Volkman, 81–116. Durham, N.C.: Duke University Press, 2005.

Zolberg, Aristide. *A Nation by Design: Immigration Policy in the Fashioning of America.* Cambridge, Mass.: Harvard University Press, 2008.

Index

Abrams, Susan, 53

Adopted Vietnamese: assimilation, 1, 38, 117–18, 126–27; community among, 129, 133, 134, 140–41; diversity among, 142; experiences of racism, 127–29; family searches, 1–3, 138–39, 145, 146–50, 152, 159; gratitude expectations, 102, 133, 136–37, 139, 143–44; later family relations, 3–4, 99–100, 120; perceptions of GI fathers, 131; public opinion on, 6; reconnection with Vietnam, 1, 119–20, 129, 130–31; as refugees vs. migrants, 5–6, 50–51; separation from ethnic community, 127, 138, 139–40; and U.S.-Vietnamese relations normalization, 118–19, 129, 130; Vietnam tours, 141–42, 145–47, 185 (nn. 62,64); and Vietnam veterans, 131, 136–38, 144. *See also* Adoption discourse re-imagining; Amerasians as adoptees; Discursive use of adopted Vietnamese; Vietnamese adoptions; Vietnamese mothers of adoptees

Adopted Vietnamese International (AVI), 140

Adoption discourse re-imagining, 119–20, 130–37, 156; cultural expressions, 133–34, *135, 136*; and cultural preservation concerns, 125–26; and discursive use of adopted Vietnamese, 131, 132, 156; and images of GI fathers, 131; and popular cultural representations, 132–33; and transnational adoption, 134–35; and Vietnam tours, 145–46; and Vietnam veterans, 131, 136–37

African American perspectives, 7, 32, 35, 53–54, 104–5

African Americans. *See* African American perspectives; Black Amerasians

Airlifts. *See* Operation Babylift

Alexander, Shana, 52

Allen, George, 42, 44

Allen, Michael, 137–38

Amerasian adult migration, 78–116; and American forgiveness for GI fathers, 89–90; and American views of family, 86, 93; and anticommunism, 85–86, 103; black Amerasians, 93, 94, 104–6; difficulties of, 78–79, 103, 111–13, 151; and exoneratve narratives of U.S. imperialism, 7–8, 82, 87, 88–89; and fraudulent family relationships, 7, 78, 92, 93–97; and GI fathers' searches, 87–89, 177 (n. 29), 180 (n. 92); media coverage of, 86–87; popular cultural representations of, 112–13, 116, 182 (n. 126); population profile, 103–4; resettlement services, 90, 93, 96, 101–3, 112, 179 (nn. 74,76), 181 (n. 113); and reunion intentions, 100–101; and searches for GI fathers, 106–11, 181 (n. 103); separation from ethnic community, 114; successes of, 114–15; U.S. expectations, 103, 110, 113; and U.S. refugee and immigration policies, 78, 83, 84–86, 91–92,

Amerasian adult migration (cont.) 94–95; and Vietnamese adoptions, 79–81, 90–91, 99–100; Vietnamese mothers, 83–85, 91, 100–101, 107–11, 114; Vietnamese policies, 89, 91, 92–93, 102, 177 (n. 28); and Vietnamese views of family, 84, 91, 92, 97–99; and Vietnam veterans, 111. *See also* Amerasians

Amerasian Affairs for International Aid, 84

Amerasian Fellowship Association, 151

Amerasian Homecoming Act (1987), 1–2, 7, 79, 90, 92–93, 113, 150. *See also* Amerasian adult migration

Amerasian Immigration Act (1982), 84, 86, 87, 88, 91

Amerasian Independent Voice, 151

Amerasian Paternity Recognition Act, 151–52

Amerasian Registry, 88–89, 177 (n. 29)

Amerasian Resettlement Program, 115

Amerasians: as accepted in Vietnam, 22–23; activism by, 151; community among, 115–16, 150–52, 154; discursive use of, 103, 112, 113; Japanese adoptions, 19–20; and POWs/MIAs, 152; as rejected in Vietnam, 73, 81–83, 92, 98, 104, 106. *See also* Amerasian adult migration; Amerasians as adoptees; Black Amerasians

Amerasians as adoptees: African American perspectives on, 7, 32, 35, 53–54; and defenses of Vietnamese adoptions, 39; and political motivations for adoptions, 32; as rejected in Vietnam, 22, 23–24; and U.S. refugee and immigration policies, 45–46; and Vietnamese policies, 25. *See also* Cultural preservation concerns

Amerasians Without Borders, 151

Amerasian Update, 105, 106, 114, 115, 116

American Council for Voluntary International Action (InterAction), 97, 105

American Indian adoptions, 37, 169 (n. 72)

American soldiers: negative images of, 16, 87, 131, 132, 164 (n. 9); varied masculinities of, 164 (n. 10). *See also* GI fathers

American views of family: and Amerasian adult migration, 86, 93; and Julie Andrews, 79, 175 (n. 4); and antiwar movement, 28; and Christian missionary work, 20; and reunion intentions, 72–73; and single parents, 17, 38, 43–44, 67, 86, 155, 168 (n. 46); and transnational adoption, 17, 20; and U.S. imperialism, 11; and U.S. refugee and immigration policies, 6, 7–8, 78, 92, 168 (n. 46)

American women: and GI fathers, 41–42; and maternal rhetoric, 8, 16, 28, 168 (n. 52); and Operation Babylift, 62; and positive adoption discourse, 64. *See also* Vietnamese adoptions

Anderson, Dave, 104

Anderson, M., 99

Anderson, Tony, 67, 98, 99–100

Andrews, Julie, 79–80, 175 (n. 4)

Anh Đào, 131, 133–34, 139, 142, 145

Anticommunism: and Amerasian adult migration, 85–86, 103; and Christian missionary work, 20; and Operation Babylift, 58; and transnational adoption, 20, 155, 166 (n. 29); and U.S. refugee and immigration policies, 7, 17, 85–86, 157, 161 (n. 7), 175 (n. 3). *See also* Cold War rhetoric

Antiwar movement, 14–15; and aid for Vietnamese children, 28–29; and maternal rhetoric, 28, 168 (n. 52); and negative images of American

soldiers, 16, 87, 164 (n. 9); and political motivations for Vietnamese adoptions, 13, 15–16, 21–22, 30–33
Armstrong, Ken, 42–44, 121, 123, *123*
Armstrong, Kien, 121
Armstrong, Ri, 42–44, 121, *123*
Asian Americans as model minority, 7
Asian war brides, 165 (n. 21)
AVI (Adopted Vietnamese International), 140

Ballard, Bert, 131, 134–36, 138, 141
Barker, Jim, 89
Barsky, Arthur, 29
Bartz, Connie and Harvey, 23–24
Bass, Thomas, 112–13, 181 (n. 103)
Beveridge, Irving C., 36
Black Amerasians: adult migration, 93, 94, 104–6; African American perspectives on, 7, 32, 35, 53–54, 104–5; and cultural preservation concerns, 7, 35–36, 120–21; and defenses of Vietnamese adoptions, 39; experiences of racism, 128–29; and political motivations for adoptions, 32; as rejected in Vietnam, 24, 104
Black Child Development Institute, 53
Black Evangelistic Enterprise, 104
Bogdanski, Joseph, 75
Bon Tempo, Carl, 161 (n. 7), 175 (n. 3)
Brenden, Marta, 91, 103
Briggs, Laura, 165 (n. 22)
Brigham, David, 110
Brodyaga, Lisa, 65–66
Brodyaga, My Hang, 65–66
Brown, Wilma, 35
Brynner, Yul, 33, 79
Buck, Pearl S., 19, 20–21, 23, 47
Burns, Bob, 125
Burns, Bruce, 89
Burns, Jane (Nguyen Thi Van), 128
Burton, Richard, 33

Cambodia, 78, 123, 129, 175 (n. 1)
Camp, Merrie Li (Than Van Thi), 67, 98, 99–100, *101*, 132, 154
Camp, Sandra, 67, 99
Capitalism, 56–57
Center for Constitutional Rights (CCR). See *Nguyen Da Yen et al. v. Kissinger et al.*
Center for International Policy, 91
Cerquone, Joseph, 90
Chaplin, Mai, 55
Char Thi Lan, 59
Chelimsky, Eleanor, 95
The Children of An Lac (film), 118
Children's Medical Relief International, 29
Child Rescue, 123
Chinese adoptions, 18–19, 166 (n. 30)
Chinook, Frank, 36, 41–42
Choy, Catherine Ceniza, 139
Choy, Gregory Paul, 139
Christianity, 19, 20–21, 27, 30, 155
Clark, Cherie, 32, 62–64, 70–71
Clinton, Bill, 130
Coburn, Judith, 52, 54
Cold War, end of, 129
Cold War rhetoric, 11, 14, 76, 120. See also Anticommunism
Colin, Don, 83
Committee of Child Welfare, 167 (n. 38)
Committee of Responsibility (COR), 28–29, 34, 35, 79
Conner, Ruben, 104
COR (Committee of Responsibility), 28–29, 34, 35, 79
Council for Rights of Adoptive Families, 66
Cousins, Norman, 165 (n. 22)
Cuban adoptions, 166 (n. 29)
Cultural preservation concerns, 32; adoptees' resistance to, 117–18, 125, 126; adoptive parents' investment in, 36–38, 117–18, 120–21, 159; adoptive

Index   197

Cultural preservation concerns (cont.) parents' neglect of, 124–25; and leftist opposition to Vietnamese adoptions, 35–36; and Operation Babylift, 53, 66; and political motivations for Vietnamese adoptions, 125–26; and post-World War II transnational adoptions, 19, 22, 166 (n. 30); and racial matching policies, 19, 22, 106, 166 (n. 30); societal concerns about, 6–7

Dai Nguyen, 100
Dang Thi Hao, 59
Daniels, Peter, 97
Dash, Suzanne, 64–65
Daughter from Danang (film), 138–39, 146, 147–48
Davis, Betty, 74
Davis, Brad, 126
Davis, Julie, 125, 126, 147
DeCamp, John, 65, 66
De Hartog, Jan, 25, 29, 121
Dehner, Marie, 60
Delaney, James, 74–75
Delevett, Kim, 126, 132, 147–48, *149*, *150*
Đêm Hoang Tu'o'ng, 182 (n. 126)
Denton, Jeremiah, 83
Dey, Carol, 27
Discursive use of adopted Vietnamese, 4–5, 8–9; and adoption discourse re-imagining, 131, 132, 156; and Operation Babylift, 49, 51–52; and reconnection with Vietnam, 118; and Vietnam veterans, 137
DNA testing, 145, 152
Doan Thi Hoang Anh, 71–72
Don Basco Center, 114
Dozier, Bill, 72
"The Dream of Meeting with the Blood Father" (Nguyen Huynh Tuyet), 106
Dubinsky, Karen, 36–37
Duling, Gretchen, 120, *122*, 128–29

Duling, Stephen Lester Ngo, 120–21, *122*, 128–29, 182 (n. 9)
Duong Bich Van, 63, 70–71
Duong Quoc Tran (Matthew David Pederson), 70–71

Edwards, Amelia Leigh, 79
Edwards, Blake, 79
Edwards, Joanna Lynn, 79
Eisenhower, Dwight D., 13
Elizabeth Saunders Home, 19
Emerson, Gloria, 53, 54
Espiritu, Ỹn Lê, 161 (n. 7)
Evacuation. *See* Operation Babylift
Evan B. Donaldson Institute, 140
Exonerative narratives of U.S. imperialism: and adopted Vietnamese, 118; and Amerasian adult migration, 7–8, 82, 87, 88–89; and Asian war brides, 165 (n. 21); and Operation Babylift, 49–50, 144; and Vietnamese adoptions, 45

Family. *See* American views of family; Fraudulent family relationships; Maternal rhetoric; Vietnamese views of family
Farrow, Mia, 33, 79
FCVN (Friends of the Children of Vietnam), 28, 71, 173 (n. 34)
Fertility rates, 17, 155
FFAC (Friends for All Children), 48, 64, 73, 75, 143
Finding Moon (Hillerman), 182 (n. 126)
FMSVC (Friends Meeting for the Sufferings of Vietnamese Children), 22, 28, 29–33, 35, 48, 63
Ford, Gerald R., 49–50, *50*, 144
Formosa Straits (Hyde), 182 (n. 126)
Fraudulent family relationships, 7, 78, 92, 93–97
Friends for All Children (FFAC), 48, 64, 73, 75, 143

Friends Meeting for the Sufferings of Vietnamese Children (FMSVC), 22, 28, 29–33, 35, 48, 63
Friends of Amerasians, 111
Friends of the Children of Vietnam (FCVN), 28, 71, 173 (n. 34)
Frontiers in Adoption, 34

Gender: and GI fathers, 89–90; and post–World War II transnational adoptions, 20; and Vietnamese adoptions, 120, 124, 182 (n. 7); in Vietnamese culture, 58, 100, 139–40. *See also* American women; Masculinity; Maternal rhetoric; Vietnamese women
"Gentle warrior" image, 16, 40–41
GI babies. *See* Amerasians
GI fathers, 39–45; adopted Vietnamese' images of, 131; adult Amerasian searches for, 106–11, 181 (n. 103); and American women, 41–42; concerns about, 44–45; conservative narrative of, 86; forgiveness for, 89–90; and masculinity, 8, 16, 40–41, 62; negative images of, 39–40, 87, 131, 132; searches for adult children, 87–89, 177 (n. 29), 180 (n. 92); and views of family, 43–44
Gilzow, Douglas, 113
Goldberg, Trista (Nguyen Thi Thu), 2, 3; adoptive parental connections to Vietnam, 124; assimilation, 1; and cultural preservation concerns, 126; and family searches, 1–3, 145, 152; and Vietnamese adoptee community, 140, 141; and Vietnam tours, 133, 145
Golding, Dominic, 145
Goodman, Ellen, 89–90
Goodson, Tiffany Chi, 130–31, 139–40, 141, 154
Grant, Wende, 33, 64
Graves, Mary, 24, 27

Hai, LeChristine, 124, 137
Hall, David, 111
Hang Thi Thay Dinh, 97
Hart-Cellar Act (1965), 6
Harverson, Stuart, 27
Herbert, Alfred, 166 (n. 30)
Hillerman, Tony, 182 (n. 126)
Hoa Bui, 114
Hoang Thi Thanh, 96
Hoang Van Thanh, 61
Ho Chi Minh, 13
Holt, Bertha, 20
Holt, Harry, 20, 21. *See also* Holt International
Holt International, 1, 30, 38, 48, 61, 140, 143, 146
Hong Kong Project, 18–19
Ho Thi Kim Nguyet, 116
Hower, Elsie, 44–45
Huebner, Andrew J., 164 (n. 10)
Hughes, Harold, 46
Human rights motivation for U.S. refugee and immigration policies, 6, 85, 161 (n. 7), 175 (n. 3)
Huntoon, Barry, 88–89
Huynh Thi Anh, 70
Hyde, Anthony, 182 (n. 126)

Immigration and Naturalization Service (INS). *See* U.S. refugee and immigration policies
Indochina Migration and Refugees Assistance Act (1975), 78
Inglese, Mrs. Tullis, 31
InterAction (American Council for Voluntary International Action), 97, 105
International Catholic Migration Commission, 92
International Conference on Children and National Development (1974), 25, 167 (n. 38)
International Red Cross, 177 (n. 29)

Index 199

International Social Service (ISS), 19, 34, 44–45, 165 (n. 19)
Interracial adoption. *See* Transracial adoption
Interracial marriages, 165 (n. 21)
ISS (International Social Service), 19, 34, 44–45, 165 (n. 19)

Jacobs, Margaret, 169 (n. 72)
Japan, 18, 19–20
Jeffords, Susan, 16
Johnson, Lyndon B., 28–29

Kalan, Jeffrey, 1–4
Kalan, Nancy and Chuck, 1, 124
Kaplan, Paul and Amy, 37
Keane, Alfred, 84, 89
Kelly, Katie, 96, 111–12
Kelner, Shaul, 141, 185 (n. 62)
Kennedy, Edward, 46
Kern, Linda Ralph, 104–5
Khanh Duy Nguyen, 146
Kiem Van Do, 97
Killingbeck, Howard, 90
Kim, Eleana, 141, 185 (n. 60)
Kim, Jodi, 139
Kissinger, Henry, 55
Klein, Wells, 23, 25
Knight, Dean (Tuan), 72
Knight, Wanda, 31
Knight, William, 72
Koppel, Ted, 82
Korean adoptions, 20, 21, 141, 166 (n. 25), 185 (n. 60)
Korean War, 18

Ladner, Joyce, 56
Lam Hoang Phuong, 63
The Last Flight Out (film), 132
Latin America, 156–57, 166 (n. 29)
Le, Lina, 90–91
Lee, Rachel, 30
Lee Heh, 38

Le Ha, 112–13
Leivermann, Christine D., 49
Leonard, David and Leslie, 37
Le Thanh Tung (Larry), 73
Le Thi Hang, 57–58
Le Thi Nga, 63–64
Le Thi Sang, 72
Levi, Edward, 55
Lieu Nguyen, 98–100, *101*
Life and Times, 182 (n. 126)
Ling Wing Yung, 18
Linh Nguyen, 139
LIRS (Lutheran Immigrant and Refugee Service), 90, 179 (n. 76)
Littauer, Virginia and Bill, 121
Lofgren, Zoe, 151
Logan, Nikki, 144
Lucas, Richard, 73, 74, 75
Lutheran Immigrant and Refugee Service (LIRS), 90, 179 (n. 76)

MacDonald, Julie, 110
Margolies, Marjorie, 38–39
Marrs, Theodore C., 49
Marshall Plan, 17
Martin, Graham, 52
Martindale, Walter, 81
Mary Poppins (film), 79, 175 (n. 4)
Masculinity: and GI fathers, 8, 16, 40–41, 62; varied forms of, 164 (n. 10)
Material advantages: and Amerasian adult migration, 87; and custody cases, 72; and Vietnamese adoptions, 53, 56–57, 66, 72, 124
Maternal rhetoric, 8, 16, 28, 80, 168 (n. 52)
McCain, John, 92
McConnell, Muoi, 55, 68–69
McDonald, Susan, 62
McKinney, Wayne, 44, 91
Memon, Angelina (Angelina Wentz, Pham Ngoc Anh), 81, 83, 93–94, 107, 108–9, *109*, 115, 150–51

Men. *See* American soldiers; GI fathers; Masculinity
Menghetti, Anita, 115
Mexico, 156–57
Michener, Mrs. Bryan P., 33
Miller, Helen, 61
Miller, Jimmy (Nhat Tung): and Amerasian activism, 151; and Amerasian community, 152, 154; mother of, 84; rejection in Vietnam, 81–82; and resettlement services, 102; search for father, 107, *108*, 109–10; success of, 114
Miller, Nhu, 38–39, *40*, 55, 57, 61, 146
Miller, Oktober, 57, 146, 172 (n. 21)
Miller, Tom, *40*; and aid for Vietnamese children, 29; marriage of, 38; and *Nguyen Da Yen et al. v. Kissinger et al.*, 55, 172 (n. 25), 174 (n. 56)
Milton, Khanh, 105
"Misplaced Baggage" (Anh Đào), 133–34, *135*, 136
Missing in Action, 182 (n. 126)
Miss Saigon, 109, 132
Mohawk Valley Resource Center, 112, 181 (n. 113)
Moss, Frank, 45–46
Motherland Heritage, 143, 146
Mrazek, Robert, 92, 94–95
Muldoon, Horace, 41
Musick, Phuong Thi, 69, 70
My Phuong, 90

National Association of Black Social Workers, 35
Nelson, Ben, 71–72
Nelson, Bonnie and John, 71, 72
Neuberger, Richard, 45
Newcomer, Peter, 89
Nguyen, Julia, 144
Nguyen Dang Tuc, 69–70
Nguyen Da Yen et al. v. Kissinger et al.: on adoption agencies, 60–61; adoptive parents' responses, 65–66; defense approaches, 62–65; and INS policies, 65, 67–68, 174 (n. 56); McConnell's disenchantment with, 68–69; origins of, 54–55; plaintiffs' approaches, 55–57; on reunion intentions, 68, 174 (n. 56); ruling in, 67–68, 76, 174 (n. 58); use for reunion searches, 59, 172 (n. 25)
Nguyen Hong Bich, 2
Nguyen Hun, 63
Nguyen Huynh Tuyet, 106–7
Nguyen Khanh Lien, 64
Nguyen Quoc Viet, 87
Nguyen Thanh Thi, 1–2, 3, 4, 94
Nguyen Thi Phuc, 59, 172 (n. 25)
Nguyen Thi Phuong, 108
Nguyen Thi Thu. *See* Goldberg, Trista
Nguyen Thi Van (Jane Burns), 128
Nhung Nguyen, 89
Nye, Patricia, 34

ODP (Orderly Departure Program), 83, 91, 92, 177 (n. 28)
Oh, Arissa, 20
Olick, Jeffrey, 49
Open Door Society, 37
Operation Babylift, 32, 48–57, *50*; and agency of Vietnamese families, 50–51; commemorations of, 140, 143–44, 154; defenses of, 49–50, 51, 62–65, 66–67; and discursive use of adopted Vietnamese, 49, 51–52; INS policies, 65, 67–68, 174 (nn. 56,64); lawsuit affidavits, 57–62; popular cultural representations of, 118, 132–33; U.S. media criticisms of, 51–54, 64; Vietnamese criticisms of, 54; voluntary relinquishment by adoptive parents, 65
Operation Babylift, lawsuit in response to. *See Nguyen Da Yen et al. v. Kissinger et al.*
Operation California, 80

Operation Pedro Plan, 166 (n. 29)
Operation Reunite, 145, 152
Orderly Departure Program (ODP), 83, 91, 92, 177 (n. 28)
Organization of Vietnam Veterans, 111
O'Rourke, Lawrence, 47
Ortoloff, Frank, 33
Out of the Dust, 182 (n. 126)

Paley, Grace, 52, 64
Pearl S. Buck Foundation, 7, 45–46, 82, 177 (n. 29)
Pederson family, 70–71
Pham Ngoc Anh (Angelina Wentz, Angelina Memon), 81, 83, 93–94, 107–9, *109*, 115, 150–51
Phan Thi My Le, 45
Philippines, 18
Philippines Refugee Processing Center (PRPC), 93, 96, 101, 102, 112
Political motivations for Vietnamese adoptions, 117, 155–56; and antiwar movement, 13, 15–16, 21–22, 30–33; and cultural preservation concerns, 125–26; leftist opposition to, 34–36; and Operation Babylift commemorations, 143; and U.S. policies, 33–34, 45–47
Popp, Hoa Thi (Lon), 73–76, 123
Popp, William, 73, 74, 76, 123–24, 175 (n. 71)
Postwar Vietnam: Cambodia invasion, 78, 175 (n. 1); economic/political reconstruction, 77–78; gender in, 58; POWs/MIAs, 129; U.S. relations normalization, 118–19, 129, 130, 137
Purdy, David, 128
Purdy, Hoang Stephen, 62, 125–26, 128
Purdy, Pam, 32, 62, 125–26

Race. *See* Cultural preservation concerns; Racial matching policies; Racism

Racial matching policies, 19, 22, 106, 166 (n. 30)
Racism, 36, 127–29
Ranard, Donald, 113
Rayor, Ann, 31–32
Reagan, Ronald, 7, 78, 85–86
Refugee Act (1980), 85
Refugee experience, scholarly exploration of, 11, 161 (n. 7), 162 (n. 13)
Refugee Service Center, 113
Rehberg, Jared, 127, 132–33, *133*, 141, 146
Re-imagining. *See* Adoption discourse re-imagining
Resettlement services, 90, 93, 96, 101–3, 112, 179 (nn. 74,76), 181 (n. 113)
Reston, James, 47
Reunion intentions, 3, 25–26; and adoptive parental responses to lawsuit, 65–66; and agency of Vietnamese families, 50–51; and Amerasian adult migration, 100–101; custody cases, 69–76; and INS policies, 174 (n. 56); and lawsuit affidavits, 57–62; and lawsuit origins, 54–55; and lawsuit ruling, 68; and Vietnamese views of family, 73, 158
Ridge, Thomas, 92
Robison, Howard, 46
Rusk, Howard, 28–29
Ryan, Matt, 134, *136*

Sandstrom, Don and Augusta, 13, 26
San Hang-Hien, 60
San Shie, 60
Sawada, Miki, 19
Schlesinger, James, 55
Schneider, Tuan-Rishard, 138
Sector, Bob, 87
Seventh-Day Adventist Church, 67, 98
Shade, John, 82
Shane, Bob, 143–44
Sheridan, Jay, 126, 137
Sibbett, Morgan, 22, 25, 30, 33

Sibble, Bree Cutting, 132
Sloviter, Dolores and Henri, 117, *119*
Sloviter, Vikki (Vu Thuy Quyen), 117–18, *119*
Smith, Desmond, 52–53
Smith, Dorothy, 37
Smith, Jean Kennedy, 33
Smith, Mrs. Donald, 31
Somewhere in the Middle (Rehberg), 133
The Sound of Music, 79, 175 (n. 4)
Stearns, Nancy, 56
Steiger, William, 46
Strand, Katherine and Dale, 66–67
Stur, Heather Marie, 172 (n. 20)
Support of Vietnamese Orphans, 54–55

Tai, Ta Van, 68
Tanous, Gary, 87
Tanous, Jean Marie, 87
Taylor, Elizabeth, 33
Taylor, Rosemary, 25, 62, 173 (n. 34)
Terminology, 161 (n. 2)
Than Van Thi (Merrie Li Camp), 67, 98, 99–100, *101*, 132, 154
Thi Toan Tran, 105
Thompson, Joan, 66
Thompson, Kimberly, 124, 127–28, 138, 139
Thu-Ha Le, 100
Thu-Hien, 147
Tiede, Tom, 47
Tisdale, Betty, 118, 134
Tjossem, Mary Ellen, 35
Torch 1975, 144
Transnational adoption, 166 (n. 25); and adoption discourse re-imagining, 134–35; and anticommunism, 20, 155, 166 (n. 29); background of, 16–21, 165 (nn. 19,22); and cultural preservation concerns, 19, 22, 166 (n. 30); home country policies, 17, 24–25, 34, 54, 166 (n. 25), 167 (n. 38); manipulative practices in, 21; U.S. policies, 21, 26–27, 168 (n. 46); and World War II, 17, 20, 155, 165 (nn. 19,22). *See also* Transracial adoption; U.S. refugee and immigration policies; Vietnamese adoptions
Transracial adoption, 35–37; American Indian children, 37, 169 (n. 72); and Operation Babylift, 54. *See also* Cultural preservation concerns; Transnational adoption; Vietnamese adoptions
Trent, Tina, 105
Tressler Adoption Services, 140
Truc Tran, 83, 98, 115
Truitt, Don, 111
Tsongas, Paul, 49
Tuan Den, 93
Tu Le, 116
Tung Nguyen, 102–3, 107, 114–15, 151, 152, 154
Tuyet Cam, 134, *135*
Tuyet Mai, 88
Tuyet Nyung, 88
Twice Under, 182 (n. 126)

UN High Commissioner for Refugees, 83, 177 (n. 28)
United Catholic Relief Services, 48
United States Catholic Charities, 102, 104, 108
United States Catholic Conference, 110
Urquhart, Carol and James, 36
U.S. Catholic Bishops, 179 (n. 76)
U.S. imperialism, 6; and Amerasian adult migration, 102; and American views of family, 11; and GI babies, 81; guilt about, 21–22, 46–47, 49, 110, 165 (n. 22); and Operation Babylift, 52, 56; positive narratives, 20, 27, 85; and transnational adoption, 16–18, 34. *See also* Antiwar movement; Exonerative narratives of U.S. imperialism; Vietnam War

U.S. refugee and immigration policies: and Amerasian adult migration, 78, 83, 84–86, 91–92, 94–95; and American views of family, 6, 7–8, 78, 92, 168 (n. 46); and anticommunism, 7, 17, 85–86, 157, 161 (n. 7), 175 (n. 3); future of, 156–57; and human rights, 6, 85, 161 (n. 7), 175 (n. 3); and transnational adoption, 21, 26–27, 168 (n. 46); and Vietnamese adoptions, 26–27, 33–34, 45–47. *See also specific laws*

VAN (Vietnamese Adoptee Network), 140
Vancena, Gary, 111
Veterans Assistance Service Program, 110
Vietnamerica (Bass), 112–13
Vietnamese Adoptee Network (VAN), 140
Vietnamese adoptees. *See* Adopted Vietnamese
Vietnamese adoptions: and adoptive parental connections to Vietnam, 121–24; and Amerasian adult migration, 79–81, 90–91, 99–100; celebrity parents, 33, 79, 175 (n. 4); extralegal methods, 44; and gender, 120, 124, 182 (n. 7); and material advantages, 53, 56–57, 66, 72; media criticisms of adoptive parents, 52–53; number of, 22; popular cultural representations of, 132–33, 138–39; and race, 6–7, 16; religious motivations for, 27, 30; Rosemary Taylor's role, 173 (n. 34); and U.S. refugee and immigration policies, 26–27, 33–34, 45–47; Vietnamese policies, 24–25, 54. *See also* Adopted Vietnamese; Amerasians as adoptees; Cultural preservation concerns; GI fathers; Operation Babylift; Political motivations for Vietnamese adoptions; Reunion intentions

Vietnamese Heritage Camp, 134
Vietnamese mothers of adoptees: as acquiescent, 63–64; negative images of, 23, 131, 132; and Operation Babylift, 51, 57–61, 62; reunions with, 2–3, 138–39. *See also* Reunion intentions
Vietnamese views of family, 98–99; and Amerasian adult migration, 84, 91, 92, 97–99; and later adoptee family relations, 4; and *Nguyen Da Yen et al. v. Kissinger et al.*, 59, 60; and Operation Babylift, 57, 61; and reunion intentions, 73, 158; and Vietnamese adoptions, 24, 39, 55, 57
Vietnamese women: agency of, 57, 58, 83–84, 100; and Amerasian adult migration, 81, 83–85, 86, 100; as invisible, 81, 85, 86; mothers of Amerasian adults, 83–85, 91, 100–101, 107–11, 114; and searches for fathers, 107–11; and U.S. refugee and immigration policies, 85, 91; victim/vixen images, 51, 57, 172 (n. 20). *See also* Reunion intentions; Vietnamese mothers of adoptees; Vietnamese views of family
Vietnam Journeys, 143
Vietnam veterans: and adopted Vietnamese, 131, 136–38, 144; and Amerasian adult migration, 111; discursive use of, 137–38. *See also* GI fathers
Vietnam Veterans of American (VNVA), 11
Vietnam War: consequences of, 5, 50–51; conservative narrative of, 7, 85; and discursive use of Amerasians, 103, 112, 113; and discursive use of veterans, 137–38; end of, 48, 76, 171 (n. 1); history of, 13–14; POWs/MIAs, 129, 130, 152; unique legacy of, 12.

See also Adoption discourse re-imagining; American soldiers; Antiwar movement; Discursive use of adopted Vietnamese; U.S. imperialism
Vo Anh Tuan, 73
Vo Huy Khan, 73
Volags, 102–3, 179 (n. 76)
Vu Thuy Quyen (Vikki Sloviter), 117–18, *119*

Waking Up American (Rehberg), 133
War Babes, 181 (n. 103)
War brides, 165 (n. 21)
Welcome Home House, 112
Welcome House, 19, 23, 24, 27, 28, 30, 48
Wentz, Angelina (Angelina Memon, Pham Ngoc Anh), 81, 83, 93–94, 107–9, *109*, 115, 150–51

"What Will We Do" (Tu Le), 116
Williams, Harrison, 46
Williams, Spencer, 67
Woerthwein, Joshua, 147
Women. *See* American women; Maternal rhetoric; Vietnamese women
Women Strike for Peace, 28
Woo, Susie, 21
World Airways, 143–44
World Vision, 20, 104
World War II, 17, 18, 20, 155, 165 (nn. 19,22)

Yngvesson, Barbara, 185 (n. 64)
Yonemura, Mas, 68

Zenk, Bob and Joan, 73, 74–75

www.ingramcontent.com/pod-product-compliance
Lightning Source LLC
Chambersburg PA
CBHW030651230426
43665CB00011B/1049